NO PLACE FOR ME

A Memoir of an Indian Doctor in East Africa

LEO J. DE SOUZA

BEAVER'S POND PRESS

ISBN 13: 978-1-64343-929-7
Library of Congress Catalog Number: 2019906424
Printed in the United States of America
First Printing: 2021
25 24 23 22 21 5 4 3 2 1

Cover and interior design by Dan Pitts

BEAVER'S POND PRESS

Beaver's Pond Press, Inc.
939 Seventh Street West
Saint Paul, Minnesota 55102
(952) 829-8818
www.BeaversPondPress.com

For more information about the author, visit www.NoPlaceForMe.com.

To Leandro and Theodolinda,
my parents

Where we love is home,
home that our feet may leave, but not our
hearts.
- Oliver Wendell Holmes

Home is the place where, when you have to go there,
they have to take you in.
- Robert Frost

HOUSE OF CAMOTH

GABRIEL DE SOUSA CAMOTH *(1815-1884)*
Joana De Sousa *(1821-1899)*
(Goa, Portuguese India)

- SEBASTIAO FRANCISCO *(1844-1920)*
  m. Margarida Eufemia Mascarenhas *(1856-1909)*
  m. Maria Felicidade Mascarenhas *(d.1929)*
  (Goa, Portuguese India)
- SERAFINA *(1846-Unknown)*
- COSME DAMIÃO *(1846-Unknown)*
  m. Maria Magdalena Santa Maria *(1862-1927)*
  (Goa, Portuguese India)
  - DOMINGOS LUIS CAITANO
    m. Ignez Elvira Severina De Souza
    (Tanganyika)
  - LEANDRO PAULO
    m. Theodolinda Claudina De Mello
    (Tanganyika)
    - MIGUEL LADISLAUS SANTOS
      m. Queenie Silvie Matilda Dennis
      - Susan Ira
      - Stanley Joseph
      - Safira Genevieve
      - Selwyn Leandro
    - LEO JOSEPH
      m. Doulat Burjorji Irani
      (Dolly Marie Therese)
      - Martin
      - Marie Louella Magdalena Paula
      - Mario Luis
      - Marie Lea Theresa
      - Maria Joanna Stella
    - MAGDALENA MAURICIA LYDIA
      m. Luis Mariano Gomes
      - Owen Joseph Paul
      - MaryAnn
  - LEOPOLDO GABRIEL
    m. Anna Dolorosa de Souza
    (Hong Kong)
  - TEREZINHA MARGARIDA
    (Goa, Portuguese India)
  - ASSUCIANA CARMELIAN
    m. Caetano Vincent Noronha
    (Hong Kong)
- ARCANGELA ANGELINA *(1859-Unknown)*
- JOAO CARIDADE *(1859-1922)*
  m. Ana Maria de Almeida *(1872-1947)*
  (Goa, Portuguese India)

Gulu
Lira
UGANDA
KENYA
Kampala
Entebbe
Lake Victoria
Nairobi
INDIAN OCEAN
Mt Meru
Mt Kilimanjaro
Arusha
Moshi
Mombasa
Pare Mts
Tabora
Lushoto
Moa
Tanga
TANGANYIKA
Dar es salaam
Lake Tanganyika
Lindi
Mtwara
Lake Nyasa

Contents

PART III

PART IV

Foreword

Leo De Souza has written a memoir that tells its own important story with great clarity and drama. My excuse for briefly detaining the reader from that story is that I can, by happenstance and good fortune, provide some background as to how the book came to be written.

I first encountered Dr. De Souza as a student in the MFA program at Hamline University. He was of an age at which most persons of his means and stature contemplate, or outright embrace, retirement. Quite to the contrary, Dr. De Souza worked away with passion that did not reveal itself in grand statements or tormented insecurities, but rather in the persistence and thoroughness of his immersion into the writing process—a process that was quite new to him, and which in many respects ran contrary to the more structured methods of surgical training that Dr. De Souza had already mastered.

It became clear that Dr. De Souza was fiercely dedicated to the telling of his life story, and with good reason—for he understood well that the racial and political realities he had encountered in East Africa had both personal and historical significance. This was not a matter of arrogance on his part. It was, to the contrary, a simple recognition of the fact that he had lived through much, and that those who had witnessed and survived those times had a duty, as well as a need, to tell what they knew.

As the primary academic advisor for Dr. De Souza's final MFA thesis—that has, years of further work later, emerged as the book *No Place For Me*—I may perhaps be suspected of mere fondness for a former gifted student if I say that this memoir is both a vital document and a beautiful memoir. But I am not in the habit of writing 'forewords' of any sort, much less insincere ones, and I am pleased to assure the reader that *No Place For Me* falls readily into both categories.

Dr. De Souza's book provides an astute social portrait of the tangled racial realities of colonial and post-colonial East Africa. It reminds insular American readers that racism takes on subtly different forms in different cultures, but leaves behind as a common residue hatred, anguish and death—just as it has in our own. But it also reveals to the reader the inner world of Indian immigrants to Africa—their weddings, sense of family, political and personal aspirations, as well as the buffeting impacts upon them of both colonial British and independent African rule. There are living persons traversing the pages of this memoir. Out of the drama of their geographic and emotional displacement, Dr. De Souza has created a narrative that renders vividly those people and their era for grateful present-day readers and for the social historians of the future who will seek to make textured sense of Africa's emergence from European colonial rule.

It should be no great surprise that an accomplished physician should be able to turn to writing and succeed convincingly. Anton Chekhov, Sir Arthur Conan Doyle, William Carlos Williams, and more recently, Richard Selzer, are examples of doctors who have excelled at literary art. One of the attributes that a doctor must possess is keenness of observation. In memoir writing it is keenness of detail that enables readers to travel to distant settings, to encounter the people there, and all the while to feel as though they are listening, watching, smelling, tasting and feeling along with the author who serves as a narrative guide. Dr. De Souza possesses the ability to capture the spirit of the times and places of which he writes. He does so through the exactitude and focus of his prose. But Dr. De Souza does more than render settings. His ear for the nuances of colonial and post-colonial dialogue—with all the embedded assumptions, fears and hatreds—is exceptional. His ability to capture the awkwardness and bewilderment of good-hearted persons, such as himself, enmeshed in racist institutions leads one to understand both the heartbreak and the rage induced by such institutions. Dr. De Souza does not succumb to cynicism or bitterness, but he does not look away from the truth. His courage helps strengthen the reader's resolve to do the same.

No Place For Me is a testament, a lament, and yet ultimately a work of hope.

Lawrence Sutin

Author of *Divine Invasions: A Life of Philip K. Dick, Jack and Rochelle: A Holocaust Story of Love and Resistance, A Postcard Memoir, All Is Change: The Two-Thousand Year Journey of Buddhism to the West,* and *When to Go Into the Water*

Preface

My memoir covers a wide expanse of time and place. The period itself encompasses a span of a hundred years. While the narrative ends in 1971 when I was forced out of Uganda, it begins with recounting the slave trade in 1871. This length of time is essential to place events in proper perspective and add understanding to how things came to be.

My parents came from Goa, a Portuguese colony on the west coast of India. In the Velhas Conquistas, life was gracious, courtly, unhurried and Catholic. However, its economy could not sustain its people, forcing Goans to seek their fortunes elsewhere, mostly in British India, especially Bombay. Some went to East Africa, some to the Portuguese colonies of Moçambique, Angola and Macao.

My father sailed to Tanga, Tanganyika, prior to World War I, when the Germans ruled East Africa. He worked at Usagara Company Limited, the foremost German firm. Germany eventually lost the war to Britain. The change necessitated that my father transfer his services to the Custodian of Enemy Property, a British government department that oversaw disposal of German assets.

My sojourn takes me to three continents.

I was born in Tanga in 1926 at the time of the British regime and, at age seven, was sent to India for my education. Although I attended a fine English school in Goa (St. Joseph's Arpora), a Jesuit college in Bombay (St. Xavier's), then Grant Medical College founded by the British, it was distressing to be discriminated against by the English, particularly as I had a fondness for their language and esteem for their literature.

On returning to Tanganyika as an adult, my first encounter with a British immigration officer on board ship at Mombasa was extremely traumatic, a baptismal rite that relegated me to second-class status. I learned that *mzungu*—a white person—was king and everyone else a serf.

Before my father's untimely death in 1957, we spent many evenings talking. My unending questions helped him recollect his past clearly: his home, marriage, hopes, aspirations. The opening account of the slave trade was recounted by Ali Aboud, legal assistant at a firm in Tanga, and his dear friend. They told me the story of the Germans, the war, the British, their friend Olenzu. A narrative of the one-day war in Tanga, when General Paul Emil von Lettow-Vorbeck routed the British and Indian army, came from my father.

My time as a doctor in Tanganyika left me incensed. The colonial system defined our status, relegating the Indian peremptorily to a position of little worth. Limitations of where we could work, live and socialise left us believing we were not quite as good as, or quite as equal to, the white man. Our wings clipped, our spirit curbed, we could not fly, we could not soar. The realms of the truly free were not for us. The innate gentlemanliness of a few good and understanding Britishers did not make amends for the injustices of colonialism.

I did not let my aspirations of wanting to be a surgeon by British standards go by the wayside. I finished my training in Britain and returned to Africa as a Fellow of the Royal College of Surgeons of Edinburgh in orthopaedics. Eminently suited to be the kind of doctor that newly independent Tanganyika desperately needed, I found out I was the wrong man. In colonial times, I was not white; now, in Tanganyika, removed from the shackles of colonialism, I was not black.

Dejected, I went to Uganda with help from my English chief of surgery who was in Kampala. In Lira I had the opportunity to work beside a renowned surgeon, Mr. Denis Burkitt, who was making significant advances in treatment of children's lymphoma, and in Gulu, with Drs. Lucille and Piero Corti at Lacor Hospital. I was transferred to Kampala at the request of Mr. Ronald Huckstep to help run the Round Table Polio Clinic and we were on the front lines of the eradication of polio. My professional life flourished and the family settled in comfortably despite an undercurrent of political rumblings. The final coup de grâce was the unexpected emergence of a boorish man at the helm of government, Idi Amin Dada Oumee, for whom violence was commonplace. It brought about my quiet and quick exit from the land I was beginning to consider my own. I realised painfully there was no place for me in this country either.

My father, brother, uncles and firstborn child are buried in Tanga, consigned to the earth. In that physical transition, they have given themselves to the very substance of the soil, altering and enriching it. I left something behind that is now part of the country.

For the years I lived and toiled there, my endeavours did not go without effecting some change for the better. I wanted, very much, to continue to give of myself, but I was not a native. If each little act is a ripple on a pond extending itself, sometimes unseen under the lotus leaves, then the ways of the people and the course of history are altered by the cumulative effect of such acts, considered insignificant at the time.

I write this story to appease my loss. Also to air my grievance that I received neither justice at the hands of the white colonial nor understanding at the hands of the black indigene. The people who shaped my life came from varied, sometimes markedly dissimilar backgrounds.

It is a story not often heard.

PART I

1

THE SLAVE CARAVAN

1. The Trek

The caravan was in the business of trading slaves as well as ivory, rhinoceros horn, lion teeth, and frankincense. The column of men set off from Tanga, a port on the East African coast, in April 1871, travelling inland to the slave market of Unyanyembe in central Tanganyika. They would return with captives to be sold and dispatched in dhows bound for the island of Zanzibar and distant Arabia.

The leader of the caravan of 150 porters and 30 *askaris* was an experienced slaver who had travelled this route and commanded respect from the entire company. Short in stature and lean of frame, Abdalla bin Salimu, the twenty-six-year-old Zanzibari Arab, had a trimmed beard and piercing brown eyes in an angular face.

As the caravan wound its way through the untamed country, the man crucial to the expedition's day-to-day success was the head porter. Strict, but caring, he kept all the porters in tow and had their loyalty. Each morning he roused them with song, then led the retinue, extracting work and keeping them in good spirits. Specially picked by Abdalla, he was the kingpin, a splendid fellow by the name of Jumbe.

Sukuma by tribe, Jumbe was tall and well built with broad shoulders. His dark skin contrasted starkly with his white teeth, widely exposed when he smiled or laughed or sang. His clothes were simple, a loose cotton wrap the colour of mud, held at the waist by a worn leather cord, and *meshadda*—shawl—knotted in front. He was barefoot like the rest.

Mostly Sukuma and *Nyamwezi*, the porters were rugged men, lugging *mzigos*—goods for sale or barter—on the way up, tusks and horns on the way

---

Askaris. (Swahili) Soldiers, policemen

Sukuma. Bantu-speaking people living south of Lake Victoria in East Africa; the largest community of Tanganyika

Nyamwezi. (Swahili) Translates as "people of the moon," but also means "people of the west"

back. And rice, *posho*—ground maize—and cooking utensils. Jumbe checked each article; it had to have a specific purpose, otherwise, it was worthless, to be tossed. Jumbe was aware, too, that each person entertained hopes for an illness-free journey, a successful end, a substantial reward. And desires. *Unafikiria nini?*—What's on your mind?—he asked as they lay looking at stars, between the time fires were subdued and sleep overcame them. *Wanawake*—women—they answered shyly.

Like a morning bird, Jumbe blew a chirpy note on his whistle at the break of dawn. The porters shook off sleep with difficulty, yawning loudly, rubbing their eyes. They put out smouldering embers, then collected their loads. Another whistle and they fell in line. Jumbe ran back and forth as the porters came to life, singing salutations to the new day.

Jambo, rafiki yango! Good morning, my friends!
Wake up to greet the sun as it rises.
And the new day as it is born.
And may God be with you.

A murmur of response rose from the awakening line.

Now up with your loads to prove you are men. You will have to wait to show it any other way. They choked on guffaws as he voiced their deep-seated urges.

Jumbe broke into a musical chant and the line, full of cheer, moved west, singing as they marched. Trekking fifteen miles a day heaving fifty-pound loads, they were especially spectacular when they changed loads from one shoulder to the other, all the while continuing to advance single file. They knew the terrain, which tribal clans to befriend, whom to avoid.

The rising sun warmed their bodies but by afternoon it would be hot enough to look for a place to camp for the night, close to water for cooking and ablutions. There, they'd pile their loads in one central spot and separate into small groups. After a short respite peppered with bantering, a few ventured out for firewood, grass and water, while the remainder stood watch. Askaris with rifles hunted wild game to break the monotony of daily posho.

Their evening meal was cooked on fires built at the edge of camp. Embers provided warmth and served as glowing eyes to keep predators away. For when the sun set, night fell swiftly, sky ablaze with a myriad of glittering stars. While the men prepared to sleep, Jumbe felt strangely protected by the heavenly constellations his ancestors had also known.

His wife's image floated before him. She had borne four children and wanted a bigger homestead, a cone-on-cylinder hut with thatched roof and more ploughing land for maize and cassava. Being head porter would make this possible. Jumbe never gave slaving a second thought. Slaves were taken in battle or sold by chiefs. Certain vulnerable areas were frequently raided for the explicit purpose of abducting unsuspecting men and women, even children. This was his first slaving expedition. He had been part of many convoys but never one that took slaves.

One day rolled into the next.

A third of the way along, the landscape became arid. The acacia trees, sprouting from bare earth, stood gaunt and bare, arms spread, heads bowed, flattened. Thorns abundant, flaying skin and ripping muscle. Jumbe covered the men's gashes with herbal paste. He recognised their fears and took time to assuage them. He helped lift their loads. Untiring, he sang to them, prancing up and down the wearied line.

You are strong as lions. You are brave as warriors.
You will make it to the end.
You are patient. You are willing.
You will have your reward. You will have your fill.
With things to choose from, with women aplenty.

He always enticed them with women, for that is what they wanted to hear, and they gave so much more of themselves. As a first-time porter, a raw young man, he too had been wild and dazzled, but no more. He was head porter and bore more responsibility.

So the men marched on as the path turned to volcanic rock. Their feet, large and used to distance, broadened out and grew callused. When rubble became powder, red dust rose to cover them in a cloud. Jumbe chanted, clear as birdsong:

You follow me.
I will lead you there.

Two-thirds into the excursion, the landscape stretching for miles into the horizon showed no sign of life, no habitation, no smoke, no sound. Jumbe knew this part of Tanganyika was endless and empty, magnificent and impossible. The place was alive, teeming with secrets but there was no time for the caravan to slow the pace, stop awhile, look and listen, and relish the moment. They walked and as they passed, unbeknownst, the impala stopped grazing, raised its head and flicked its left ear; the slothful lion stood up and looked regal again; the warthog's snout quivered as she stopped the family trotting behind her, and black-and-yellow birds in trees ceased chattering.

On the twentieth evening, they rested in the middle of a central plateau, an oasis in that inhospitable bush country. They were a day's trek from Unyanyembe. The restless porters could hardly sleep. Where were the women Jumbe had promised?

Jumbe had always raised their spirits to urge them on, but on this night, reversed himself.

You must conserve your strength. We have just arrived. Our real work begins tomorrow when *Bwana* Abdalla will lead you. Once we finish, you will have your reward. For tonight, sleep early.

Jumbe was pleased everything had turned out well. They had walked for three weeks. Now the difficult task would begin, not with tusks or horns but with the men, women and children they would buy. Unpleasant work . . . he was relieved he was not Abdalla.

2. Bargaining for Slaves

The caravan arrived in Unyanyembe in good time and camped close to the slave stockade.

Leaving Jumbe to watch the restive porters, Abdalla went to meet the slave traders, Arabs with whom he had previous dealings. He donned a loose brown robe belted at the waist, pistol on the right side of his belt, curved dagger on the left. A traditional Arab headdress held in place by the *agal*, covered his head and thick leather sandals were strapped to his feet and ankles. Abdalla had led two earlier convoys, though smaller, each one enhancing his reputation for toughness as a shrewd slaver who could bring fortunes to his patrons, influential *Akidas* and monied Indian merchants.

Bwana. (Swahili) Boss or master, often used as a title or form of address

Agal. (Arabic) Cord, usually of goat's hair, that Arabs (as the Bedouins) wind around their heads to hold down the kerchief-like headdress

Akidas. (Swahili) Chiefs

He was aware traders wanting the best prices would sing praises of slaves, same as they would of their horses: their flanks, their carriage. For his part, he would talk them down; he was used to bargaining and was good at it.

The market, spread over many acres of open land, was located on an elevation meant to show off slaves in a better light. At one end stood men, six to eight shackled to each other with iron chains; women and girls herded together at the other. Boys, half of whom had been castrated, were in between. If they survived the mutilation, they would fetch large profits serving as eunuchs in harems and bedchambers of women in Arabia.

Effusive greetings and coffee refreshments done, Abdalla was taken to view the slaves. As a matter of routine, he looked closely at their limbs and orifices for strength and stature in men, for firmness and looks in women. They started with the women, clean-shaven and oiled.

Open your mouth. Spread your legs. Turn around.

The overseer patted their rumps, making a clapping sound. The women recoiled.

They are good, the headman leered. Whatever you want them for.

Abdalla inspected closely—their calves, their thighs, their buttocks.

Raise your arms.

He ran his eyes over their mounds, bellies and breasts. *Are they firm? Are they sagging?* Next he walked to the men, unbound, under the eye of a rifle.

Walk . . . Jump.

A quick look at their shoulders and backs before a final cursory look at the boys, eyes wide with fear, faces joyless.

We'll take sixty women, sixty men, forty children.

Abdalla and the traders remained closeted, drinking strongly brewed coffee and negotiating price. He spoke animatedly, gesticulating often, but was unable to lower the amount. There were more buyers than slaves and little he could do.

I have bought 160 slaves. Jumbe, can you manage that many?

Ndiyo—Yes, Bwana.

Tomorrow we go farther inland. Tusks and horns waiting for us. We will try for more slaves.

He did not tell Jumbe he was planning a devilish trick in an attempt to add more slaves to his collection without having to pay.

The caravan rested for a day before resuming its journey. The vast countryside turned green and soft, rolling woodland with outcrops of rocky hills. On the fourth day, they reached east of the bend in the Malagarasi River where Abdalla was fortunate to obtain huge tusks, each requiring to be hoisted by two porters.

Abdalla was exhilarated; the monies this would bring dazzled him, as did the thought of more profits from additional slaves. Late that afternoon, he received an unusually good supply of rhinoceros horn, which, ground to powder, was used by the Chinese as an aphrodisiac. Abdalla knew a good horn or tusk when he saw one and was always prepared to pay for prime value. Traders sought him out as a fair buyer not given to undue haggling over merchandise of quality. Eventually, he knew, his profits would double.

By the end of the day, he was content yet restless. He thought of his wife ardently waiting. It was a long time for a woman to be without a husband but such was a woman's lot. He went on slave caravans; others took to the seas in dhows; still others peddled carpets in distant towns. He missed her scent; her body fragrance, jasmine *attar*. He thought of her hands, expressive, animated; fingers, long and slender. Even so, it would be nice to have a second wife, another woman to make him happy. He imagined burying himself in her roundness; he was aroused, warm all over. His entire body tingled.

He would tell his mother, I want a chubby wife, different from Fatima. His mother would be so proud of him. *So young, so successful, and in time, two wives!* Rhinoceros horn, fetching a handsome price, could make this a reality.

The following morning, Abdalla met Jumbe and the chief askari and told them he was working on a plan to get more slaves but had serious issues to resolve.

Too many slaves die on the way. There is profit to be made but not if they are dead. Take good care of them. I shall reward you well.

Abdalla's eyes narrowed into slits, aware the operation could be crippled unless tightly controlled.

And there is another problem; it is to do with our porters.

His men had not been close to a woman for a month and their desires grew stronger each night. Coarse men who toiled each day, eased hunger with food, tiredness with sleep, while their loins swelled. They were primed to explode . . . stallions ready to mount. The men believed these women were receptacles for their desires. Abdalla had no problem with that. No one could tell them otherwise. Captured women were chattel. So what if they were uprooted, forcibly taken, dragging and screaming? So what if their faces were wet with snot, eyes red from crying? A little mating would do them good. Abdalla's concern was the women might be hurt from sheer physical force or lose their will to live.

Attar. (Arabic) Fragrant essential oil, typically made from rose petals

The men will quarrel over the women. There will be two to every woman. Keep your eyes on them. Settle claims amicably. Use little bribes, force if you have to, or shoot your rifle in the air. But no harm is to come to the women. I want all slaves alive when we reach Tanga.

Yes, Bwana.

Crossing the river, Jumbe led the way to the *Vinza* chief. Following customary greetings, Abdalla presented him with a bundle of *merikani* and knives, and trinkets for his women. The chief thanked the visitors effusively, then voiced his problems.

Our neighbours, the *Ha*, are evil, ungrateful curs who eat our food, then bite our foot. They steal our land. They are too many and too strong.

Abdalla gave him a firearm with a promise of more to come to fight the Ha.

We leave tomorrow and need food. We are here looking for tusks. Can you help us? We will compensate you well.

He left more fabric, more ornaments, more hoes.

At daybreak, twenty women bearing baskets of food and one young girl carrying special cakes for Abdalla arrived at camp. Abdalla signaled to the chief askari to act on his instructions.

Two men who plied the boat were surreptitiously seized, hands tied behind and to each other. The women were abducted.

3. Oju, Whispering in the Wind

Mama, can you hear me? You are already so far away that I am afraid you may not. But soft winds of our village will carry my voice to you. It must, for you are waiting to hear and I must talk to you.

Two boatmen took us across to the far side of the river where the big caravan was waiting. We felt proud to be selected by the chief. Everyone was so excited.

Bibi was there . . . not the one from across, but Bibi your sister. She said to me, You lucky one. All of us have baskets of food but you were chosen to present a basket of gifts to the headman. I felt so important.

They took our baskets. I handed maize cakes to the Arab. He smiled, but I was afraid.

Vinza. Tribe based in Kigoma region, Tanganyika

Merikani. (Swahili) Printed cotton fabric

Ha. Tribe in the Kigoma region in northwestern Tanganyika

Suddenly, it was as if an earthquake shook the ground. They tied our boatmen and fired a shot. They grabbed our wrists and pulled . . . herding us like cattle, askaris behind with guns. Auntie Bibi screamed. Other women screamed, bent double, flailing their arms as if possessed by demons. But I knew what it was; they were frightened of these men.

Just looking at them, I couldn't move. I became stone. The Arab kept looking at me. I couldn't open my mouth. I shivered and felt cold. There were shouts, shooting, screaming, wailing. We were fighting to get away; they pushed us in the other direction.

I heard myself howl, afraid they would kill me. I cried louder.

Mama, please come and get me. Mama, please come and get me.

I didn't stop calling for you. Did you hear me, Mama? You must have. Soft winds must have carried my voice to you.

Please talk to me, Mama. I am on this road leading away from home to nowhere.

Dada—sister—it is the second day and I am so lonely.

The women are kept away from me. I cannot even talk to Auntie Bibi. She is out there wanting to hold my hand but I cannot see her.

This Arab man does not let me out of his sight. He has large eyes and a hooked nose. He looks at me, places his hand on the nape of my neck, my shoulders, sometimes on my buttocks. He tries to talk to me but I do not understand what he says. So he smiles. But I don't smile. He pats my cheek.

I don't know what to do. I am afraid, so afraid he will kill me.

I wish you were here with me. You were always so strong and you knew what to do when boys were teasing, wanting. I remember Baba saying, Keep close to your dada.

I miss you. Send me a message on the soft wind.

Little brother, I was supposed to play with you when I left.

How I wish I had not gone. But I thought they would give us cakes. And when we got home, I could share these with you.

I don't know when I will get back. But when I do, we will go out to the woods to pick berries, visit Juju and her brother.

Here, there is time for nothing, only walking, walking, walking away.

Mama, I am heartbroken. I cried all day yesterday. I want to see you but this road they have taken leads us away from you. What shall I do? I could run away but these men are cruel and have guns. They will shoot me. Besides, the Arab man keeps me close to him, all the time.

Mama, what shall I do? Tell me. I shall die if I don't see you. I shall die.

There is only soft wind joining us now.

4. Bibi, Marching in a Hostile Land

It is already the second day. A whole day and night have passed since we crossed the river, bearing baskets of food for these travellers who turned out to be traitors.

What is happening? Where am I going? Whatever this is, it isn't real. It is a nightmare. When I wake up, it will all be gone. But is this a nightmare? No? Then what am I doing here?

All I can remember is walking. Walking, walking, walking. There's Maju, cousin to my husband, in front, guarded by a man with a gun.

Where are the others? I see a long line in front and I know there is a long line behind but I'm afraid to turn for fear of looking at another man with a gun.

Where are we going? How did I come here?

I remember. We crossed the river and handed them baskets. It was peaceful. Then a thunderstorm broke over our heads. Gunshots split the air. A man put his arms around me to drag me away. I pushed him but he was strong. I tried to squat but he pulled me up. My sweat smelled of fear. My chest hurt, my throat closed. No sound would come. Suddenly, a shriek came out of me and pierced the air. Everyone howled. But the men prodded us on with rifles and our crying became hopeless.

I want so much to talk to Maju. My mouth is so dry I cannot get her name past my tongue. I am a gazelle chased and caught with dry spit at the nostrils and none on my tongue. Do my eyes look startled and unseeing? Will they kill me?

I don't think Maju will talk to me. I want to ask her where they are taking us. Will they kill us? What do these men want with us anyway? The men with guns? They are cruel. The others hauling loads? They are savages. The short-bearded Arab?

My God, I clutch my breast, digging my nails into my skin.

He's got Oju, my sister's little girl . . . God, what is going to become of her? I haven't seen her since yesterday when she was with him. He seemed a kind man then, smiling at her. But surely he cannot care for her as he would his own daughter. That is impossible. And yet, Oju is just a little girl.

There will be wailing at my sister's house. Women will come to comfort her, wail with her. Men will stand outside, brooding, making plans to kill if it will bring back their women. The medicine man will use his powerful skills; pungent smoke from burnt white feathers will reach up to our ancestors. A goat will be killed to soothe the spirits. A black rooster, spouting blood from its cut neck, will plead for Oju's return and the burial of a dead dog will shut away evil and force the Arab to release her.

My sister will beat her chest. Oju is her favourite. She often helped pound corn, powder dried bananas into flour and tend goats with her younger brother. In another year's time when her blood flow begins, she will be given to a man for a herd of goats as bride price but not before her older sister. It will be an occasion of great joy, eating sweetened cakes, drinking *urwagwa*—banana beer—and dancing for days, often into the night.

If we keep trudging this way, we will never get home. Oju will be lost to her family and leave an emptiness as big as the sky. All my poor sister will have are memories that ended when Oju left to take cakes to the Arab.

Though my sister cannot see Oju walking, her feet sore from the stony ground and face swollen from crying, she can hear Oju's heartbeat with fear and longing, for these two are close.

But what is to become of Oju? Poor girl, barely fourteen, forced to walk with this man in a world she does not know. She is young and innocent. And without her mother. Does it mean I am now her mother? Yes, I am. I am. My ancestors, please listen to me. Your little child, not yet a woman, is in grave danger. She needs you; I need you.

I never imagined such misfortune would befall us. We heard these stories when strangers came and took you away, but it always happened to people we did not know. I cannot think of what will happen tomorrow. We may be dead. For Oju, it will be bewildering. If only I could protect her somehow.

My husband will not miss me. The past ten years we have been married did not yield a child. My family felt I let them down. After the big bride price my husband paid, it was shameful of me not to reward him with a son or even a daughter. I subjected myself to him all the time, to his slightest whim. I slept with him as often as I could. I tried but it didn't work. I cried often.

You cheat, you are no good. Where is my son? You want people to call me a crippled man?

His friends thought he lost his manhood; women blamed me and said my soil was arid, desolate, dead. His family shunned me, saying I ruined their son.

You are as good as a harlot, they whispered. Why don't you leave him so he can marry another woman who will give him a son?

I cringed every time they passed. But if I left him, where would I go? I did not know if another man would want me, a woman who cannot conceive a child. I would end up becoming what my husband's family said I already was, when I'm not. And what would I become if I gave myself to several men to keep myself together? Would that make me a *mchawi*?

My sister tried to take care of me. She took me to many *waganga.* I ate and drank every medicine they gave me. I rubbed my body vigourously with whatever they advised. I shaved my hair, walked naked in the woods. I cultivated friendships with mothers who had borne several children. I adjusted myself even more to him, the better to receive his seed. But to no good. My sister finally said, You leave your husband and come live with us. We will build you a hut.

Now, there is no need for it. I am not stumbling in a shallow pond anymore where I can pull myself out. I am in a fast-moving river without hope of being saved. I am heading to unknown waters where I shall drown. I will be battered against rocks. Tossed over rapids. I am not scrap. I am not deadwood.

I hear women in front saying we are slaves. Slaves, I think. Me, a slave. I never imagined such a thing. I was going to ask Maju more about slaves but dare not. She has shunned me. She would say, You barren woman, are you ignorant, too?

The thought of what will happen must be on everyone's mind. We will be sold, condemned to work. The younger ones kept for sleeping with the master. They talk of Oju as if I do not exist. Being young is in her favour. The Arab will keep her; she has many years of pleasure to give. When her time is ready, the first man to enter her will pay a lot to the one who owns her.

My sister will surely die if she hears of it. I need to do something for Oju. But what can I do? I am her mother now. I should talk to the Arab. But he does not speak my tongue. That important porter does. I will wait till we stop and approach him.

What do I tell the Arab after saying I am her mother . . . that she is my only child, that there is no one to care for her very ill father, so please send her home? What if he shakes his head? Then what? Maybe I should offer myself to him. *Aay!* Has the craziness of the mad hyena got into me? I don't know. I need to have a plan. I shall throw myself at his feet. And then . . . even if it is the worst thing . . . if I have to save Oju, if that is what he wants, how can I say no? I deny myself to him, I deny Oju her only chance . . . and how much

---

Mchawi. (Swahili) Witch

Waganga. (Swahili) Medicine men

worse could it be than the humiliation my husband has heaped upon me? I shall do it. I shall go see the Arab. I will get Oju out of his scheming clutches. My ancestors, I am ready.

Bwana Abdalla, the mother of this girl is here to see you.

What does she want?

Abdalla listened to Jumbe's translation of Bibi's distraught request.

No, I cannot turn this caravan around to deliver the girl to the village. She stays. And no, I don't want the mother; tell her I will take care of the girl.

5. Returning with Booty

The caravan returned to Unyanyembe on the sixth day after the capture of the Vinza women.

Abdalla settled what he owed for slaves with merchandise. It was a fair exchange. He did his utmost not to part with even a tithe of tusks and horns, as he greatly anticipated a profitable sale, large enough to get himself another wife.

Later that day, as Jumbe set out with porters and askaris to collect the slaves, he heard mournful wailing and high-pitched ululations in the distance. When he got closer, he recognised it as anguish, coming from wretched-looking men, women and children whose hope was in staying together, as close to each other as possible. Jumbe could not decipher the language or words but the agony was unmistakable. While some groaned as in the throes of death, others looked up to the sky, arms raised, desperately crying for help. Faces swollen, hands intertwined, bodies close, skin to skin, the moaning continued, a sustained dirge.

Soon, four, large towering men, immune to the crying, began the task of dividing the throng. As they tried to separate wives from husbands, sons from fathers, and sisters from brothers, mothers clasped their children, husbands would not let wives go. Clinging became their salvation, even for the minutest fragment of time. But the burly captors continued their task of division and separation; they swore, they pushed, they dragged slaves apart. Keening ripped the air. Shrieks arose akin to a pack of wounded animals. The earth quivered with their cries. When it was all over, a haunting quiet remained.

Jumbe had never been on a slaving expedition or seen slaves wrenched from each other, screaming in desperation. With the plaintive sounds still dinning in his ears, he stood rooted to the ground, grappling with the measure of their sorrow. It was without end, hopeless. His cheerfulness left him. His throat, his lungs, the progenitor of songs, lay inert. His ingrained determination to lead vanished. He doubted he could rouse the porters.

The caravan, currently exceeding 360 men, women, boys and one girl, set out at daybreak for the weary trek to Tanga. Weighed down with tusks and horns and a fresh supply of food, porters and askaris were jubilant and intoxicated by the presence of women.

The captives, burdened with heavy hearts, had lost their will to move. The male slaves were reined in with metal halters that yoked them in pairs, one behind the other, hands bound securely at the wrist. The women were unrestrained unless they attempted to get away. Abdalla kept the young girl by his side.

The first week was trying. It was difficult to get the slaves to pick up any speed. Jumbe could not sing anymore. The porters' patience became stretched, as did their nights. There was great unhappiness. Some men were sleeping with women by the first evening but there wasn't enough sweetness to be had without fighting amongst themselves. Abdalla had to jump into their many frays. He drew his dagger on a porter who threatened to kill another planning to take a woman for the second time. On another occasion, he pulled out his pistol, fired in the air.

I will kill any mother's son who dares to harm a woman on this caravan and throw his worthless carcass to wild dogs.

The week had hardly ended when slaves began to die. Two or three each day, then six, even seven. It began with the boys whose tiny testicles had been removed by an old bearded butcher. Their empty scrotums puffed with infection. They burned with fever and died in excruciating pain. Women pined away, ate nothing, gave up their spirit and never woke up. Jumbe was certain it was melancholy that killed them but Abdalla blamed the porters. Of the yoked males, those behind lead walkers could not protect their feet from thorns. Poison spread, tainting circulation, and they died frothing at the mouth.

Abdalla was afraid that in spite of all his attempts to protect the captives, he might arrive with little more than horns and tusks. His hopes began to fade. He groped for ways to prevent impending calamity and wondered if he could pick up some more slaves.

At sunrise, the caravan arrived at the edge of the forest. Abdalla's ears picked up women's voices, doing their washing by a running stream. Jumbe was set against taking any more slaves but that did not deter Abdalla. With help from the chief askari, he had the entourage let up, directing it towards the quiet stream. In the melee that followed, the women's cries went unheard, their desperate pleas unheeded. They simply became part of a line of people heading steadily away.

One day merged into another and each day brought them closer to the coast. Jumbe became progressively quieter. He led the caravan but did not exhort, did not sing. The loud laughter that usually boomed from him was infrequent. His broad smile, however, remained; he owed it to his porters who still looked to him for guidance. He kept a protective eye on Bibi. He could not do much for Oju, but was certain Abdalla would not touch her, at least not here.

For the first time, he observed the amorous advances of the men with distaste. A *Swahili* porter crouched noiselessly to get close to a woman lying on her side. In one swift move he lay behind her, put his hand on her waist, then between her legs. He rolled her over. She tensed, moaning softly. Another porter followed a woman going to the pond. As she bent, flexed at the hips to collect water with her cupped hands, his right arm snaked around her and his left securely covered her mouth as he dragged her into the nearby copse.

Jumbe could not alter the course of events. It had always been that way. He had promised porters exactly that on their way up. But the voices of screaming women haunted him.

On the sixtieth morning, the caravan smelled the sea. The salt tang born of the ocean filtering through thick mangrove swamp was unmistakable. Not even the dust that clogged their nostrils could keep it away. The wetness in the air soothed parched, callused skin. Except for the slaves, the mood was one of elation. The end was in sight. Tanga was not far away. For the captives, the journey would continue.

Abdalla and his patrons inspected the trophies—size of tusks, number of horns, sex of slaves—and were immensely pleased. Akidas bussed him, Indian merchants praised him. They supervised the loading of the dhow bound for Zanzibar with the *nakhoda*—captain—whose shrewd eyes ran over the collection of listless slaves, skipping the men, curiously looking over the boys, and lingering over the women. His gnarled hands twitched at anticipation of softness.

Abdalla relieved his longing for the fragrance of his wife whom he had fantasised over night after night. Exultant, Fatima gave all, letting herself be possessed. Abdalla, however, soon tired of her, became despondent, and began to look for new thrills.

Swahili. Bantu-speaking people of Zanzibar and adjacent coast

I have the means, so why not?

He approached his doting mother.

I have a request from your loving son. He desires for you to have a second daughter-in-law, someone with good flesh on her so she won't tire taking care of you.

Abdalla kept Oju for himself, entrusting her to his reliable friend, chief of the *Bondei,* for safekeeping until more practical arrangements could be made. His family would not accept her. She would be a kept woman, not a wife. At Jumbe's insistence, Abdalla let Bibi stay with her.

You have not been yourself these past few days.

Husbands dragged from wives, mothers from daughters. Heart-wrenching cries. I could not bear it.

But that is slaving. I don't do that. I simply buy and sell.

What about the Vinza slaves and the women by the stream?

Oh! You have to cheat sometimes to ensure profits. Otherwise, what's the use?

Jumbe went home to his wife, to the land by the big lake, happy he would not go again into the business of slaving. Tusks and horns, lion teeth and frankincense, yes. Slaves, no.

It was too much for him, the red dust, the keening.

Bondei. Tribe in the Usambara Mountains of Tanga region

2

NOW THE GERMANS

Magaya, the eighteen-year-old son of the Bondei chief, became smitten with Oju. She was only fourteen, but beautiful. The young man had not experienced the throbbing, tingling excitement of falling in love.

The chief suspected his son's mounting attraction for the girl and issued strict instructions he keep away from her. But this was impossible. She was on his mind all day; he dreamed of her in his sleep. Every time she came into his view, his eyes wandered longingly over her. He was devoured by desire . . . her eyes, always looking at something but seeing nothing, held him. She wept without tears; it broke his heart.

He wanted to comfort her, tell her he cared, that he would do his best to provide a loving home. He wished to be her parent, her sibling, her lover. Magaya knew he would not have his father's support and, in desperation, eloped with Oju to the coastal town of Pangani, thirty miles south, where his father's sister lived.

My aunt will understand me, help me, he assured himself repeatedly. He had stayed with her often; it was his second home and she was partial to him.

He taught Oju Swahili as well as customs of the Bondei. Sea and sandy beach were new to her. He was patient with everything, unusual for a lad of eighteen, but his heart dictated all he did. In time, he restored her spirits, her laughter, her sparkle. Her eyes looked for him; he became her world. They had a child, Olenzu, and Magaya's aunt wisely suggested it was an opportune time to return home. The gift of a grandson as a peace offering would be irresistible. Besides, a male child assured conduit to posterity. She was right. There were celebrations and ceremonies. Bibi was there to accept the bride price and all customs were honoured.

Oju was aware it was over two years since she first set eyes on this town, where her past had been forcibly torn, her future crushed, and providentially, she had been rescued by Magaya.

Magaya learned avidly from his father—his store of knowledge, his exercise of judgement. Narratives set his mind thinking, for inside the amusement of the tale was a lesson to be uncovered. He listened to accounts of embezzlement and witnessed his father delving into laws of inheritance and how these were invoked to remedy misappropriations; to justice meted to a man who slept with his wife's sister and to resolve the murder of a man stabbed by a drunken friend. He joined his father and elders in deliberating with neighbouring chieftains on how to deal with ruffians molesting women working in *shambas.* While he learned tribal laws and customs from his father, his mother and aunts tutored him on respect for the elderly, silence before strangers and courtesy to everyone.

The slave caravan of 1871 that brought Oju to Tanga was one of the last from the interior to the coast. For more than fifty years, the British had been demanding abolition of slavery, but it wasn't until 1873 that Sultan Seyyid Barghash bin Sa'īd of Zanzibar signed the Treaty for the Suppression of the Slave Trade. In 1876, all slave markets in East Africa closed.

Magaya was overjoyed by the turn of events for he could not banish from his mind the heartbreak Oju endured. Even now, five years later, her face, contorted with fear and grief, often appeared before him.

When Magaya became chief, he heard rumours about a *mgeni*—foreigner from across the seas—who was personally exhorting chiefs to sign away their lands in return for protection from his white nation. Magaya thought it strange that someone would want to rule another country and hoped the chiefs would not do anything foolish and agree to this unheard-of arrangement.

It was autumn of 1884. An ambitious adventurer, a German by the name of Carl Peters, set foot in Zanzibar, obsessed with the idea of a colony for the fatherland and dreams to rule Africa. Peters, who spent some time in London, was astounded by Britain's global power and imperialism and wished to emulate her exploits.

When the twenty-eight-year-old upstart came to Tanga, Chief Magaya prepared to meet him. Bwana Peters extolled the virtues of his kaiser and said if German rule were to be extended throughout the land, benefits would descend and prosperity and progress would follow. He praised Magaya's stature as leader, his wisdom, his concern for his people, and how, as their good chief, he would sign the proposed treaty. With that, Peters presented a parchment that said:

Shambas. (Swahili) Cultivated plots of ground, farms, or plantations

Kimeri Magaya, chief of the Bondei on the coast of Tanga, transfers the sole and exclusive rights of his territory to Dr. Carl Peters, representative of the Society for German Colonisation for the exclusive and universal utilisation of German colonisers . . . for all time.

Magaya did not know how to read but surmised what was in the parchment. His immediate reaction was one of loathing, though he repressed the feeling. Standing up to his full height, white cotton *kanzu* cascading to his sandaled feet, he looked Peters in the eye and said in a clear, firm voice:

We do not need rulers from across the sea. My people are content as they are.

Peters rose sharply. His hands shook and his eyes spat venom. Wiping his reddened face, he walked out without shaking hands.

I hope we never meet again. If we do, you will regret it.

Chief Magaya's response did not hold Peters back. He travelled inland, plying illiterate chiefs with liquor and their wives with trinkets, having them unwittingly cede their lands without realising what they were doing.

By the end of the year, Peters was able to obtain treaty rights giving him exclusive sovereignty over 2,500 square miles of the mainland. When he returned to Germany, Chancellor Otto Eduard Leopold von Bismarck ratified these treaties and, in February 1885, Kaiser Wilhelm officially proclaimed a German protectorate over the lands annexed by Peters. In this way, Tanganyika became a German colony—Deutsch-Ostafrika, German East Africa—and Tanga, a military post.

The German government placed Peters as director of German East Africa. Peters's rapacious appetite for brutality, bloodshed and barbarous punishments earned him the sobriquet *Mikono wa Damu*—Man with Blood on his Hands.

Bewildered by the sudden change, Magaya could not believe that Peters, a seeker of signatures to amass foreign land, was ruler of his country. There was little he could do but go along with the new rulers who had little empathy. An African could be conscripted at any time, without consent, to work twelve to sixteen hours on private plantations or town projects. He carried loads on his head an entire day for inadequate remuneration and insufficient food. If he complained or stayed away, he could be punished by flogging. Many died from overwork and excessive discipline, lack of nutrition and disease. After conferring

---

Kanzu. (Swahili) Long white cotton or linen robe worn by East African men with other chiefs, Magaya approached the German district commissioner to obtain redress but met with little success.

Never had Magaya known anything like this; an alien race promising protection, moving in and unleashing harsh, tyrannical domination. He was angry, frightened. There was widespread discontentment. His people, Arab traders and Indian businessmen, were outraged and forged an alliance to fight the intruders. Overnight, there was a spontaneous popular revolt. Bismarck took this as a personal affront, believing natives should be thankful for the patronage afforded them. In exasperation, he sent experienced soldier Hermann von Wissmann to quell the uprising. In 1891, after three years of intense fighting and much shedding of blood, German cruisers and superior firepower suppressed the rebellion, which led to the recapture of Tanga and the rest of the country.

The Germans did not attempt to understand the natives and made the grievous mistake of cruel subjugation. Severe and inflexible laws, meant more for beast than man, chafed the easygoing people. World opinion was swift—a scorching censure of the German colonial administration—which stung Bismarck. Peters was recalled, indicted and dismissed from service.

It took a while for Tanganyika to come around. While uprisings continued in the south, Tanga began to settle down. Once the Germans put away their whips and treated the Africans more benignly, they were compliant workers. Magaya and chiefs of *Segeju* and *Digo* tribes insisted on legislation to safeguard Africans from exploitation.

The hinterland behind Tanga was right for growing sisal, coffee, rubber, cotton; the higher ground for planting tea and, somewhere in between, cinchona for its quinine. The rulers, too, were ready to work with their hands, dirty their boots and sweat in the heat, but required their beer at the end of the day.

Commerce and growth began to flourish and expand. Tanga's small port expanded to accommodate German steamships and export goods. The Usambarabahn line was laid, creeping north like a snake to Moshi. Then came roads, buildings, bridges, a hospital and the first school. In time, the sleepy fishing village acquired an urban shape.

Magaya's strapping fourteen-year-old son attended the new school. Standards for education were unmatched with exceptional teachers and curricula. Discipline was strict and corporal punishment common. Shoddy

---

Segeju. Tribe from Mkinga District, Tanga region, Tanganyika

Digo. Bantu tribe living in southern Kenya and northern Tanganyika along the coastal strip students were caned, insubordinates kept in chains and those who were lazy went without dinner. Parents were elated; where else could you get an education like that?

During this period of prosperity, Magaya's family provided him with a haven, a source of great joy. Oju became a contented mother with three more children. Bibi lived with them and she and Oju spent many lively hours reminiscing about their home in Vinza. The news they craved from the village never came. Magaya was grateful the aspect of Oju's youth that he had not been a part of was brought to life by Bibi. He did not know what he would have done without her.

While Magaya remained intensely resentful of the Germans, he gradually softened his stand and came to accept their presence as inevitable. There was nothing he could do but he remained perplexed and wrestled with many recurring questions.

How did this come about? Could it have been avoided? Was it a good thing for us?

He had no doubt putting an end to slavery was morally upstanding. But another form of enslavement immediately followed. What the Germans were doing was not much different from what had been done to slaves.

Could slavery in any form be beneficial—being kidnapped and sold to a life of bondage or, alternatively, a foreign power colonising your country and demanding to be served?

The answer was a most definite no.

Magaya grew melancholy. He wondered if there was anything he could do as an emasculated leader. It dawned on him he could not, for he himself had been enslaved.

3

A SHORT-LIVED BLISS

Life on the coast of Tanga had a sweet languorousness until the arrival of Europeans at the end of the nineteenth century. Two worlds collided and change came abruptly. However, a compromise of sorts evolved between ruler and ruled whose lives, separated by a palpable distance, came together when the African worked for the European.

Even as Magaya and his allies mourned their country's loss to white intruders, the Germans, following initial mistakes, gained knowledge necessary to adjust to the needs of natives. They were firm without being cruel and concerned rather than callous. In time, the indigenes came to see advantages accrued from this shifting relationship: opening of schools; a remarkable collection of storied buildings replacing the marketplace; the ingenuity of the iron snake that slid on rails taking people and goods across distances; and the marvel of cables coming off cranes by the wharf doing work no man could.

With the unfolding of the twentieth century, the Germans needing merchants, masons, mechanics and junior personnel brought in two communities of people to the country—Indians from India, a British colony, and in smaller numbers Goans from Goa, a Portuguese possession on the west coast of India. These groups, too, remained insulated from the European and African.

Leandro Paulo De Souza was twenty-eight years old when he sailed to Tanga in 1911 from his ancestral home–Casa Camoth–in the sleepy village of Parra, Goa. The cultivation of rice, coconuts and cashew nuts from inherited lands was not enough to sustain the family, and young men, to the dismay of their mothers, found it necessary to leave home in search of work in distant Macao, Hong Kong, or East Africa. Leandro crossed the wide ocean to a world he knew little about because of the prospect of getting a job with help from cousins in Tanga. Brothers Leopoldo left for Hong Kong and Domingos joined Leandro later.

Tanga, after many uprisings, was looking forward to a period of calm. The Germans zealously established trade between the new colony and the fatherland. Entrepreneurs set up a business establishment, the Usagara

Company Limited, named after a small village on the Mukondokwa River. It was the very village where German coloniser Carl Peters began his single-minded drive in 1884, collecting signatures from unsuspecting African chiefs to cede their land. Usagara, the largest venture in town, was in the business of importing and exporting. A site of ceaseless activity, German ships transported merchandise from safety pins to machinery, cutlery to cameras, and farm tools to lenses while the company exported such staples as sisal fiber, tea leaves, cinchona bark and coffee.

Leandro recently began working at Usagara, having been taken on within a month of arrival. Section Manager Paul Krause, surprisingly active in spite of a large beer belly, was kindly disposed towards newcomers. On that morning, there was more than the usual flurry of energy, for a cargo ship from Hamburg was due the next day.

Mr. Souza, can you look into whether tea thermometers are in the consignment? Amani Tea Estates needs them *sasa hivi*—right away. They are in a hurry to start production of black tea. Oh, another thing—Kurt Staedtler is getting married. You know Staedtler, yes? Chief accountant, yes? We plan to give him Dresden china at his wedding. Can you check if it is in? *Danke*—Thank you.

Mr. Krause liked Leandro's enterprising nature, diligent effort, neat appearance and the fact he was also extremely good at figures. Leandro did enjoy his work, never leaving a day's assignment unfinished. Tall and lanky, he walked with a slight slouch, giving the impression he was not in a hurry. His dependability appealed to the Germans and his keenness to learn their language found favour. Mr. Krause, in his normal stance, fingers hooked around suspenders, suggested Leandro get together with Olenzu, Chief Magaya's eldest son, who spoke fluent German.

Olenzu studied at the German school and became a teacher but was persuaded to join Usagara as a liaison to his people. He was thirty-eight, married and ten years senior to Leandro.

A week of continuous action ensued after the arrival of the German ship. The consignment was unusually large, requiring it be entered in ledgers, precisely stored, correctly priced and prepared for dispatch or sale. Thermometers had been sent to Amani Tea Estates and Dresden china located and carefully kept aside, ready for Staedtler's wedding.

As the workload was winding down, Olenzu came by Leandro's desk.

So you want to polish your German, *ja*, Bwana Souza?

Ja.

Then we shall meet often.

If you did not see Olenzu, you could not tell the German was spoken by a Bondei, except it was an octave lower and followed by an infectious chuckle. He was as tall as Leandro with a firm handshake and wore a white cotton kanzu beneath a grey jacket.

Had it not been for Olenzu, Leandro's relationship with Africans would have been perfunctory. Leandro found him warm and gracious, fond of people and eager to know his neighbours and their customs. They became friends and traded learning and traditions.

Olenzu lived with his wife and children in the African section on the south side. His home was neat and comfortable with a *makuti* roof of plaited dried coconut palm leaves and an all-round *baraza.* Leandro shared a house on the west side with two unmarried Goan émigrés. It was a modest home with cement floors, finished walls, wide verandah and corrugated tin roof. The men shared expenses and took turns preparing meals.

Leandro's cooking was a strikingly novel experience for Olenzu who had eaten rice but not curries. He was intrigued by the mixture of spices that, added to chillies, made a variety of different curries for fish and meat. Scraped coconut and its milk added body to the *masala* and toned down its piquancy. He found them pungent but in time learned to relish them.

Olenzu's wife introduced Leandro to tribal food such as *ugali*—a semisolid porridge of maize flour cooked to a soft consistency and served with a meat sauce; *samaki*—freshly caught fish—steamed whole; and *kashata*—a sugary snack with peanuts or grated coconut. Leandro tasted *pombe*—a sourish beer made from malted millet—and strong *tembo*—wine from fermented palm sap. He was captivated by African drums and found when rhythm rolled off the drums, feet leaped to keep time, bodies became lithe and moved in unison, stopping only when the drums ceased. He understood why *ngoma*—a voluptuous undulating dance—started at sunset on Saturday and didn't end till sunrise; it was the hypnotic beat that beckoned the natives.

In two weeks, my daughter is getting married at my father's home. Please come.

Leandro was excited; this was his first local wedding.

Magaya's house was close to the sea. Tall, graceful coconut trees grew all around but their soft swishing did not keep the steady sound of the sea breakers

---

Baraza. (Swahili) Verandah

Masala. (Hindi) Combination of spices ground into a paste or powder for use in Indian cooking away. As Leandro neared, he heard the haunting tune of the *zomari* being played by men in long robes. Women, veiled in *buibui,* chanting, clapping, swaying, stopped at the house and sought out the young, radiant bride. They showered her short-braided hair with jasmine blossoms, then sprayed her with perfume.

Karibu rafiki yangu—Welcome, my friend. I was hoping you would come. You have made us happy.

I would not have missed your daughter's wedding. I am honoured to be here.

From a distance came the sound of music: faint drums, rattles, tambourines, singing. The beat became a throb as a throng of men surrounding the groom approached. Music-makers handed the groom a new gourd with beer. Guests clapped wildly as he took the first sip. The earth pulsed with rhythm. Drums, primeval, mysterious, dramatic, drew guests into movement, their motion flowing, animated. Music, intense, persistent; dancing, wild, frenzied. Cadenced pelvic rolls, shudder of chests, random shrieks of joy. Round and round, forward, back, together, apart. His feet keeping time, Leandro was mesmerised by the tempo, the explosiveness, the repetition. Suddenly, he felt a hand on his shoulder. It was Olenzu.

Come, meet my mother.

Inside the coolness of the house, Oju was seated on a low divan. She beckoned Leandro.

I Mama Oju. Karibu. Olenzu tell me about you. A ship brought you here over the waters. I also come from far away. As far as your legs carry you.

A wistful look crept into her eyes. She grew quiet for some time, then took Leandro's hand.

It was a long time ago. Even though I try to remove it from my mind, it remains as strong today as yesterday. An Arab slaver snatched me, my auntie Bibi and other women from my village. I was a young girl who had never been away from home. But here we were, forced to leave everything we had known, under the eyes of guns and the Arab, who would not let me out of his sight.

She tensed, tightening her grip on Leandro.

We were so afraid, our bodies would not move. They treat us like animals. All I could do was cry and call out to Mama to save me. I did not know what

---

Zomari. (Swahili) Woodwind instrument

Buibui. (Swahili) Billowing black ankle-length gown with head covering worn by Muslim women, on the East African coast the Arab would do to me. After two months of being on our poor feet, we reach Tanga. It was here Olenzu's father miraculously saved me.

Leandro was aghast. He had heard about slaves but had never met one personally.

Have you been back?

In my mind many, many times. On foot, no.

Have you any news from home?

There is nobody to bring news. I have only memories.

Leandro thought how much better off he was, able to receive letters from home even though it took six or more weeks, and to look forward to returning to his family one day. He felt a strong compassion for Mama Oju.

God will bless you.

He already has. This is my world now. It will be yours too.

4

WAR, AND THEN THE BRITISH

In 1914, Tanga and the rest of German East Africa was settling down to the routine of everyday life; children in school, women busy planting in shambas and men gainfully employed. Germans seemed part of the country now and locals close to accepting a ruling tribe of lighter colour. Expectations ran high the future would hold better days.

Africans could not have known their fate would be tied to Europe's; that a conflagration building overseas would spill over into their land, distant though it was, and when done, permanently alter their lives by forces beyond their control.

There was no radio or newspaper to report what was developing abroad. On the twenty-eighth of June 1914, Archduke Franz Ferdinand Carl Ludwig Joseph Maria, heir to the throne of the Austro-Hungarian empire, and wife, Sophie Maria Josephine Albina, riding in a royal motorcade through the streets of Sarajevo, Bosnia, were fatally shot by a young Serbian nationalist, Gavrilo Princip, who resented Serbia's annexation by Austria. The assassination set off a chain of condemnations and strife. Germany, ally of Austria-Hungary, sent Serbia an ultimatum seeking immediate redress. Russia mobilised to protect Serbia, which drove Germany to declare war on Russia on the first of August and, two days later, on France. Great Britain was drawn into the uneasy dispute after Germany invaded Belgium while marching to France. Britain, bound by treaty to protect Belgium, declared war on Germany on the fourth of August. Thus, the fury of World War I was unleashed in Europe.

Africa was immediately thrust into the conflict because the warring nations possessed significant colonial territories. Two main adversaries, Germany, in possession of Deutsch-Ostafrika (Tanganyika, Burundi, Rwanda), and Britain, with Buganda (Uganda) and British East Africa Protectorate (Kenya), were neighbours sharing a common border along the Great Lakes region.

From the outset, Britain's main objective was to acquire German East Africa. They chose Tanga, the second most important town with its large, busy port and terminus of the Usambara Railway, as a strategic entry point. Because Britain had very few troops on the continent, they planned more recruits from India and promoted Brigadier General Arthur Edward Aitken, leader of Poona Infantry in India, to the rank of major general. He was given command of the Indian Expeditionary Force B with orders "to bring the whole of German East Africa under British authority."

Aitken, with thirty-five years' experience but none in combat, felt certain victory would be his and assumed the assignment was not much different from skirmishes England was continuously involved in across its vast empire. His blustery overconfidence arose from contempt for the enemy and conviction his troops would sweep away "racial inferiors."

My men will make short work of a lot of niggers.

On the sixteenth of October, Major General Aitken set out from Bombay on the SS *Karmala* with a convoy of forty-five ships, fourteen troop transports and some eight thousand Indian and British soldiers. The voyage across the Indian Ocean was horrific. Indian sepoys packed in overcrowded, infernally hot transport ships got seasick and suffered from diarrhoea and malnutrition. Morale was low and the men, weak and dispirited.

After two weeks at sea, the convoy reached Mombasa, a British East African port north of Tanga. Aitken met with the Admiralty to finalise plans and though he had scant information, chose not to spend time learning about the enemy or terrain. When advised to rest his exhausted soldiers, Aitken decided this was an "unnecessary fuss," thus losing the opportunity for his men to recoup and be ready for battle. He also refused loan of Kenyan askaris familiar with the rough topography, despite their knowing about the excellence of the Schutztruppe, the German colonial army.

The German is worse than we are, his troops are ill-trained, ours are magnificent, and bush or no bush, I mean to thrash the Germans before Christmas.

The convoy sailed for Tanga on the night of the first of November. Aitken ordered the landing of troops and supplies and, by the evening of the third, disembarked at Ras Kazone Beach unopposed. Tanga could have been taken that night without a single shot fired if Aitken had mounted an attack, but he had not sent reconnoitering patrols and missed a golden opportunity when he opted to wait until daylight. This was all the time the Germans needed.

General Paul Emil von Lettow-Vorbeck, a seasoned commander trained at leading military schools in Germany, had served in more places than any other officer of his rank. A rare combination of gentleman and soldier, he insisted on his men giving their best, recognising that all were not equally gifted. The askaris, in return, gave unquestioned loyalty because Lettow-Vorbeck sincerely believed in the ability of the person rather than the colour he carried, in a land where he was part of the ruling elite.

Lettow-Vorbeck resolved to defend Tanga. He arrived from Moshi by rail at three o'clock on the morning of the fourth with his Schutztruppe of one thousand men and then set off on bicycle with two officers to check the goings-on at the harbour. Picking their way down to the beach in the moonlight, they saw British troops going ashore with no attempt at covertness. Alerted to their arrival, the intended assault lacked an element of surprise and when Aitken launched his attack at noon, Lettow-Vorbeck was ready.

With no knowledge of the area, Aitken's men followed the shoreline, wading through mangrove swamps. Lying in wait on the outskirts, German forces quickly attacked. Many British troops bolted in confusion but an equal number went down, unaware of what was happening. A day later, Aitken's best regiments entered Tanga, captured the customs house and hospital and hoisted the Union Jack. Elsewhere, Indian soldiers, caught in dense patches of rough bush, encountered accurate, unremitting and deadly fire from German machine guns. These men, primarily new recruits, were badly trained with no battle or bush warfare experience and poorly equipped with obsolete rifles. They fought valiantly but, in the absence of a coherent plan, became disoriented and hopelessly lost. Askaris then fired into hives hanging from baobab trees, agitating swarms of angry bees who descended, viciously stinging soldiers. Panic set in as they fled, dragging themselves to the beach by nightfall.

Major General Aitken, on the bridge of the SS *Karmala*, watched the sorry spectacle unfold. He could hardly believe what he was seeing: his men falling back, the battle approaching his ship. It was difficult to accept and he speculated regrouping and attempting another attack by moonlight, but continuous reports of the day's disasters overwhelmed him. Wearied beyond measure and sickened by the outcome, Aitken simply wished to get away.

Lettow-Vorbeck, on the other hand, was keen to keep going and push the British into the sea. His men were showing signs of exhaustion, and for reasons of safety, he pulled his troops. It was eerily quiet as night descended. This was the second time Aitken could have seized Tanga, if only he had attempted. But he was whipped.

On the fifth of November, Captain Richard Meinertzhagen, carrying a white flag, requested the fighting be stopped. The Battle of Tanga, the first major battle of World War I in Africa, was a crushing blow to Britain and it was several months before the government released news of the defeat. Casualties included nearly a thousand men killed or wounded.

In May 1916, a year and a half after Lettow-Vorbeck's spectacular victory, war was still raging in Europe, and Britain began its second advance into German East Africa. Forces led by General Jan Christiaan Smuts decided to invade the country from multiple points.

Leandro was immersed in work and life was acquiring a pattern he came to enjoy. His German was steadily improving and his friendship with Olenzu thriving. By late June, Mr. Krause warned staff at Usagara to be prepared for another British invasion.

You know, Mr. Souza, I fear trouble. We expect the enemy to attack us from the sea. Maybe in a week's time, maybe sooner. So I tell you, play safe and move your family out. You yourself leave in the afternoon and come back to work in the morning. Maybe I go too, *ja*?

Tanga emptied itself after the day's obligatory work was done. Harried residents left, some on bicycles, but most on foot. With each passing day, the inevitability of the attack bore down with great certainty, forcing residents to leave homes, markets, shops and offices. Olenzu and Leandro cycled two hours on rough roads to Muheza, a village twenty-six miles west. Uncertainty ripped through the even tenor of their day-to-day lives.

If it were not for the war, this might be an enjoyable outing. So many of us have to run away. How many people do you think live here?

I would say about one hundred thousand, including Europeans, Arabs, Indians and Goans.

That's a lot. Indians have the biggest problem leaving because they have shops and live above them. Arabs less so. Tell me, are Goans a separate tribe of Indians?

You could say so. We were conquered four centuries ago by the Portuguese on their way to the Far East for spices and silks. They converted some of us to Christianity and we adopted many of their customs.

What about the British?

They have been in India for a hundred years but didn't change people's religion or customs. India is too large for that. They are simplifying the country, trying to give them one language, one government.

I wonder how it is going to be for us? The only rulers I've known are the Germans. I don't want anyone else.

They are all rulers and some are better than others. The Germans are a fair people. From what I've heard, the British keep a distance from their subjects.

At break of dawn on the third of July, continuous salvos of deafening gunfire heralded the presence of three warships outside Tanga's harbour. Upon hearing the roaring guns, Leandro and Olenzu promptly pedaled to Muheza as fast as possible. They attempted returning over the next few days but were prevented by thunderous volleys from the artillery.

Steady bombing persisted until the seventh of July. Unexpectedly calm, a force of five hundred troops from Fifth Indian Light Infantry cautiously crept into town, finding it empty. They were suspicious the evacuation was a ruse, that Lettow-Vorbeck would descend from an unknown quarter, attack them where they were most vulnerable. So they remained hidden, ready to repulse any counterattack, and sent spies in every direction to detect German contingents. The Germans had evacuated Tanga and the British failed to get Lettow-Vorbeck.

Tanga was captured without a fight, without a single casualty. It was now in British hands. Once they cleared a fifty-mile radius and posted scouts, soldiers were commissioned to reassure local inhabitants that no harm would come to them, that they should register themselves at the newly established town commandant's office and hand over all weapons.

The next day, Leandro and Olenzu strained to listen for the bombardment with every mile they covered. There were no guns to be heard. Everything was quiet and ominous. Bodies bathed in sweat, feet tired from pedaling, their anxiety grew. The closer they got, the tenser they became. They looked at each other. Should they proceed? Would they have to face the British, or would they be among their own? Leandro and Olenzu soon found out. Destruction was restricted mainly to the town; they were relieved to see their homes safe.

Leandro's connections with everyone and everything he had known were severed. Usagara was closed and staff placed under temporary arrest. He was not allowed to meet Mr. Krause or others at the firm. With them went all his years in Africa. The town was at a standstill, the marketplace deserted, shops shut. Vendors hawking daily necessities by his house—fish, chicken, eggs, bread—had disappeared. Trains ceased running. Communication with the outside world was cut off. There was no mail from home, no news to sustain him. The port was silent.

With the Germans out of the way, the future was a blank. Would German rule be restored? When would the war end? What would become of their jobs, their contracts, the leave they had accumulated? When would life revert to normal? It was an unsettling time.

Leandro was given leave to return home, overdue as it was by two years. World War I ended on the eleventh of November, 1918. He left for Goa the following day.

5

SUDDENLY A BRIDE

Although the journey ahead was long and arduous, Leandro was eager to return to Goa. It was November, season of short rains, time of *Kaskazi*—southerly monsoon winds—that made sailing north difficult. Leandro boarded a dhow to Mombasa. The turbulent waters mandated a sturdy boat, the contrary winds an experienced crew with more than a modicum of good luck. The drenched dhow ploughed its way close to the coastline, taking a full day to reach Mombasa.

Leandro stood with his few belongings a short distance off the quay where the passenger ship SS *State of Bombay* was berthed; he watched it bob in the choppy sea. The voyage stretched across the vast expanse of the Indian Ocean in an easterly direction. It took twelve days to reach the port of Mormugão, a natural harbour on the southern coast of Goa. He then travelled twenty-five miles along small inland channels in a canoe paddled by two boatmen to Betim across from the capital, Pangim. There, a *boilanchi gaddi*—two-wheeled carriage pulled by oxen—brought him to Parra.

Home at last! His mother, Maria Magdalena, and two sisters, Terezinha Margarida and Assuciana Carmelian, ran out to greet him. They held him in a long embrace and wept.

My son is back! Our brother is back!

They climbed the broad steps up to the porch. His uncles, aunts and cousins poured out of Casa Camoth, the large ancestral house. No one could believe he had been gone seven years! Neighbours came, followed by village folk. He should have been exhausted from the long, rough journey but was not. He laughed, he cried, he was happy to be home and regaled them with anecdotes of the passage and of life in Africa. Family and friends insisted he eat and drink and toasted his return. His mother looked at him, shut her eyes briefly, and remembered to thank God.

It took a few days to come down to earth. He felt tranquil sipping coffee and watching the early-morning mist lift slowly with the rising sun. The delicate orange-pink *abolim* spoke of love and his thoughts wandered to the neighbour's daughter, Anna, who had blossomed into a lovely lady. In Tanga, there were no suitable unmarried women. It was a place men went to earn a living.

His mother never tired of asking about Africa and how he fended for himself. One day, she said, It is time you got married.

I don't know anyone here.

Anna's image flashed through his mind.

I shall find you a good girl, one you will like. I have already received many proposals for you.

Leandro blushed. The quest for a wife would have been more acceptable if initiated by a male relative. But his father, Cosme Damião, had long since died and his mother was closest to him.

Everyone wants you. Some are offering big dowries. You are an eligible man.

Marriages among Indians are exclusive affairs marked by age-old Hindu rituals that formalised unions between those of the same caste. Goan Catholics, despite colonial Portuguese influence, retained the Hindu caste system of their ancestors. This practice made for peace of mind. No rules were broken, no customs transgressed, all deities appeased, and all relatives kept content. Few among those getting married select their own spouses; they are picked by their parents. In arranged marriages, caste plays an important role, and families make sure betrothed couples marry in their caste and religion.

Maria Magdalena had someone in mind, suggested by her brother Michael Santa Maria. The girl was from Camurlim village, from a household well known to his uncle. She was an only daughter, just eighteen, whose father died before she was born. It had fallen to her mother, Cândida, to bring her up. Life was difficult, but family assets of rice fields and produce, and three sons—Jorge, Fortunato and Eugênio—working abroad, helped. The time had come to get her daughter married. It was a heavy responsibility, even though she had jewellery and money saved towards the dowry.

The girl was well mannered and fair complexioned, a colour universally desired by relatives of young men looking for women to marry. Brought up with little male influence, she was quiet, almost shy. Laughter did not come easily, yet her face could light up with a sudden smile. Of gentle disposition, modesty came naturally.

Abolim. (Konkani) Firecracker flower, also known by its scientific name *Crossandra infundibuliformis*

Her given name was Theodolinda. Since the shortened version Theo sounded too masculine, the family settled on Theodolin.

One evening at the dinner table, her mother said softly, There is a proposal for you—a bachelor from Africa who is here for three months. He is from a good family. Same caste as us, *Kshatriya*.

I don't know, Mai.

Theodolin knew marriage was initiated through the formal process of matchmaking. At her age, she experienced stirrings of emotions deep within, of love and passion that lay dormant. It was inevitable one day she would be a wife and mother.

Cândida did not press further, hoping for the best outcome and praying God would take care of it. If nuptials were delayed, the likelihood of getting a good husband would lessen as her daughter aged. However, she didn't want her to marry just anybody. Once married and gone, it would be lonely in the big house, but still preferable to watching Theodolin's prospects diminish by the year. Cândida started a novena to Our Lady of Perpetual Succour.

Mai's words slowly sinking in, Theodolin became very anxious. She had not thought much of settling down, but the issue was imminent and being away from Mai saddened her.

The next day, Cândida gently brought up the subject again.

They are good people. Dowry isn't important to the young man and we don't have much. Think about it.

Theodolin lay wide awake that night, tossing and turning. She was uncertain about this man, never having seen him and not knowing what he was like. And Africa was so far away! To say *yes* opened possibilities; *no* denied them. There may be no other offers or men not quite as desirable. Mai was not coercing her but eventually would expect the answer to be *yes*, for she was aware that girls like herself, once they came of age, were given away in marriage.

Theodolin and Cândida were invited to Sunday afternoon tea at Leandro's uncle's house in Maina, Siolim. Mother and daughter rode in a private gaddi that usually accommodated four people. The carriage, its square wooden frame colourfully painted orange-yellow with gold edging around the windows, jogged along the crest of the hill before descending into the valley where the village nestled. Cândida placed a reassuring hand on Theodolin's knee.

Kshatriya. (Sanskrit) Second of the four Hindu castes, the warrior caste; the traditional function of the Kshatriya is to protect society by fighting in wartime and governing in peacetime

I wish your papa were here. I'm sure he is keeping an eye on us . . . on you.

As they neared Maina, Theodolin, heart beating wildly, palms clammy, began to perspire and her eyes brimmed with tears.

I'm no good, Mai. Take me back. Where is he?

Who?

Papa. He should have been here today. I need him.

Cândida put her arms around Theodolin and let her cry until the tears stopped, then got a fresh handkerchief from her black handbag.

Here, wipe your face. Stop crying. Remember, you are Assiano's daughter.

Leandro, Maria Magdalena and Uncle Michael were seated in the *sala*—living room. Before Michael welcomed them and commenced introductions, Theodolin's eyes nervously swept from son to mother, back to son, resting there awhile. *Not bad looking, neatly dressed in his Sunday best!* She was relieved.

Leandro was impressed. Theodolin was comely and unassuming. Her complexion appealed to him. He noticed she seemed lost on occasion and sensed it was a difficult choice to leave home. His heart went out to her.

Michael suggested the couple spend some time on the verandah getting to know one another while the elders discussed matters of family, compatibility, dowry and possible wedding dates. Theodolin felt awkward. He was thirty-six, older than expected. Twice her age. Eighteen years her senior! They were only together because someone *arranged* it. He was tense, a feeling she shared. Neither expected love at first sight and would soon find out if they were suited.

Leandro set out to tell her stories of Africa: when he got there, his job, his friends, how the war affected Tanga, what he was returning to. She listened intently. He fervently hoped she would accept his proposal, as he did not want to go through the formality of meeting other prospective women.

Over the next two days, Theodolin relived that evening—his tone, expressions, silences, from the time they were introduced to the time they bid each other goodbye. She remembered his soft-spoken voice, gestures, considerate manner. She recalled when they exchanged glances for the first time. His friendly eyes were a chestnut brown. His age didn't matter much. Africa disturbed her more. She'd rather remain in Goa. If he were the man with whom she was destined to spend the rest of her life, how could she be certain he would love her? There was a good chance he might, for the beginning was promising and that was all she had for now.

She knew her answer was *yes. Kazarachem utor zalem*—a verbal commitment was made. *Mudi zali*—they got engaged.

The wedding, by mutual agreement, was set for Monday, the ninth of December. Preparations moved quickly. Banns were read at church, invitations printed, and the village goldsmith summoned. No marriage was complete without the forging of exquisite twenty-two-karat gold to adorn the bride.

Sonu Lotlikar took off his well-worn *topi* and old jacket and sat down, settling his white *dhoti* around his legs.

Porab ditan—I offer you felicitations. Our lovely Theodolin-*bai* goes to a good house. Long lineage. Family once owned a lot of land. Their goldsmith, my brother-in-law. He says *nouro* very nice. I pray for good health and many children. Where is Theodolin-bai? Let's see what she likes.

With suggestions from Theodolin, Sonu drew several intricate jewellery patterns on flimsy pink paper as a guide to creating her bridal ornaments. For the engagement, a fine set of four bangles for her and two rings for the groom. For the wedding, a heavy necklace set with oval pendant, earrings to match and six thick bangles. The trousseau was next. Three tailors, in the sala for four full days, were busy sewing clothes, including the wedding dress, a rose-coloured dress for the *muino* and light cotton dresses for Africa.

Cândida began immediate preparations to deliver large quantities of *vojem* as tokens of appreciation. Balancing large woven baskets of sweetmeats on their heads, women from the *vaddo* distributed the formal gift to all the groom's relatives. Vojem included large plantains, jackfruit, coconuts and *bol*—a sweet, brown flatbread of semolina, shredded coconut and palm jaggery, especially prepared for this happy occasion.

Mai requested Theodolin visit neighbours for the accustomed prenuptial *bessaum;* it would provide a final opportunity for her to see each one personally.

Topi. (Hindi) Lightweight cap worn in tropical countries for protection from the sun

Dhoti. (Hindi) Loose piece of clothing worn by Hindu men, wrapped around the lower half of the body and tied around the waist

Bai. (Konkani) Polite form of address for a woman

Nouro. (Konkani) Bridegroom

Muino. (Konkani) Return of bridal couple to the bride's house for her relatives to welcome the groom into the extended family

Vojem. (Konkani) Basketful of Goan sweets distributed by the bride's family to relatives and neighbours of the groom

Vaddo. (Konkani) Subdivision within a village in Goa

Bessaum. (Konkani) Blessing

Wearing a soft pink dress, *chuddo*—green and yellow glass bangles—on both arms from elbow to wrist, the bride-to-be walked to each house beneath the shade of a large red umbrella carried by a *sotrekarn* to protect her from the sun. They blessed her and quietly slipped a gift of money or small gold trinket.

Ever since the subject of marriage was brought up, Theodolin had not been able to think clearly. There was always something to plan, something to do. From the start, she was the centre of attention. It worried her immensely she might make a mistake, say the wrong thing, wear the wrong dress, forget to recognise a face, shake a hand, thank a person. If only she had additional time at her disposal, if only she were not so pressed, if only she could see Leandro more often. It was a dizzying period with little time to dwell on apprehensions.

Mudi—engagement ceremony—was a week before the wedding. When Leandro slipped the ring on her finger, she noticed his hand tremble, beads of sweat on his face. The moment had the opposite effect on her: it calmed her down. She felt optimistic for what lay ahead.

I think he will understand if I make mistakes. I like this man, she mused and smiled. Grinning affectionately, he took her hand.

On their way home, Mai remarked, Leandro is very considerate. He made certain somebody took care of me all the time. He was always attentive to his mai and his sisters. Did you see that? Your papa would have liked him.

Theodolin smiled, less trepidatious in the comfortable darkness of the gaddi as it jogged in the dim light of a single kerosene lamp, wheels creaking, cowbells jingling. She leaned back, relaxed, and dozed off to the sound of hoofs pounding rhythmically on the stony road, waking when the carriage stopped at her house, marking the end of an overwhelming day.

They were married at ten o'clock at Santa Ana *Igreja* in Parra. The 230-year-old baroque church, a beautiful white landmark, sat between rolling green hills and terraced rice fields. On that cool morning, while the nuptial Mass was being

---

Chuddo. (Konkani) Special ceremony where the *kakonkar* (bangle-seller) comes to the house and fits bangles on the hand of the flower-bedecked bride in the presence of other women. The bangles are to be worn in the following order: *folli* (green background with yellow lines), green, red, yellow, folli, and green, red, yellow. Bangles should not be broken, and as such, the bride is not expected to do any work, lest a bangle breaks and cast evil on the betrothed. (Source: www.goanwedding.com)

Sotrekarn. (Konkani) Woman who carries a red velvet umbrella at weddings, religious ceremonies, processions and receptions of dignitaries

Igreja. (Portuguese) Church

recited, the sound of 'Ave Maria' sung at communion amidst a multitude of violin strings, rose on the fragrance of incense towards the high ceiling adorned with paintings of Christ from the time of nativity to his death and resurrection

The *vor*—reception—was in a specially erected *mattou* on the grounds of the groom's house, with waxed bamboo matting for the floor and plaited coconut leaves for the roof. It was a time-honoured occasion with music and dancing, spirits and food aplenty. *Cervejo, tinto,* cognac, scotch. Bowls of *caldo*—chicken broth with crushed cream cracker biscuits and a black olive. The customary toast to the bride, groom and their families given, trays of finger foods were passed around—petite sardines on deep-fried rectangles of bread; dainty sandwiches of coriander, coconut, and green chilli chutney; and *forminhas*—little cups of chopped sardines mixed with mayonnaise, topped with chopped beetroot, green peas, and carrots. The banquet continued—*ishtu*—a mixed meat stew of pork, beef, chicken, cubed potatoes, tomatoes and elbow macaroni—and *pulao*—spice-infused rice with saffron threads. The sumptuous feast ended with the bridal couple cutting the traditional wedding cake—a rich fruitcake covered with a layer of soft marzipan paste and royal white icing.

Old, old *Konkani* songs, sung only at weddings, provided entertainment. One song after another. Of love, marriage, joy and sorrow. The groom joined in, surprising his bride at how lustily he sang. She did not sing but listened to the words of the ballads.

> *Tollem sukolem*—The pond has gone dry
> *Bhokem mhojem, babuddem rê zalem*—And my stork is now lonely
> *Tollem suktokoch*—After the pond dries
> *Bokheak mhojea, mannik melltolem*—My stork will find a gem
> *Mannik melltokoch*—When she finds a gem
> *Bokhem mhojem, girest zatolem*—My stork will become rich
> *Girest zatokoch*—When she becomes rich
> *Bokhem mhojem, Kazar zatolem*—My stork will get married
> *Kazar zatokoch*—When she gets married
> *Bokhem mhojem, tantiam ghaltolem*—My stork will lay eggs
> *Tantiam ghaltokoch*—When she has laid eggs

Mattou. (Konkani) Pavilion

Cervejo. (Portuguese) Beer

Tinto. (Portuguese) Wine

Konkani. An Indic language spoken mainly in Goa and adjacent parts of southwestern India

Bokhem mhojem, pilam kaddtolem—My stork will hatch chicks
Pilam kaddtokoch—When she hatches her chicks
Bokhem mhojem, manan bhoumtolem—My stork will go about with great honour
Manan bhoumtokoch—When she goes about with great honour
Bokhem mhojem, matrem zatolem—My stork will become old
Matrem zatokoch—When she becomes old
Bokhem mhojem, moron vetelem—My stork will die
Bokhem mortokoch—When my stork dies
Tollem mhojem, portun bhortolem—My pond will fill up again

Weddings were relaxed affairs extending over many days with the final celebration, muino, at the bride's house a month after nuptials. This time, however, the celebration took place within a few days to accommodate Leandro's itinerary.

At the end of the muino, as was custom, the couple and best man stayed on, while the groom's family and guests returned to Parra. Theodolin would be in her own home for the last time before leaving for Tanga with her husband.

A bride now, she moved around the house with familiarity, taking care of the day's programme—what to serve for lunch, when to visit neighbours, whom to invite to dinner. Most importantly, she made time to spend with her new husband, taking him to Chapora River where they found a quiet place to sit comfortably and watch small fishing canoes. He put his arm around her. She held it there and smiled.

Theodolin was a new woman, confident and content. Leandro's kindness and patience brought a calmness to her life. He seemed to be with her, even when he wasn't. In the kitchen, while cooking, his face materialised. Before the mirror, trying a new dress, she heard his appreciative laugh telling her, *Tu bore dista*—You look nice! Daydreaming, his eyes were all she thought about. A month ago, she wouldn't have believed this was possible. It was a happy time.

In January, they moved to Casa Camoth. For the first time, Theodolin was separated from Mai and all she had known. Her heart was sad. She was a new wife in a new home, with an extended family and many new customs. She tried hard to fit in and wondered if all new wives felt this way. In one month, they would leave for Africa. What would that far-off land be like? How different would her life be? The signs had been propitious: a good start and everything proceeding well. She prayed it would continue.

6

AN UNEASY VOYAGE

Leandro would always remember the year 1918. World War I came to an end; Germany lost the war; he went home; he got married.

It was time to return to Tanga, accompanied by his new bride. The family began feverishly packing provisions for Leandro and Theodolin, none of which were available in Tanga. There was mackerel seasoned in spices and vinegar, salted sardines, roasted cashew nuts, *channa,* jaggery and *caju feni.* His mai and sisters painstakingly prepared the cherished *choris* —loops of pig intestines meticulously cleaned, filled with air and sun-dried served as casings; choice pork, cubed, seasoned and marinated in masala, stuffed into casings, then knotted in intervals to form sausages. After drying for a few weeks, these were packed in large tins and sealed. This was like carrying a little of Goa to East Africa. It would be another five years before Leandro would return.

They took enough food for themselves and for friends whose long absences from Goa had whetted their appetites for delicacies from the mother country. Theodolin was not fond of seasoned sausage or tart pickled fish but involved herself in the elaborate process, knowing her husband would savour it. She was apprehensive of the voyage ahead; the closer the day of departure, the more anxious she became.

They left the second week of February, taking a canoe to the SS *Karanja* berthed in Mormugão. Theodolin was terrified of boats and waves. She couldn't bring herself to hop into the skittish vessel from the gently swaying old wooden pier. Before Leandro could come to her aid, the grinning boatman deftly picked her up and, in one swift move, deposited her in the lurching boat.

Channa. (Hindi) Chickpeas, usually roasted and eaten as a snack

Caju feni. (Konkani) Spirit produced in Goa, distilled from the cashew fruit

Choris. (Konkani) Sausages

All women same. Afraid of water. *Bhiye naka,* I take you to big ship.

Leandro helped her to a plank seat and sat by her side. She realised painfully that, at the end of this ride, she would encounter the same problem. Tears came to her eyes. *I hope I do better than this. My husband will think he has been stuck with a useless woman. I cannot let this happen again.* She calmed herself and struggled to put a faint smile on her tear-stained face when asked if she felt better.

Their luggage, mainly large trunks and wooden boxes, had been delivered to customs and immigration the previous day. At the docks, a cacophony overwhelmed her—porters shouting to make way, creaky handcarts, raucous swearing and rebuffs, pushing and shoving. Around mounds of belongings, there was intense haggling over fares, pleas and promises, offers and counteroffers for prompt transfer of baggage past customs to the ship.

As Theodolin looked around, her heart sank. The size of the ship astounded her—she had never seen anything so big! *Thank God I am not travelling alone.* For all its vastness, sleeping arrangements were disappointing—an area on the open deck no larger than two single beds. Surrounded by luggage and people speaking languages she had never heard, there was no privacy. This was their space for the entire voyage.

Going from a protected childhood to sudden marriage was one thing. It was life. But her present situation, where she became part of a motley travelling group, roughing it on a ship, was more than she could take. It was unacceptable.

You never told me it was like this!

Leandro hadn't minded deck class too much when he was single and, knowing how impossible it would be to get anything else, presumed it would be all right with Theodolin. He had not given any thought to the voyage itself.

I'm sorry, I should have booked a cabin. But there wasn't enough time to get one. Please don't worry. I'll do all I can to make you comfortable.

She did not blame him but found it difficult to relax. He understood her predicament, for he, too, was ill at ease. Any hint of intimacy was out of the question. As night fell, lights dimmed. Babies cried and unruly children couldn't be quieted. Seasoned travellers began to play cards. Snatches of conversation floated by long past bedtime. People constantly picked their way between sleeping families and belongings, seeking lavatories located in the middle of the deck.

Bhiye naka. (Konkani) Don't be afraid

Every morning, the deck was hosed down. This meant getting up early, rolling up bedding and moving luggage. The chlorinated water mixed with disinfectant along with the ship's smell of tar and turpentine nauseated Theodolin. The gentle pitching of the vessel as it ploughed through an increasingly restless sea made it worse. She became seasick. Disheartened, and unable to conceal her discomfort, she sank into moments of intense loneliness, crying to herself as she remembered Mai and home.

Leandro sat by quietly, unsure what to do.

The slow, unchanging routine of each day eventually brought a rhythm of normalcy. As the ship raced along, Theodolin spent hours watching the ocean and noticed the soft sky join the sea in the distant horizon.

On the twelfth day, they docked at Kilindini Harbour in Mombasa. By the time they got through customs and immigration, it was midday and scorching. Sweat dripped down her forehead.

I didn't know it would be so hot.

Leandro smiled apologetically. February is the hottest month on the coast.

Theodolin couldn't keep from perspiring. Her damp undergarments clung to her uncomfortably. She was embarrassed and longed for the cool comfort of an airy house, for a wash, a change of clothes. Leandro's mind was racing with pressing problems . . . finding accommodations for the night, safe transportation of baggage, and Theodolin's comfort, considering there was capricious sailing ahead.

They rode in a rickshaw to the waterfront on the opposite side of the island where Leandro found a dhow leaving the next morning. The wind, still the south-blowing Kaskazi, would be in their favour. A boatman transferred their luggage from the docks to the dhow. Theodolin and Leandro then headed to a guesthouse run by a Goan hotelier. After a short nap and tea, they felt so much better.

Let me show you around Mombasa.

As they slipped out into the hot and humid late afternoon, they heard the cry of the *muezzin* calling the faithful to prayer. The voice, high-pitched and haunting, caught Theodolin's attention. She sensed an urgent message in its tone.

Allahu Akbar—God is the greatest. *Hayya'alas salah*—Come to prayer.

She did not know the muezzin's call was as common as the Angelus bells in

---

Muezzin. (Arabic) Man who calls Muslims to prayer from the minaret of a mosque her village reminding them of the Annunciation. For Muslim men, it was heard five times a day, at dawn, noon, midafternoon, sunset, and nightfall.

By the seafront, Arabs in long white *thobes* with embellished waistcoats and women in buibui sat with their families watching the sun go down. Theodolin was startled to see women covered in black flowing robes from head to feet, just their eyes exposed.

Are they in mourning?

The question surprised Leandro as he had seen this form of dress among Muslim women before and not given it a second thought.

No, it is their custom. Muslim women cover themselves for modesty. Husbands don't want other men looking at their wives.

But they must be so hot in those clothes!

The harbour was noisy and busy, smelling of smoke and salt fish. Some dhows were being loaded with hides, tusks and frankincense, while others, on stilts, were being repaired, scraped down, oiled and limed.

They sauntered through the old town. It was stifling even in the shade. Everyone moved slowly, passersby, shoppers, handcart pushers taking time to greet each other, their movements languid. Arabs in *dukas* selling carpets, carved wooden chests, and brassware; Indian silversmiths forging their wares. Theodolin noticed people in a little café slurping, with audible pleasure, tea poured into saucers, and flies feasting on small brown cakes in the open display case. I wouldn't eat those, she murmured.

They were drawn to a tiny kiosk where small pieces of marinated meat on skewers roasted on a low charcoal fire.

Let's have some . . . Jambo. I'll take two sticks. This is my wife's first day.

Karibu, memsaab—Welcome, madam. I give you one as gift.

Asante sana—Thank you very much.

They chewed on the kabobs while they strolled, the air filled with the aroma of coffee coming from a large brass pot on a charcoal brazier.

Coffee?

I'll try, she said with a sense of adventure. The coffee was strong, served black in small cups with neither sugar nor milk. It tasted bitter and she handed the cup to Leandro, who laughed as he gulped it down.

Thobes. (Arabic) Ankle-length, long-sleeved, gownlike garments worn chiefly by men of the Arabian Peninsula

Dukas. (Swahili) Shops, stores

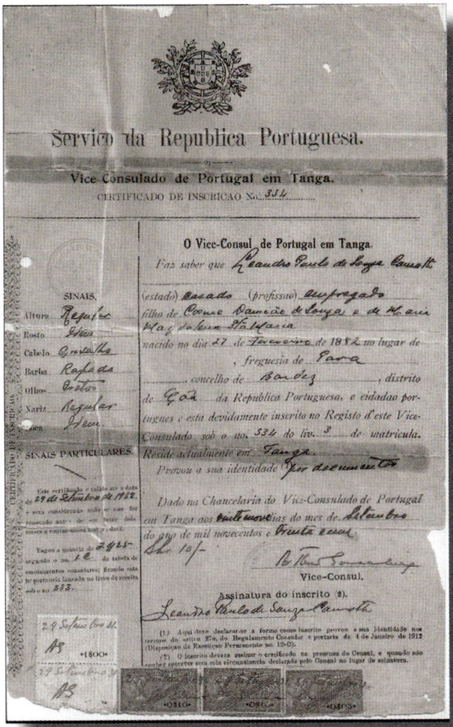

Serviço da Republica Portugueza.

Vice Consulado de Portugal em Tanga.

CERTIFICADO DE INSCRICAO No. 334

O Vice-Consul de Portugal em Tanga.

Faz saber que Leandro Paulo de Souza Camotti

(estado) casado (profissão) empregado

filho de Cosme Damião de Souza e de Maria Magdalena Sta Maria

nascido no dia 27 de Fevereiro de 1882 no lugar de , freguesia de Parra , concelho de Bardez , distrito de Goa da Republica Portuguesa, e cidadao portugues e esta devidamente inscrito no Registo d'este Vice-Consulado sob o no. 334 do liv. 3 de matricula.

Reside actualmente em Tanga

Provou a sua identidade por documentos

Dado na Chancelaria do Vice-Consulado de Portugal em Tanga aos vinte e nove dias do mes de Setembro do anno de mil novecentos e trinta e um.

Vice-Consul.

Assinatura do inscrito (2).

SINAIS.

Altura Regular

Rosto Idem

Cabelo Grisalho

Barba Rapada

Olhos Pretos

Nariz Regular

SINAIS PARTICULARES.

Este certificado é valido até a data de 29 de Setembro de 1932

Pagou a quantia de 2425

SERVIÇO DA REPUBLICA PORTUGUESA

Passaporte de Viajante

Miguel Joao Martins

No. 63/46

Vice Consul da Republica Portuguesa em Dar es Salaam

Faço saber aos que este passaporte virem que desta cidade de Dar es Salaam faz viagem para Goa via Bombaim

o cidadão português

estado casado de anos de Idade

natural de de profissão empregado

filho de Cosme Damião de Souza

e de Maria Magdalena Sta Maria

com os sinais e assinatura à margem, levando em sua companhia

Sinais

Estatura

Cabelo

Olhos

Rosto

Nariz

Bôca

Barba

Côr

Sinais Particulares

Assinatura do Portador

Peço portanto a todas as autoridades civis e militares, a quem êste passaporte fôr apresentado, que não ponham impedimento algum ao portador, antes lhe prestem todo o auxilio e favor de que êle possa necessitar para seguir a sua viagem. Ida e volta.

Este passaporte é pessoal e válido pelo tempo de um ano.

Vice Consulado de Portugal em Dar es Salaam, aos de de 1946

Pagou a quantia de segundo o No. da tabela ficando esta importancia lançado no livro da receita sobo No. Vice-Consulado de Portugal em Dar es Salaam de de 19

Vice-Consul.

Leandro's Identification Certificate, issued by the Portuguese Consulate in Tanga

One-year travel document to Goa, issued by the Portuguese Consulate in Dar es Salaam to Leandro

Leandro Paulo De Souza

Plaque erected to soldiers at the Battle of Tanga

Michael Santa Maria and sisters; Maria Magdalena is on the left.

Gaddi

Casa Camoth, Parra, Goa

Gharry outside Casa Camoth

Theodolinda Claudina De Mello

St. Anne's Church, Parra

Family photo, 1933:
Theodolin, Leo,
Magda, Leandro

St. Joseph's High School, Arpora, Goa

Bust of Father William Lyons, founder of St. Joseph's High School

Leo and Santos,
Arpora, 1936

Christmas concert at St. Joseph's. Leo is the fourth angel from the right.

Terezinha Margarida (Bai)

Mama and children

Leo and Santos
with Bai

At dawn, they set out for the old port to board the dhow. It was a ninety-ton sambuk, a spry little vessel with a sixty-foot deck. Her rough mast stood tall and towering. The long yard, to which the lateen sail would be attached, lay prone on the deck, taking up almost its entire length. Compared to the SS *Karanja*, this craft was ragged and frighteningly unsteady. Theodolin tightened her grip on Leandro's arm.

Do we have to get on this boat?

Don't be afraid. I'll help you.

He picked her up gently while she placed her arm hesitantly around his neck, then stepped onto the dhow as if carrying her over the threshold.

Wasn't too bad, was it?

Lowering her eyes, she was mortified at being carried by a man in open view. Shyly, she murmured a soft *I'm sorry*—both for herself and him, considering he was the only man who had to help his wife. The rest of the women were seasoned travellers, something she distressingly wasn't.

By the time they navigated out of port, the sun was up and a steady breeze came from the northeast. The crew pulled the triangular sail and attached it to the heavy yard, scrambling to hoist it to the mast with ropes. Pulling with a rhythmic chant, muscles straining and bodies glistening with sweat, the ivory-coloured sail slowly rose against the blue sky. Once aloft, it instantly billowed, trapping the Kaskazi.

The boat rolled and pitched the first half hour, then sped smoothly, never leaving sight of the shoreline. To Theodolin, the sailors looked like a band of ruffians—sweaty faces covered in several days' stubble, faded turbans, dirty *kikois* knotted at the waist, and daggers hanging from belts.

Theodolin did not feel any queasiness when the crew served breakfast: platters of *khubz*—unleavened bread—and sweet tea in thick glasses. She was unnerved by the man with a large scar on the left side of his face, which ran from the corner of his mouth to the lobe of his ear. But he spoke gently, reassuringly:

Memsaab, afadali, kula hi khubz, ni mzuri—Madam, please, eat this bread, it is good.

He returned with another plate. *Tahere, ni tamu*—Sweet dates.

The crew spent most of the morning taking care of daily chores. Some put out fishing lines, others sat comfortably mending nets. Leandro, an avid fisherman,

---

Kikois. (Swahili) Distinctive East African striped cloths with an end fringe joined them, tending the lines while the sailors filleted and salted the catch. They ate fish, steaming hot rice and seasoned stew, with glasses of sweet tea.

Relaxing after lunch, Leandro took his turn with the hookah, inhaling deeply. The unroasted tobacco gave off a pungent aroma and smoke gurgled as it passed through water.

Ahhh . . . smoother than a rolled cigarette.

Overcome by the sultriness of the afternoon, Theodolin curled up and dozed, awakening as the crew brought down the sail and directed the dhow to the pier. Leandro heaved a sigh of relief. They arrived in Tanga at last.

We are here!

Kwaheri, keti salama—Goodbye, and stay well.

In awe, Theodolin gazed beyond the swaying coconut palms. Somewhere out there was her new home.

7

UNFORESEEN CHALLENGES

Great Britain was officially confirmed the new ruler in 1919 and German East Africa renamed Tanganyika Territory in January 1920. More than a hundred thousand of the one million Africans serving as askaris and porters for the Germans and British perished in the war. Those fortunate to return found their families starving as lands destroyed by General Lettow-Vorbeck's scorched-earth policy produced no maize, no cassava, no sweet potatoes, no vegetables. Although most food shortages were temporary, hunger stalked the land.

The military had not expected continuing allegiance to the Germans and strove to strengthen its grip on the region while trying to restore services and win the confidence of the people. English replaced German as the colonial language and soon became widespread at government offices, hospitals and other places of service. At churches, clergy spoke English and schools hired English-speaking teachers.

Usagara Company was seized by the Custodian of Enemy Property and its assets liquidated. Most Germans, including Mr. Krause, repatriated following incarceration. Leandro's savings, all Deutsch-Ostafrikanische rupien, was not worth the paper it was printed on. Both he and Olenzu were retained to be part of the new unit.

You will now have to teach *me* English, Leandro!

Over the next few days, Leandro's friends and neighbours dropped in to meet his new wife. They lamented the bad situation.

It's not like before, *yaar*. The British don't know what they're doing. Who the hell is in charge? The Germans were strict but at least we knew where we stood. It's all very confusing, and to top it off, now we have no jobs.

Disheartened and worried, Leandro had a hollowness in his stomach, tightness in his throat.

Yaar. (Hindi) Friend

After a fitful sleep, he woke early, promised Theodolin to be home in good time, and retrieved his bicycle from the back for his customary ride to the office. Fastening clips above his ankles to prevent trouser ends getting caught in the chain, he mounted it, throwing his right leg over the bar and pushing off the right pedal. It was an odd way to start riding, but he was a tall man and that was how he did it.

Leandro, a portrait of composure—taupe cotton suit, stippled blue tie, white pith hat—was too preoccupied to greet colleagues as he usually did.

You're Leandro, I take it? Well, sit down for heaven's sake.

The mzungu sitting behind the desk did not look older than twenty-five. A singularly ungainly man, Mr. Whitmore was a soldier with the Fifth Indian Light Infantry who quit upon discovering the benefits of a colonial career where he could rise rapidly to a high position.

So, you were at Usagara when we took control? A mess it is. Whoever said the bloody Germans were orderly? If you are one of those who still love the Germans, you're a bloody fool. Make a list of all their assets and present worth. Report your progress to me daily. Well, get along then. We haven't got time to waste.

Yes, sir. *A bloody fool yourself,* Leandro thought, struggling to compose himself.

Leandro went about work with great thoroughness, making necessary inventories of materials in stock, checking corresponding bills of entry at the customhouse and assessing current value. The Indian rupee, which had been used as local currency, had to be converted to shillings. Goods ranged from pins to sisal decorticators, from pens to grass slashers, and putting a price on each item was not easy. The holdings of the Usagara were too vast for Leandro to manage by himself.

Mr. Whitmore, is there anyone who could help me? There is a lot of stock. I can do it myself but it will take time.

What? Who do you think you are? Bwana mkubwa? Big boss? You want help? What next? *These bloody wogs! Help them once, they think they're our equals. Can't do that. Never!*

So Leandro worked longer hours, leaving home earlier and returning late. What disturbed him was not just the change of guard but lack of civility in day-to-day dealings. He was not used to mzungus who had little respect for nonwhites. He found the British condescendingly aloof, unlike Germans who, in spite of being rigidly disciplined, were affable.

The job slowly eroded Leandro's spirit. He lost his easy, good-natured demeanour, growing quieter and withdrawn. Mr. Evans, deputy chief of operations, noticed the change.

Cheer up. It will be all right. You're doing splendid work. Don't let anybody tell you differently. If you have any problems, come see me.

Leandro had an ally in Evans. However, it was unlikely Evans would countermand his English colleague's directives on behalf of a non-British employee. Leandro's relationship with Whitmore remained uncomfortable, sometimes humiliating. He could not afford to resign, with a wife, and a family in Goa, to support. Times were bad and there was a dearth of jobs.

Evans eventually left for Dar es Salaam to oversee the entire Custodian of Enemy Property operation and was replaced by Simons, a recent arrival from South Africa known for his booming voice, loud laugh and passion for everything English. Like Whitmore, Simons had been in the army. One afternoon, waiting to update Whitmore on a consignment erroneously earmarked for Ruanda-Urundi, Leandro overheard Simons.

It's a bloody good thing Tanganyika is under British rule. Every country in Africa should be speaking English. Our standards must be enforced across the continent. And why not? Every morning, I remind myself that it is wonderful to be born an Englishman, not a native or a bloody Indian.

Deflated, Leandro held on to his file and quietly left. He was unable to revive enthusiasm for his work or superiors for a long time. He also missed his good friend Olenzu who had left Usagara to go back to teaching.

It was an exciting time for Theodolin as they unpacked trunks and boxes and began the task of setting up a home together in Chumbageni. Leandro, an attentive husband, proudly showed her around town, walking through the market, meeting neighbours, going to church. Filled with exhilaration and trepidation, she took in everything, and stories Leandro told sprang to life.

Shortly after their arrival, Leandro formally presented Theodolin to the Souza-Bencett family, who had helped him immigrate and acclimate to his new life. He had not forgotten the favour or their kindness in caring for him. The Bencetts, amongst the earliest Goan settlers, lived in Mambani, a coconut plantation by the coast.

While tea and biscuits were being served, he gave much-appreciated gifts of choris, seasoned mackerel, cashew nuts and caju feni. Knowing the Bencetts would like to hear about Theodolin's upbringing, Leandro talked about her village, house and family.

Mrs. Bencett took Theodolin outside to see the view. The house, built high on a cliff, overlooked dark craggy rocks jutting into the ocean. Enormous waves crashed on the rocks, sending a thousand droplets of white spray towards them.

You have such a lovely place.

Come visit us any time. Leandro, you must bring Theodolin again.

The rickshaw ride home took them through the heart of the shamba, thick with coconut palms gently swaying in the breeze. Passing through a small village of mud-and-wattle huts, their unexpected arrival caused a commotion: squawking chickens, bleating goats, naked children squealing delightfully.

Jambo! Jambo! greeted mothers, babies swathed in kangas on their backs.

These are Olenzu's people, the Bondei.

Theodolin slowly began to adapt to the new place and its ways. The Bencetts sent them a houseboy. Twenty years old, with no schooling, this position assured him of regular meals and wages.

Juma would learn to cook Goan food, clean and help with daily chores. Theodolin's routine was confined to running the home, preparing meals and being a good wife. She craved companionship, an occasional chat, walk, tea perhaps, with a neighbour or friend. Picturing Mai all by herself, she wished she were close by; her presence would be a tonic for loneliness.

Standing on the verandah one morning, she saw a young African woman wearing a one-piece orange-yellow wrap—*kanga*—knotted above her breasts, shoulders bare, red beads encircling her neck and cropped curly hair in tight tresses. With a broad smile, the woman waved.

Jambo, memsaab.

Jambo. Theodolin had learned that word in Mombasa.

Karibu—Welcome.

Asante—Thank you. Another word she picked up.

The woman said something Theodolin did not understand. Not knowing what to say, she nodded several times.

Kwaheri—Good-bye.

The language barrier became more evident when neighbours visited. Sushiben Patel brought *ladoos*—a delicious round yellow Indian sweetmeat made from gram flour, sugar and *ghee*. Amina Alibhai, mother of two girls, came with a platter of *samosas*—triangular pastries of chopped curried meat—a

---

Ghee. (Hindi) Form of clarified butter

special *Bohra* snack. Theodolin longed to ask about their families, *what did they do every day, how long had they been here, were they homesick, how did they make ladoos and samosas*. . . but besides Konkani, she was not conversant in any Indian language. Asante sana and a multiplicity of gestures were not enough.

What can I do? They all speak Swahili. I must learn it. But how? Is there a school? For children, yes, but for housewives? People will say Theodolin is going to school instead of looking after her husband and having children. They'll think I'm mad!

Leaving Juma to prepare lunch, Theodolin put on comfortable sandals, chose a scarf and ventured out, hoping to browse through dukas. In her haste, she forgot a parasol.

A hint of frangipani in the air and fluffy white clouds amid a clear aquamarine sky made for a pleasant walk. The streets, broad and sandy, were divided by a median of widely spaced *kungu* trees. She passed an austere, single-storied, ivory building with a fluttering British flag. In front, a police squad in khaki uniforms, *puttees* and *fezzes* marched to crisp orders of a forbidding headman. On the opposite side an imposing structure that looked like a fortress belonged to the Office of the Provincial Commissioner, the most powerful mzungu in town. It was close to eleven and she had not come across any shops. *Leandro will be home for lunch soon. I must start earlier next time.* Disappointed, she turned back.

The strong African sun directly overhead made it impossible to escape the insidious heat and humidity. Its blinding brilliance hurt her eyes. Hoping for relief, she tied the scarf around her head and tried walking faster, without much progress. The scorching sand got into her open-toed shoes. The only shade lay under large kungu trees. *Can't rest here . . . must go home. Didn't know it would be this bad.*

Stepping up to the verandah, she felt light-headed. Legs weak and shaky, she struggled to hold on to the jamb, didn't succeed, and slowly went down. Running towards her, towel and jug of water in hand, Juma cried out, *Memsaab, hawaendi nje wakati wa jua kali*—Madam, you can't go out when the sun is so hot!

Bohra. Sect within the Ismā'īlī branch of Shia Islam

Kungu. (Swahili) Indian almond tree

Puttee. (Hindi) Strip of cloth used as a covering for the lower part of the leg from the ankle to the knee

Fez. (Turkish) Felt headdress in the shape of a short, cylindrical, peakless hat, usually red, and sometimes with a tassel attached to the top

In April came the incessant rains, cooling the place by the evening. Everyone was relieved as sweat and dust washed away, the air refreshed. In the darkness of night, frogs set up a continuous litany of prayerful croaks and, when done, another group would respond in a lower key, stopping suddenly after a long series of rhythmic chants. Theodolin registered the ferocity of the rains by its loudness on the corrugated tin roof, lines of wet clothes in the house and peskiness of mosquitoes. Illness was common during this season, especially malaria. She detested the bitter white quinine tablet she was obliged to take every night and the discomfort of sleeping inside mosquito nets. The long rains were as dispiriting as the heat.

The next few months were a struggle. It was exasperatingly slow getting to know people. Apart from Olenzu and his family, Theodolin's interactions with locals were minimal. She haggled with vendors at the market and hawkers who came door to door selling fresh fish and vegetables. Her exposure to Europeans was limited to church, where the front two rows were reserved for whites. There was also a matter of distance. Anyone living beyond her walkable perimeter remained outside her circle of contact. She didn't cycle—no woman did—and rickshaws were not readily available.

She gradually realised there was little chance her world would be different. Tanga could not take the place of Camurlim, where people knew each other and spoke the same language. Theodolin slowly turned her focus inward, resolving to make home a priority . . . a haven for Leandro to recoup and relax.

8

SCHOOL TIME

As the years passed, Theodolin and Leandro's family grew, providing a deep sense of satisfaction. Over the next decade, they had three children, two boys and a girl.

I was born on the eleventh of April, 1926. Family tradition dictated our names include the Saint of the Day and our godparents. And so, I was named Leo Joseph after St. Leo the Great and my godfather, Joseph D'Mello. I remember my mother telling me the long rains expected in March had been delayed, resulting in a drought. Days were simmering hot, nights unbearable, until I arrived amidst welcome rains. Mama always believed this to be a good omen.

My older brother, Miguel Ladislaus Santos, born the first of November, 1921, *Todos Santos*—All Saints' Day—had a mind of his own. Mama laughingly tells the story of how he freed the brass horse:

> In our sitting room, we had a small horse on a stand. Your papa liked it very much. That boy, Santos was very upset the horse was stuck and badly wanted it to be free. So do you know what that boy did? *Ai saiba! Malkiryad cheddo!* He found a wire, and every day, he sawed that wood stand. After months, it finally came off. He was so proud and ran to show Papa. *Saiba bhogos,* Papa was so angry, he whacked him on his bum!

I was three when Papa and Mama took us to Goa for Santos to begin his Portuguese studies at the Municipal Lyceum in Mapusa. In those days, owing to lack of schools, families routinely sent children to boarding schools in Goa for their education. I have no recollection of the trip. However, I do remember when my sister was born. I was five. My parents were delighted to have a girl. Papa reminded us that none of his siblings had daughters, only sons. They

---

Ai saiba. Malkiryad cheddo! (Konkani) Oh my goodness. Naughty boy!
Saiba bhogos! (Konkani) Literal translation is *God forgive me*; colloquial translation is *Oh my God!*

named her Magdalena Mauritia Lidia in honour of his mother. Thrilled to have a new plaything besides Ponki, my furry toy monkey, I promptly called her *Bada Ponki*.

In 1934, I began my schooling in the first standard at St. Anthony's School, run by Irish priests and nuns of the Rosminian order. A year later, my parents decided the time had come for me to join my brother. Papa took his six months' home leave and we went to Goa. I was enrolled in the English day school, Sacred Heart of Jesus, at Pinto Vaddo, Verla, in Parra, while Santos continued at the Lyceum as a day scholar. The dichotomy in selection of schools, Portuguese for Santos and English for me, rose from the fact that while we spoke Konkani at home, we needed to be proficient in Portuguese, the official language of Goa, and English was best for life in British East Africa.

When it was time for Papa to leave, they decided Mama should stay behind with Magda, Santos and me. This scenario was all too common. Husbands and wives, fathers and children, endured years of separation as the pressing need to earn a livelihood abroad required mothers to relocate to care for the children. These were devastating times for families.

We rented a house in Khorlim where we planned to stay for a few years. I missed Papa. I remembered his large, gentle and loving presence—the smell of his rolled cigarettes, gunpowder from his hunting rifle used to bag guinea fowl, his fishing gear. At dinner, two tots of brandy with water left a mellow bouquet on his breath. I loved seeing his clothes hanging neatly and his slippers by the bed. In Khorlim, there was nothing to remind me of him. I wanted him with us but knew this was not possible.

Santos and I settled in but Papa wasn't doing well. Life, unexpectedly, turned out to be difficult. He had been in Tanga a year without us, and in spite of having Juma's help, found it challenging to take care of the house. He was lonely and missed his wife. Sensing my father's anguish in his letters, Mama made up her mind to go back with Magda. She had no choice but to register us in boarding school.

Mama worried endlessly over me. I was frail and sickly, susceptible to recurrent colds and coughs that settled in my lungs, causing chronic bouts of wheezing. My chest was rubbed with coconut oil before I bathed. She made sure I had beaten egg yolk with honey every morning, a tablespoon of cod liver oil at lunch and tonic after supper to make me strong. When I was ill or off colour, a *dixttikarn* would be summoned to remove the evil eye my mother suspected had been cast on me. Holding a big dried red chili and mumbling prayers, the woman slowly ran her hands down one side of my body, from head to toe, and up the other side. After several circles around my head, she flung the chili, always intact, into the flaming fire. The crackling sound assured me the evil eye had been drawn out and dispelled. *Dixtt geli! The evil eye is gone!*

St. Joseph's High School in the village of Arpora, the oldest and finest English school for boys, accommodated approximately five hundred students, a third of them boarders. Built on a low, laterite hill bestrewn with cashew trees, the two-storied building housed classrooms, a dormitory for seniors, teacher quarters, chapel and library. At the entrance stood a marble bust of founder, Father William Robert Lyons, a Jesuit scholar. Up the hill, separated by a private road, lay the dormitory for younger boys, refectory and kitchen. The playground and football pitch were at the bottom.

A day before Mama left for Tanga, she called for the gaddi to take Santos and me to St. Joseph's. The driver strapped our two black metal trunks to the roof. My aunties bid us good-bye amidst tears, prayers and a promise to have us home for our holidays. Riding in the gaddi, Mama gripped my hand tightly.

Write a letter to us every month on aerogramme. Santos, keep an eye on Leo. If you have any problems, go straight to Father Mendonca.

The school loomed into view. We stopped at the junior dormitory, unloaded our trunks, and went to meet Father Felipe Neri Mendonca, the principal, for whom my parents had the utmost respect. A portly man, fortyish, he wore a white soutane and sandals.

Pushing us forward, all my mother could say was, My boys.

He understood. Behind black-framed spectacles, his eyes were keenly observant. He was familiar with such situations.

Don't worry, Mrs. De Souza. They will be all right.

Repeating her never-ending list once more, she told me how to care for myself.

Wear your woollen singlet, *babu.* It will keep you warm. The monsoons are coming. Change your clothes if you get wet. The showers don't have hot water. You'll catch cold. Dry your hair completely. If you get a cold or cough, go tell Santos or Father Mendonca right away; otherwise you'll start wheezing. Your cuts and blisters take a long time to heal. Go to the dispensary.

Dixttikarn. (Konkani) Person who performs ceremony to remove the evil eye or curse

Babu. (Hindi) Term of endearment for a male child

In the end, she could only stroke my cheek. Take care of yourself, babu.

My world was going to change and my heart went out to Mama. I wanted to console her but didn't know how. I felt like crying. Santos did too, but he had been to boarding school before and was more independent. Mama hugged and blessed us but could not pull away.

I'll try and come tomorrow.

It gave her solace, delaying the finality of the moment. Although it was not possible for her to return, I kept a watch for her the next day, anyway.

That evening, I sat on my bed, an iron cot with thin mattress, sheet, pillow and folded grey blanket. Lights were out and I clearly heard the *thump-thump* of the generator outside. A locker by my head held my books and personal items. A torrent of tears rolled down my face. Santos was in the senior dormitory. I don't know how long I sat on the edge of the unfamiliar bed, looking into the dark and seeing nothing but Mama's drawn face going home without me.

At five thirty, the morning bell woke me. Seeing boys making beds, changing clothes and saying prayers, I couldn't tarry under the blanket. Ablutions done, we headed, single file, to the chapel for Mass. Bleary-eyed, hair uncombed, shirt collars unturned, few were prepared for this first day. Staying attentive took great effort. I was hungry and wondered what sort of breakfast would be served.

Following Mass, we bounded over the many steps to the refectory. Hot porridge, buttered slices of bread with jam, and tea with milk and sugar tasted good.

Lessons began at half past eight. The ringing of the bell informed us we had five minutes. I joined the melee of students in khaki shorts and short-sleeved shirts, jostling to fall in line. Being one of the youngest, I stood in the front. Santos, who had chosen to be in my class to improve his English, was at the rear. At the close of morning salutations and announcements by the principal, we filed into our classrooms.

School was dismissed at half past four, and the day scholars went home. Boarders were expected to be on the playground and pitch, but my body felt languid, and all I thought about was running away. I could be in Parra before dark but neither Santos, Mama, nor Magda would be there.

I went for a quick shower. The cold water made me shiver. Older boys returning from play guffawed, shouted and splashed around. The biggest among them, noticing I was quiet and new and small, yelled through the spray of water, Hey you, missing your mama's milk?

The rest took up the chant. Missing his mama's milk, missing his mama's milk.

I struggled not to let their taunting upset me and when it didn't get the response they hoped for, the chanting stopped as suddenly as it started.

The quiet study period preceding dinner was designated for reviewing the day's work and completing homework. My mind wandered to Mama during the entire forty-five minutes. I ran my fingers through my hair, which was still wet, and heard her voice. *Dry your hair, babu. You'll get sick.*

Fortunately, the days were busy, allowing little time to think, to mope. I looked forward to the unscheduled hour wedged between dinner and turning in for the night. On cold evenings, we built a fire and sat around telling stories, ragging on each other, or just relaxing and doing nothing.

This hour acquired special meaning when Father Mendonca chose to join us. He could recognise which boarders were settling in and those who were unhappy and needed help. He was aware younger boys, in their first few months, still pined for their families, and had an uncanny knack of drawing out what might be bothering them. Twirling his keys on a short chain around his finger, as was habit, and bantering with us, he would find out if any new nicknames were making the rounds, ask if we had heard from our parents. He knew I was homesick and spent time giving me tasks I enjoyed, to keep me busy and my mind off home. It was comforting talking to him and we loved his warmth and kindness.

Father Mendonca involved his students in debate and theatre. At the annual concert, he gave me and six others the part of angels. We were so well made up that a group of nuns attending the concert mistook us for girls and wondered how Father Mendonca had managed this. It became a joke, and shortly thereafter, he said:

You looked so much like an angel that I shall have to change the Latin declension for you. The new one will be *leo, leonis*—feminine, angel.

The Latin declension of the noun *lion* was *leo, leonis*—masculine, lion. My spirits soared when I realised Father Mendonca, my Latin teacher, was attempting to change the great masculine lion to a feminine angel.

In the matter of languages—English and Latin—I felt obliged to excel as a way of expressing my gratitude. Mathematics, however, gave me problems. I could not grasp the fundamentals and did poorly. Santos began to tutor me, since he had studied mathematics at the Lyceum. I applied myself diligently to prove he was a good teacher.

Renowned for its academics, St. Joseph's also prided itself on having an exceptional lineup of athletes who performed well at interschool competitions. The annual sports event was a local highlight. One hundred and fifty students performed a torch drill at dusk before large, excited crowds of parents, villagers and special guests. Our imaginations fired, in the days following the event, we worked hard like our glorious athletes, running, jumping, throwing the shot put and javelin. When we failed to see any tangible results, it was football and field hockey again.

We had holidays three times a year: October, after the monsoons ended and rice paddies turned gold; Christmas season; and two months in summer. Santos and I stayed with our spinster auntie, Terezinha, whom we fondly called Bai. She fussed over us, cooking our favourite meals and making sure we ate well.

Kind and well loved, Bai was my godmother and I was very attached to her. No sooner were we home, she reminded us of our obligations—a visit to the neighbour's ill son . . . condole with a distant auntie who lost her husband . . . call on the elderly gentleman living alone. Before long, we visited everyone in the village. A devout woman, Bai attended Mass every morning, walking five minutes to St. Anne's Church in simple long dresses and black Italian lace veil. She never insisted we go with her.

Sleep, babu. You're on holiday.

Santos was an early riser; I slept late. In the mornings, armed with *cattys*—slingshots—we rambled over hills that rose gently behind our house, exploring valleys, climbing trees, swimming in wells and quarries. During siesta hours, I read whatever I liked and borrowed many books, mostly adventure, from the library. On occasion, we played field hockey and football, though my small stature kept me off teams. So I joined the girls for hopscotch or seven tiles and got teased by my cousins, but didn't mind.

Going back to school was hard and the last day, worse. We wandered around, brooding and counting down the hours. Bai would hover, grumbling she had been unable to do everything she'd planned. Despite the sadness, we all eagerly looked forward to the next holidays.

Six years later, I finished at the top of my graduating class, obtaining distinctions in the subjects Santos and Father Mendonca taught me.

Santos and I went to Bombay in June to begin college at St. Xavier's, established by German Jesuits. A bustling city of two million, it derived its name from Mumba Devi, goddess of the local *Koli* fishing people. Going to Bombay from Parra was an enormous change. Trams clanging in the middle of the street and towering red double-decker buses droning along. Trains bringing hordes of commuters, pushing, shoving, in colourful *saris, salwar kameezes, kurtas,* dresses, dhotis, and a cacophony of dialects. Honking taxis, clip-clopping horse carriages, vendors shouting their wares, policemen blowing whistles all made me afraid to cross the roads. I couldn't walk straight for fear of colliding with pedestrians, handcarts, beggars with bowls, and stray cows.

We stayed with our cousins in Khotachiwadi, Girgaum, a southern neighbourhood of Bombay. It took some time getting used to the city and its teeming millions. I was mesmerised by the constant motion of *Chira Bazaar,* its stunning array of jewellery dukas; dilapidated tenements with clothes strung window to window, hanging out to dry; narrow cobbled lanes of wooden houses that reminded me of Goa. The smells were just as diverse, from the strong, briny odour of the *Chirabazar* fish market to the aroma of piping-hot tea poured into a saucer at an Irani restaurant, from fresh droppings of horses tethered to carriages waiting for a fare to the scent of incense emanating from a sari shop.

In the midst of this dynamic theatre of sound, sight and smell, St. Xavier's College was a refuge. Founded in 1869, the three-storey, grey-stone campus, built in the Indo-Gothic style, enclosed two quadrangles and a chapel. It was an imposing institution with arching vaults, marble artistry, classic gargoyles and stained glass. I was profoundly impressed but would not allow the grandeur to beguile me.

Father Mendonca instilled in us the need to hold our own outside of Goa. He did not want us feeling at a disadvantage merely because we were from a vaddo. I came from a fine school. Now, I looked forward to a fine college where classes were stimulating, the library inviting and the ambience intellectual and cozy.

Sari. (Hindi) Traditional garment worn by Hindu women consisting of a long piece of cloth, five to nine yards in length and two to four feet in breadth, typically wrapped around the waist, with one end draped over the shoulder or head

Salwar kameez. (Hindi) Kameez, long shirt or tunic worn over a salwar, loose trousers, wide at the waist narrowing to a cuffed hem, held up by a drawstring, which causes pleating around the waist

Kurta. (Hindi) Loose collarless shirt tunic

Chira Bazaar. Neighbourhood in Kalbadevi, Bombay, famous for jewellery

Chirabazar. Renowned fish market in Girgaum, Bombay

PART II

1

HELLO, AFRICA

The year is 1952. The month is May, season of the elite mango and earthborn watermelon. To bite into the flesh of the mango is bliss; to crunch into the watermelon, ecstasy. The sun is brilliant, shade nowhere to be found, air heavy with humidity no fan can move. Nights are uncomfortable, sleep impossible. Only the monsoons coming down in torrents, day after day after day, will cool the city.

I am now a doctor and it is time to head home. I have lived in euphoric, post-independent India and not given much thought to Britain and its colonies. There was no occasion for it. On the verge of change that will bring me face-to-face with a land of black locals and white rulers, apprehension seizes me. I do not know what the future holds.

I board the SS *Karanja,* pride of the British India fleet. The steamship that sails seasonally between Bombay and the East African coast will cross the Atlantic once more before the heavy monsoon rains of June roil the sea, making it impassable.

As the vessel slowly pulls away, I find a vantage spot on the upper deck and wave to friends who are here to see me off. Most are companions from medical school, all dear to me. Among them is the love of my life, Doulat "Dolly" Burjorji Irani, whom I plan to marry the following year. I leave behind her closeness and the promise of a life together. All I carry is blind faith that Africa will recognise and accept me and that this young woman will join me when she is done with her residency.

Dolly, bravely attempting to be cheerful, wishes she were accompanying me. But her home is Bombay, mine Tanga. She belongs to the Parsi community, I to another. She is Zoroastrian; I, Catholic. Yet we have dared to fall in love. This is not accepted in the land of arranged marriages. We are aware problems abound for both of us. But how could I not love this vivacious, empathetic lady? Will my father and mother approve? I am not sure.

The whistle gives two long blasts and the steamer picks up speed. I stand frozen to the railing. Though there are myriads of people on that bustling wharf,

I keep my friends in sight. As they became smaller and smaller until mere specks, I get a lump in my throat and my eyes grow misty.

The ship swings south to round the pulsating island of Bombay. For the first time, I observe its large busy port, piers reaching out to liners of every size from every nation. A magnificent arch of yellow basalt looms through the bright haze, the Gateway of India, commemorating the 1911 visit of King George V and Queen Mary. The iconic Taj Mahal Palace Hotel follows. A sense of awe slowly gives way to regret that I may not pass this way again.

The yaw of the ship is unsettling, the cabin oppressive and berth hardly bigger than me. I am alone, my thoughts my sole companion. Five years at Grant Medical College being groomed for a profession where much was expected; those glorious years held a rich store of memories.

The graduating class of 1951 was an extraordinary collection of 150 students, a third of whom were women. We came from different communities—Gujaratis, Marathas, Parsis, Anglo-Indians, Goans—and religions—Hinduism, Islam, Sikhism, Zoroastrianism, Catholicism, Judaism. Most of us were middle class, some well-to-do and a few wealthy. Our backgrounds did not matter as we were socially and intellectually compatible. Everyone was proud to be part of the medical school, privileged to be an alumnae in the making.

There was a happy mix of enthusiasm, rapport and competition, combined with innocent flirting and high fashion. Our motto was to grasp life in its fullness. We'd finish round-the-clock clinical terms and burn the midnight oil. Spurts of intense application alternated with periods of relaxation. Sports thrived—cricket, football, field hockey and tennis. Serious discussions on Bertrand Russell, Mahatma Gandhi, independence, and the folly of the British in partitioning Pakistan and India were plentiful.

Friendships flourished and weekends were spent on daylong picnics, watching cricket, or at the cinema. My roommate Aziz Kazi, a tall, handsome, popular Indian from South Africa, and I did yoga headstands in our dormitory at the old hostel. A daily morning ritual, we stood inverted facing each other, running through a quick revision of the anatomy dissection from the previous day.

In 1946, a year before the British left, the air was charged with fiery nationalism and demonstrations. I marched with a band of student protesters outside the college gate, chanting, shouting slogans and waving *Quit India* placards. Our fervour could not be subdued. There was nothing beyond the scope of our resolve and nothing we could not achieve. We were invincible. Suddenly, the sound of firecrackers. *Pop-pop-pop.* It was the police opening fire.

We ran in all directions, seeking safety. Later that day, I tossed my expensive tie into a bonfire to rid myself of all things British. An eloquent protest.

With simmering tensions, communal rioting was common. One evening, six of us, all second-year medical students, were in a streetcar heading back to campus. Someone shouted riots had broken out. My insides twisted. I knew this meant stabbing, killings, revenge. Hindus and Muslims settling old scores. We fled the tram, jumping into a *gharry,* only to be intercepted a couple of blocks later by Muslim rioters.

Tum kon hai? Kaham jatai?—Who are you? Where are you going?

Our Hindu companions shrank visibly. Our Muslim friends, helpless, yet wanting to protect us, mustered enough courage to say we were doctors on our way to the hospital.

Ham, jau, JAU—Okay, go, GO.

I step outside and look intently at the ocean. Judging from its long V-shaped wake, the ship is making a straight run. My mind churns with thoughts of the years spent in Goa and Bombay as an adolescent and young man and I realise the enormity of my father's investment in me. Dutifully sending money to cover my expenses every month, I never had to worry on that score except for a situation of my own making.

Euclid de Souza, my avid race-going friend, convinced me there was a fortune to be made if we played the horses intelligently, so we go to Mahalaxmi Racecourse. Programmes in hand, we made meticulously calculated choices as we watched the beautiful horses at the paddock. It was an intoxicating afternoon, emotions peaking and ebbing with each race. I wagered all my money on *Her Majesty!* Dashing up the stands, eyes glued to her streaking form, wildly waving, cheering, yelling, and screaming, *Her Majesty, Her Majesty*, I was one of hundreds hoping our horse would win. In the lead from the start, I was ready to burst at the thought of my payoff. Down the home stretch, she began to falter and it was over before I knew it. I was ready to collapse. I could not see beyond the evening. We had no way to pay for a cab or bus to take us to the campus.

Cheer up, Leo, there's always another day, my friend!

Following medical school, I spent a year doing my internship at Gokuldas Tejpal (GT) Hospital and felt important as patients called me *Dr. Sahib.* That

---

Gharry. (Hindi) Horse-drawn cab

designation placed me on a pedestal, though our professors constantly reminded us as young doctors we had a long way to go in acquiring competency in our chosen fields.

Over the next few days, I find my sea legs and begin mingling with other passengers. My social circle, determined by our customs, consists of men. We gather prior to dinner, pleasantly whiling away time as we drink scotch and become friends. They tell me about their families and new lives made for themselves in East Africa. I am amazed at how they survive and prosper while keeping their connection with the motherland strong and unbroken.

Praful Shah, a quiet, shy, well-to-do gentleman in his forties, is in the cotton ginning business.

How long have you lived in Uganda?

Oh, I born in Jinja, Dr. Sahib. Went for holiday to Gujarat. I look for husbands for my daughters. Two girls, one eighteen, one seventeen. No good men in Africa.

Did you find any?

Yes, yes. He blushes.

Anthony de Mello, short, balding, and friendly, never lacks for an opinion. He is one of several hundred hard-working Goans recruited to man the civil service. Starting at an entry-level position, he worked his way up through years of transfers in the undeveloped countryside of the British Protectorate of Uganda. After earning the trust of his superiors, he is promoted to accounting officer in the treasury department at Entebbe, Uganda's colonial administrative and commercial centre.

How was your holiday in Goa?

Enjoyable. I retire when this tour of service ends. Then I will go to Goa for good.

Won't you miss Uganda? You've been there most of your life.

Yaar, Goa is *susegad*. I won't know what to do without work.

Ismail Badruddin, a jovial Dawoodi Bohra Muslim, whose grandfather emigrated from Kutch in western India to the island of Zanzibar, sells second-hand car parts in Nairobi, Kenya. He recently expanded his business to include a taxi service and had gone to recruit his younger brothers for his latest venture.

Susegad. (Portuguese) Restful; (Konkani) Carefree.

The fourth man, Mohandas Virgee, a shopkeeper, has a duka in Tabora, the interior of Tanganyika along the railway line. Tall and stout, with a moon face and engaging smile, he is a likeable person who tags along quietly, his presence benign. I enjoy his company, even though he says little.

I cannot wait to hear about East Africa. I want to understand what it is like to live there. To work. To play. In India, it was the British and Indians. Now it will be the British and Africans with us thrown in.

How is life with the British?

After a palpable silence, each one has an opinion.

You work, you be good with African, you all right. No need mzungu.

I not go to mzungu clubs. I stay with my friends. I okay.

They not shop at my duka, so I no worry. Mzungu let us stay in Africa. We work, earn money, have children, send money home.

And the Africans?

They live separate from us like we live separate from the mzungus. We don't socialise outside work.

They have not much training and do simple work.

I go all way to Gujarat to marry my daughters. I not go to Nairobi to ask Ismail's sons. Why? Ismail Muslim, I Hindu. Same with locals. Many things different. Our people, our religion, our customs. Harder than you think.

It is the eighth day, our last, yet none of us mentions it. We stay up later than usual, vowing to meet again, though we know this is unlikely.

I wake up unusually early, dress slowly and deliberately in my favourite attire—white, long-sleeved Arrow shirt, light rust polyester trousers and matching Tootal tie. I have no time for breakfast, just a cup of coffee. I rush to the deck. After seventeen years, I will land on African soil again. Inhaling the salty tang, I cannot suppress my excitement. *It will be nice to see where the sky and sea touch Africa. This is the land of my birth.*

As the island port of Mombasa materialises into view, I catch sight of delicate greens and dots of red; a mantle of grass, shrubs and lush creepers, through which peep tiled roofs of hidden bungalows. A long sandy beach, backed by coconut palms, rolls out in either direction. The sky glows brilliant orange and red. The grey ocean becomes a blue sea. The ship drones softly as seagulls fly alongside, guiding it to port. The day is unfolding, the town awakening.

At nine, the SS *Karanja* touches Kilindini Harbour on the south side. I will soon be with my father, brother and uncle, who are driving from Tanga. Time drags and impatience devours me.

It occurs to me I have to meet the immigration officer to rectify the date of birth in my passport, erroneously recorded as my baptism date. Issued by the British Embassy in Bombay, it identifies me as a British Protected Person of Tanganyika Territory. One of those unique creations of British ingenuity, I am neither British nor Tanganyikan. It is not even a true passport, mainly serving as a travel document. Any deficiency or irregularity raises concerns about the holder's bona fides. If there is an error, as in my case, it would create suspicion, which I wish to avoid. I want to start on the right foot the first day of my return.

The officer will be British and that makes me apprehensive. If I confer with him early enough, I might avoid stalling the queue of passengers needing to fulfill immigration requirements.

I bound up the narrow, steep stairway to the captain's office at the ship's prow. A door, with a board marked IMMIGRATION, is open, and a tall Kenyan askari stands sentinel. On his head sits a fez at an angle. It is red with a black tassel hanging from the right side and metal insignia on the front. Tribal scarring marks his unsmiling face. Pressed khaki shorts, collarless khaki shirt and matching puttees cover his hefty, motionless frame. An old rifle in an at-ease position hangs from his left shoulder, and his feet are bare.

I hesitate at the door, then peer in. Seated at a cluttered desk, smoking a pipe and leafing through the *East African Standard*, is the immigration officer. He wears the customary white shirt with short sleeves and immigration badges where epaulets should be. I knock softly and prepare to step in.

The askari comes alive. He shoots his right arm across the door, barring entry.

Hakuna ruhusa—No permission, he says sharply.

All I am aware of is a giant blocking arm; everything else is blurred. Startled and shocked, I grab his arm with both hands and pull it away from the door. He loses his balance and falls. Rising, eyes wide and wild, he lunges and grabs me by my collar and tie. Unintelligible words sputter from his mouth.

That's all right, let him go! Come in.

No, thank you, I don't care to, I answer stiffly.

Struggling to control myself, I stumble away barely finding the way to my cabin. *What just happened? Was I such a threat that physical interception was necessary?* I have never been subjected to this kind of affront. The immigration officer could have easily prevented the ugly development by simply asking me to enter the moment I knocked at the door. He made himself inaccessible by sitting inside and placing an askari outside. I had expected an imperious attitude from the British but had not factored in the element of insulation exhibited by the African. It is not the pain of physical injury but the dreadful anguish of indignity. I am thoroughly shaken.

Among the many faces on the pier, I see my father trying to spot me. Santos is by his side, Uncle Robert behind him. I rush down the gangplank straight into Papa's arms. We embrace. His face beams as tears of joy roll down.

You're here, he whispers.

Santos, not demonstrative by nature, gives me a quick hug and enquires about the voyage. Uncle Robert, my father's first cousin, pats me on the cheek. He is fifty-two, unmarried and from our ancestral home.

By noon, we are on the dusty road to Tanga. Uncle Robert is at the wheel of his regal 1938 black Ford. Santos sits next to him. Papa and I relax in the soft, plush back seat. Depending on weather, it will take us three to five hours.

We exit Kenya at Lunga Lunga, crossing the unmarked border into Tanganyika. The landscape is rugged, vegetation thick. The road begins to slope gently and Uncle Robert brings the car to a slow stop. He turns around, one finger on his lips, the other pointing to the road in front.

Resting in the middle is a pride of four lionesses and five cubs in one massive tawny heap. Three lionesses lie peacefully on their sides, asleep; the fourth keeps watch. Even in repose, they are astonishingly majestic and powerful. We watch quietly, waiting . . .

They must have just had a big feed, my uncle murmurs.

Half an hour later, the lions rouse, stretch lazily, look around and walk slowly into the dense bush.

Uncle Robert is relieved. The Swahili say if you wait long enough, even the lions will let you through the bush.

The lions, I am certain, will be no problem. They are, after all, my namesake.

But the mzungus?

2

A MATTER OF ACCEPTANCE

As I enter the house, my mother walks up to me with deliberate steps, savouring my return. A shy smile makes its way across her face, a shimmer of tears in her eyes. I hold Mama tightly.

Babu, you're home! After all these years! You're looking so *theen!*

I stay with my parents and sister in their new home on Goan Street in Chumbageni, a neighbourhood deriving its name from *Nyumba ya Wageni*—House of Guests. Santos lives down the road in their former house from where he runs his radio repair shop. Attired in work clothes—short-sleeved white shirt, khaki shorts and white stockings—he is immersed in a maze of tiny wires and tubes that make up the convoluted innards of radio and sound equipment. His work is meticulous, his reputation beyond reproach. For that, he is much sought after. In up-and-coming Africa, the radio brings news, politics, music and sports into the intimacy of the home, making it as indispensable as electricity in the town, as firewood in the village.

My father proudly presents me to friends of the family. These visits, a ritual born of closeness and shared memories, bind émigrés together and are reason for congratulatory drinks and celebrations. Because I am a doctor, the community treats me with deference. Santos inducts me into the Goan Gymkhana, which provides a setting of familiar faces and conviviality away from our homeland. There I eat, once again, the warm *njugu karangas*—roasted peanuts—sold in small newspaper cones by *ting-ting wallahs* and savour their delicious smoky flavour and mildly salty skins. We get together for badminton or billiards, darts and cards, or merely for the camaraderie of having a smoke, enjoying the popular local Tusker beer, and talking politics, sports and highlights of the day. Weekends, after picnicking, we dance the night away to Jov's Blues. Surrounded

---

Ting-ting wallah. Nickname given to man selling snacks from a pushcart. Ting-ting is the bell he rings to let people know he is there.

by the gaiety of social activities and competitiveness of sports, I know I have arrived home.

Tanga retains its simple charm and unhurried pace. Each morning, a *Mwarabu* peddles strongly brewed coffee, steaming hot on a portable coal brazier, and a *shiri* hawks fish and live shrimp in season. Tanga is a British coastal town but I find it to be unequivocally stamped MADE IN GERMANY. A statue of Major Hermann von Wissmann stands in the middle of town, keeping an eye on the orderly flow of traffic. German colonial architecture includes a smattering of coral-coloured structures from the imperial provincial commissioner's office to the post office, from the stern courthouse to the exclusive European Hospital. Rows of attractive segmented arches and columns make for airy verandahs. The German presence is alive, dormant but breathing.

Predating the Germans is a small old Muslim cemetery by the squat stone clock tower on King Street, overlooking the harbour. Peaceful, unadorned, elevated grave sites carry lingering passersby into an era when the monsoon winds brought Arab dhows to these shores, along with trade and their way of life.

The town's main activities centre around vibrant picturesque Market Street. Shops with open barazas welcome patrons and provide shelter from sun and rain. Banks, hotels, offices, eating establishments and car repair garages are interspersed. A large open-air market comes alive with the hustle and bustle of local vendors selling prominently displayed wares: freshly laid eggs, jackfruit and custard apple, fruit twisted and plucked from its stalk, cassava, sweet potato, brown beans, *moringa*, vegetables picked from gardens, kingfish and mackerel caught at dawn, mutton and beef from animals slain the same day, and live chickens strung by their feet. Amidst buzzing flies and cawing crows, there are warm greetings, loud laughter, sour deals, swearing and clamorous offers of low prices. Here is where the three races—European, Asian, and African—converge and blend.

Business operates on two tiers. The British, virtually unseen, conduct wholesale trading, importing and exporting goods. Business is brisk. Sisal and tea sell well on the international market. In offices administered by secretaries, heavyset moustachioed bwanas, powerful potentates, direct with insiders' know-how. In contrast, Indian retailers, with small family-owned shops, are

---

Mwarabu. (Swahili) Arab

Shiri. Vendor, usually Arab

Moringa. Popular vegetable in Asian cuisine, also known as drumstick always in the public eye. The *muhindi* does not answer to the white man and, not constrained by strict regulations of time or place, can stretch working hours to suit customer needs.

Opportunities for Goans are limited to civil service and the professional sector. Portuguese rulers discouraged the Goan Catholic from taking up trade in favour of government white-collar jobs. *Empregado*—Portuguese for *clerk* or *civil servant*—carries an aura of importance. Most Goans occupy senior clerical positions, but colour bars their rise to administrative or managerial levels. Professionally, some are teachers and a few enter the medical field.

The average African, in the eyes of the British, has no marketable skills. Menial servitude is the extent of his capability—shop assistant, domestic for mzungus and *wahindi*, and labourer in the shambas. Of an unhurried culture, they are easygoing, given to quick laughter that rolls out rich and infectiously.

Haina neno. Itakuwa mzuri tu—Not to worry. It will be all right.

When work is done, everyone returns home, an allocation put in place at the start of German rule: mzungus, east to Ras Kazone; Goans, west to Chumbageni; Arabs and Africans, south to Ngamiani. The majority of Indians live above their shops on Market Street.

After my first month, assailed by moments of anxiety, I have to decide how I will earn a living and be independent. My options are either to enter private practice—an uncomplicated way of beginning a career since there are few doctors who have their own dispensaries—or be attached to the government-run Tanga General Hospital, where I can ask to be placed on the surgical side.

Friends advise me to see the medical director at the Government Medical Service in Dar es Salaam. All hospitals in Tanganyika belong to this group, so I could be assigned anywhere in the country depending on need. I will request Tanga because I have been away from my family for many years and wish to intern with the surgeon who is expected to join the staff shortly. However, after my encounter with the immigration officer, I am uneasy about meeting another British official. To put me at ease, my father offers to ask Dr. Armando Nazareth, a friend of the family, if he would accompany me.

Dr. Armando and his wife, Lydia, the only child of the Bencett family, live in Makarora, a large coconut plantation outside of Tanga. Although trained at the famed Universidade de Coimbra in Portugal, his credentials are not recognised

---

Wahindi. (Swahili) Plural for Muhindi, Indians

by the Government Medical Service. The sole concession made was to permit him to treat labourers on his plantation. An extensive library keeps him well read and up to date with journals and newspapers. I take to him readily and sense I can divulge my worries. He has faced similar problems and his guidance will be helpful.

It will take some time before you get used to life here. When I got married, I thought I would practise medicine and manage the plantation. Did not happen. The government did not allow me to pursue my profession and my in-laws never gave up control. But I got used to it. I had no choice.

Was it difficult?

Yes . . . in the beginning. What can you do? The bureaucracy is too firmly established. For now, if you want a job, take it one step at a time. Like going to Dar today.

As soon as the Dakota Douglas DC-3 aircraft takes off, I am unencumbered. Talking to Dr. Armando lifts a load off my mind and makes me view my misgivings in a more practical light.

Medical Director Dr. John Evans is courteous and proper, though not quite ready to make an exception. He understands my position; however, appointments are made on the basis of need. I would hear in due course.

Four weeks later, which seems like a lifetime, I receive a yearlong contract at Tanga General Hospital. Papa walks on air. Mama cannot contain her joy. Beer flows at the Gymkhana.

Congratulations, Dr. Leo!

Tanga General Hospital, commonly referred to as European Hospital, is an imposing two-storey edifice facing the sea. Built by Germans at the beginning of the century, its grand, well-serviced European ward is staffed by European doctors and nursing sisters. The African section, added on during the British rule, is a complex of half a dozen one-level buildings spread around in no particular order. Built to hold thirty people, fifteen on each side, the ward overflows with patients curled in mud-coloured sheets, which, though clean, look dirty. At the first sign of recuperation, they leave their beds and are out on the hospital grounds sitting under the shade of mango trees. The isolated Indian ward—a large, solitary, derelict room sprouting inconspicuously on the south side—has a reputation for indifferent medical coverage. European nurses do not visit the wing with any alacrity and physicians occasionally stop in to oversee Indian doctors and African medical assistants. Indians keep away except when in dire need and there is no recourse. Most of the time, it is three-quarters empty.

The three wings accommodate standards of living and individual customs with quality of care as disparate as the colour of the patients.

On my first day, anxious and perspiring, I remind myself I have been trained well.

You are all right. Don't worry. Be yourself.

I am introduced to Hospital Superintendent Leonard Pike, who remains seated behind an imposing desk. A big man with a handlebar moustache, he does not ask me to sit.

Senior Medical Officer Dr. Liam Delaney welcomes me, bids me sit down, talks mostly about trivial affairs, alludes vaguely to what I will be doing, returns to inconsequential chatter, then stands to shake my hand.

Dr. Donald Currie is the medical officer in charge. Recently arrived, this is his second tour. His wife, Ysobel, is the anaesthesiologist. Like all British doctors, he wears a short-sleeved shirt, white shorts with white stockings turned down at the knee and brown shoes. He has a kindly face, warm smile, and speaks to me at length as an equal, without affectation. I hear he is a good listener and an understanding man.

I am assigned to the African wing and meet the team of four Indian doctors—Somabhai Patel, Madhusudan Datar, Shashichandra Dalal and Naresh-Kumar Dave. These men have spent the best years of their lives in remote areas fighting disease in the bush—blackwater fever, sleeping sickness and yellow fever. After years of hardship with uncomplaining wives and growing children, they are at a big hospital in a town with amenities.

Indian doctors are classified sub-assistant surgeons, the lowest rung in the rank of physicians, which does not make them surgeons. Their practice is limited to treating Africans and they are denied access to the latest procedures and prescribing new medications. Compensation is miniscule compared to their white counterparts; in fact, a recently arrived English nurse stands taller in estimation and salary. Respect in the eyes of staff and patients is low. Not perceived as full-fledged physicians, this lack of recognition is dispiriting and they bide their time until retirement.

I am given the designation of assistant surgeon, one notch above sub-assistant surgeon status. No Indian is a medical officer; that appellation is carried only by a white doctor.

There are no African physicians, only medical assistants. In the eyes of their people, they are neither foreign medical practitioners nor *wagangas*—witch doctors—and do not measure up to local expectations.

I settle in at a slow pace—*pole-pole*—sharing night call at the Indian ward, assisting with some surgery and seeing patients at the African clinic Mondays, Wednesdays and Fridays. It is not unusual for them to stand in long, sinuous queues, earnestly hoping their afflictions, fevers and colds, abdominal worms, twisted feet, burning urination and swollen scrotums, can be relieved with one visit to Bwana *Daktari*. These patients have immense faith in the immediate efficacy of the white man's medicine and hope I will prescribe an injection. *Sindano*—the needle—holds magical powers! Much as I sympathise, it is difficult to convince them it would do little good for their hernias or roundworms.

We see male and female patients on different days. The women, although ailing, carry sleeping *mtotos* on their backs and continue tending to their toddlers. I sit in with Dr. Patel, a kind, avuncular gentleman with more experience than all the medical officers combined. He can intuit a disorder before the patient finishes relating his story. I watch expressions and listen carefully to their stories. I try to decipher Swahili, happy to get the gist by putting two and two together. I begin to feel more at ease, establishing rapport and understanding my patients' progress. Are they better? Worse? Any complaints?

The operating theatre is a freestanding, single-level structure with the anaesthesia room on one side and recovery room on the other. Today, I am assisting Dr. Jan Lommerse of Dutch descent and recent arrival from Britain. The patient, a man in his twenties, has a hernia on the right side of his groin. The perforation is long-standing and the sac protruding from the abdomen has adhered itself to the surrounding soft tissues.

Dr. Lommerse attempts to separate the sac and accidentally ruptures a vein. Bleeding ensues. Sponging and suction fail to keep the wound dry and blood obscures the anatomy. As slow bleeding persists, tissues lose detail. Dr. Lommerse severs the vas deferens. Inadvertently. The vas is a slender, thick-walled tube that transports semen from the testicles to the base of the penis. The surgeon remains unfazed.

You cut the vas, I say softly.

What?

You cut the vas deferens.

Oh!

Daktari. (Swahili) Doctor

Mtotos. (Swahili) Babies, children

He looks over his green cloth surgical mask and seeing my discomfiture, tries to allay it.

Happens. In the best of hands.

I make no response, though I have never seen this mishap.

The patient is breathing regularly under spinal anaesthetic and sedation. The nurse drops a pair of scissors in the kidney-shaped metal dish and snaps open a glass vial containing catgut, suture material. I snip off the ties as Lommerse places them around bleeding vessels. The anaesthetist at the head of the operating table suppresses a cough.

You aren't saying much. You should be tolerant of unforeseen occurrences.

I don't answer.

You know, I didn't cut your tongue. All right, I'll put the vas together. In any case, this young buck will impregnate as many women with one vas as two.

The operation done, the patient is off the table. We peel off our gowns and gloves and walk into the changing room.

What's eating you?

You could have been a little more careful.

Who the hell do you think you are? Professor of surgery? You come from some damn bloody university in India. Hardly started here and you think you know it all?

I have not repaired a hernia myself but I have assisted. I am just . . . just. . .

Just what? Shocked? My dear fellow, you learn from experience. There's no good surgeon who hasn't made mistakes. If you've not made mistakes, you've not operated enough.

There are mistakes and mistakes. Some are bad.

Oh, shut up! You people from India are all the same. Always moralising. Think you're so superior! I'll tell you what you are. A bloody sniveling opportunist. All you want to do is make money. You mention this incident and I'll have you transferred. In any case, there is nothing to talk about. Who's going to believe you anyway?

Trembling with rage, I try to steady myself. I want to tell him he is a fool, ignorant and biased, but am too angry to respond adequately. His threat to have me transferred unnerves me. I slowly slump into a chair as I see the year promised to me fading away. I go home.

I'm going to leave the hospital. Chuck it! They can get some other yes-man, lackey. I've had it!

It takes my father a while to understand me. I am incoherent, unable to clearly describe what took place.

Bos baba—Sit down, son. Have a drink. Everything will be okay. Try and forget it.

How can I? After what he's done and said?

There will be many situations like this. You can't afford to leave now. Later, maybe.

I glance at Papa. There is a look of concern, a squint of sadness. All the medical officer needs to say is that I cannot get along with the staff and I will be dismissed. My father is aware of that too.

At work, days are drawn out and strained. A fortnight goes by. Dr. Delaney receives notice that Dr. Lommerse is being transferred to Iringa in the southern highlands to fill in for their surgeon who is returning to England on holiday. For me, the news announces the end of a tumultuous period.

3

YOU NEED SHOES? I HAVE.

In his usual sports shirt and longs, Santos, affable as always, is seated at the bar of the Gymkhana with a glass of beer, talking to his companions about getting more youth to the playing field.

Leo, come play hockey with us. You've been hibernating for too long.

Four months have passed since my return, and almost all that time has been taken up seeking employment. With a job secured, I can now join friends for some recreation.

Official Tanga shuts down at four. By five, all pitches take on lives of their own. Football is East Africa's favourite sport, and any vacant lot is an open invitation to kick a ball around, but I haven't touched a football in a long while. Cricket is very British, prim and proper, popular in the colonies from India to Australia. I don't play cricket. I am good at hockey, most often at the right half position. However, Santos has always been a better athlete and was on the formidable second eleven team at St. Xavier's College.

I don't have any equipment.

Go to Tanga Sports on Market Street and buy yourself some shoes and whatever else you need. It's a good place and I know the owner, Mr. Sampaat.

As sports secretary for the Gymkhana, Santos, with his friendly, helpful nature, is familiar with all sporting goods merchants. If he knows the Sampaats as well as he says, I can probably get in and out of the shop in a trice.

Friday after work, I drive over in my dove-blue Volkswagen Beetle. Mr. Sampaat, a dark, stocky Indian man in his mid-fifties, is appraising cricket bats with a customer. There are four on the counter. The Englishman picks one out, takes a step back, places the end of the bat gingerly on the floor, positions himself as if receiving a ball from the bowler and goes through the graceful motion of swinging the bat forward in a mock defensive stroke.

There is no one else to help me. *This cricketer isn't going to be long. He is almost ready to buy.* The Englishman picks up another bat and goes through the motions again, this time attempting to drive the ball forward through a full swing. He cannot decide and finally leaves, stating his preference for English willow over Pakistani bats. I am relieved. Mr. Sampaat walks towards me, raising his bushy eyebrows.

Yes?

I need shoes . . . for hockey.

You need shoes? I have. What your size?

Nine and a half.

I bring.

He goes into the adjoining room returning with an oblong cardboard box. Taking the pair out, he wipes the soles against his rounded middle from habit and hands them to me. I barely take the shoes when a lanky European boy, not more than sixteen, comes in. Sampaat sees him through the corner of his eye and quickly goes to assist him.

I'd like a white pair, not blue.

He does not hear me. I am annoyed but since this chap is Santos's friend, I decide to have a little patience. My eyes wander around the room. The left side is stacked from floor to ceiling with sporting merchandise, shelved in rows. A movable ladder stands at the corner, giving easy access to the highest rack. The right wall is similarly stacked. An alcove in the middle holds two large colour photographs, one of King George VI looking rather staid and the other of Queen Elizabeth II, resplendent in coronation robes. Below the photographs stands a tiny statue of Ganesh, the Hindu elephant-headed god, garlanded with a string of marigolds. The ceiling fan chugs away, attempting to cool the space. It is hot and humid and I perspire under the collar, chafing at the delay.

The lad goes through a selection of shorts and swim trunks, unsure of what he wants.

They good, sir. No shrink or lose colour. Made in England, sir. You use long time.

Sampaat's eyes haven't left the boy's face other than a furtive glance or two at the discarded pile of clothes. His thick lips remain slightly parted in anticipation of a sizeable sale.

When he sees some hesitation, he adds quickly, I give very good price, sir.

I am still standing with the shoes in my hands, vying for Sampaat's attention. He remains focused and when the lad decides not to buy, his jaw slackens.

Very good, sir.

Excuse me, Mr. Sampaat, I've been waiting . . .

He doesn't glance in my direction and instead greets another person entering the shop. She is white.

Good afternoon, madam.

I want to start netball at the African girls' school. Show me a net that you won't charge me too much for.

I stand taut, observing Sampaat's every gesture. My hands tighten their grip around the shoes, squeezing from them a whiff of factory rubber.

Yes, madam. I show you different qualities.

He scurries into the back room.

Damn. I will never come here again.

I toss the shoes on the hard polished wooden counter, turn around, and leave.

The next morning, Santos reminds me, By the way, we play hockey at five. Only a practice game. Today, you'll play as a back. Isn't that where you play?

No, but it doesn't matter because I don't have shoes.

How come? Didn't you buy a pair from Sampaat?

I went, but the fellow had no time for me. He was too busy serving mzungus.

Was he the young Sampaat or the old man?

How would I know? It was my first time there.

I recount my visit.

Must be the father. If you don't buy from him, you won't get them anywhere.

Then I don't get shoes.

A week goes by. I miss two games.

You still don't have shoes?

No.

A few days later, Santos hands me a package loosely wrapped in newspaper.

Your shoes. These are from Old Man Sampaat. He's very sorry and will not charge you.

Santos has lived in Africa longer than I and is familiar with how things work, how people behave. He is also more understanding, less likely to become agitated. His way of dealing with this impasse was to drop in at the shop, greet the old man, mention how poorly the Tanga football team fared against Dar es Salaam, enquire solicitously about his business, and nonchalantly bring up the fact that his brother had been there to buy a pair of shoes.

I'm in a quandary. If I return the shoes, it will be childish. If I keep them, I will be able to play, but my main issue would remain unresolved.

That week, I play hockey twice. Driving past Market Sports, I am unable to bring myself to stop in. I don't care for Sampaat or the Europeans he serves, but since he sent me a pair of shoes, gratis, I need to thank him and find out if he will accept payment. I feel awkward. Gradually, my anger wanes. I drop in at his shop. Sampaat looks perplexed, then recognition registers in his eyes.

Dr. Sahib, good afternoon. Come in, come in. I very sorry. Please, please sit down.

He calls for Bikhu, his assistant, to bring two cups of tea, and immediately leaves to attend to a customer.

Shunned again. Why did I listen to Santos? Bikhu returns with tea and Sampaat joins me.

I very sorry, Doctor. But this Africa. To have business, I make *salaam* . . . very sorry. You excuse me.

I sit down longer than intended, sipping spiced Indian tea while he tells his story.

Sampaat came from the enterprising coastal district of Kutch in western India. After World War I, as a young man, he sailed across the Indian Ocean in a dhow to East Africa. The long and treacherous journey took more than thirty days. His father's elder brother, a dealer in grains—rice, wheat, lentils—helped him. When Sampaat learned more about trade and business, he decided to import small items that Europeans would readily purchase.

First, I bring balls and bats, slowly grow, now sports dress. English buy most my stock. They spend money but you must say, *Very good, sir; yes, sir; no, sir,* give lots attention. Indians no have time for play and they want cheap. If English go tomorrow, my shop close.

I am embarrassed I have not been more understanding. In trying to cater to the needs of the Europeans, he was hoping I would be tolerant. I view his actions the only way I know. I am a prisoner of the times as much as he, but we look at the same thing from different perspectives. He has accepted the status quo. I am fighting it. He will not accept any money.

Salaam. (Arabic) Peace, greeting

4

HEY, YOU

It is Saturday, a light day at work, and only a few weeks before Christmas. I finish rounds at eleven and, on my way home, drive past a surprising collection of churches—the unpretentious Catholic Church of St. Anthony with its tall, slender steeple and affiliated primary school; the impeccably white Greek Orthodox Church, its domed entrance and latticed front topped by two rounded and asymmetric steeples; and the sprawling Anglican Church of St. Albans, seemingly unconcerned about its peeling paint and need to update its appearance.

I park my car and decide to visit Santos to go over plans for a picnic at Pangani Beach. A decrepit, antiquated town, Pangani was once a prosperous centre for smuggling slaves. It is quiet now, memories of those harrowing times buried in the anonymity of its past. The beach is beautiful, and casuarina pines ruffled by gentle sea breezes produce soft whispers that are among the most soothing sounds in the world.

Walking absent-mindedly to my brother's house, an impressive grey Bentley drives towards me on the metalled road. It slows down, then stops. Behind the wheel is a large, clean-shaven European dressed in a tan-coloured suit and tie, with neatly combed hair. His right elbow rests proprietarily on the open window.

Crooking his pointed index finger, the man imperiously beckons me. Intrigued, I hasten to the car, my feet carrying me against my will.

Looking past me, he brusquely asks, Where is the Anglican church?

St. Albans?

Yes, of course, he retorts impatiently.

Turn right at the end of this street. You'll see the entrance.

He presses on the clutch, slides into first gear, and speeds off without a thank-you! I recognise him to be Arthur Barnett, a private-practice physician. Overwhelmed by his insolence, I am disgusted and indignant at myself. How could I have responded to a man who solicits attention by authoritatively curling his finger, *Hey, you, come here*? I squirm at my response. Unacceptably obsequious. That could not have been me. It couldn't have! *A white man crooks his finger and I run . . . I run to him.* When Dr. Barnett summoned me, he saw an Indian and based on skin colour, respect was denied instantly. Would his disdainful behaviour have been different had he known I was a doctor, just like him?

When I am somewhat composed and less ashamed, I mention the incident to Santos.

That's how it is, Leo. Mzungus have this mind-set. Happens all the time.

Back home, my father tries to console me.

He was not out to insult you personally. If he knew you, he would not have done that. He's just used to treating our people that way.

But I *AM* my people.

We are quiet, brewing in our silence.

At work, plagued with contrary emotions, I become overly sensitive. If a white nurse merely says, *Doctor, about the medicine Husseini should have . . .* I bristle at the questioning of my competency, until she finishes, *You forgot to write down the prescription you suggested at rounds.* I know I am being needlessly unfair and then go through another type of fire.

I am quite certain I will go abroad for my surgical training. There is nothing to hold me back. The only way to overcome inequity is to train where the colonial himself comes from. Then he may be willing to accept me, believing implicitly as he does, that whatever is British is the best in the world.

Like the leopard who cannot change its spots, I cannot change my colour.

5

MOTHER'S BLESSING

It is a warm September evening. Outside, the cicadas chirp persistently, the high-pitched droning welcome and hypnotic. After dinner, I am ensconced in an easy chair in the living room buried in the *Tanganyika Standard,* the local daily. In Dar es Salaam, the Goan Hockey Eleven are due to play the Sikh Union, both teams among the finest exponents of field hockey. The Mau Mau in Kenya are portrayed as a militant guerilla band committed to violence in order to obtain independence for the *Kikuyu.* In America, General Eisenhower is girding himself for the campaign leading to the elections.

There is a hand on my shoulder.

Babu, my mother whispers. I have a letter from Bai. There is a proposal for you. The girl comes from a good family and they are prepared to give a big dowry. She is fair, nice looking, and educated.

Saying no more, Mama turns around and returns to the kitchen.

I go back to the newspaper, eyes riveted to the page, not seeing anything. The question of a woman in my future is suddenly thrust into the open. I am an eminently eligible young man now, a doctor, much sought after by families with suitable daughters.

I get up from the chair and mechanically walk through the door to the verandah. All I see is Dolly. Her wavy locks tumbling over her forehead, her soft brown eyes, her high cheekbones, her smile . . .

We have been corresponding weekly. Letters delivered to Santos's post office box 316 help keep our relationship secret.

My thoughts go back to the night I proposed. We were riding in a gharry on Marine Drive, along Bombay's western sea face. The New Year's Eve Ball at the Catholic Gymkhana had ended and I was taking her home. The breeze was playing with Dolly's hair, blowing it into my face. My lips found her ear and I whispered, Will you marry me? A half nod and simultaneous tightening of her

---

Kikuyu. Bantu tribe who live in the highland area of south-central Kenya, near Mount Kenya.

arm around my waist was her immediate response. I understood. The answer was *yes*, but she didn't want the world to know. I leaned back, blissful, listening to the rhythmic trot of the horse. *Clip-clop, clip-clop,* clean and clear, like bells ringing out our secret.

Three weeks later, Dolly's older sister Tehmi came to see me at my resident quarters. Although startled by her presence, I was not entirely taken by surprise. I had been going out with Dolly for some time and expected this would happen.

Tehmi felt it would be best if we gave up the notion of marriage. The family was distraught about Dolly's future. She was planning to marry a man not of her faith or community, a man who would eventually settle down in Africa. Her mother and father were heartbroken.

Do your parents know about this? What does your mother have to say?

It would be irresponsible to say I had not told them, so I hedged as truthfully as I could.

It will be all right with my family.

Will you promise to stop seeing her?

That's not my decision to make. It's Dolly's.

The encounter plagued me through the rest of the night. It must have taken a great deal of resolve to seek me out. The only reason for her visit was to protect her sister from what might befall her in unknown Africa. Dolly's parents were apprehensive about the challenges she would face without family or friends. Yet, I could not oblige them. I wished there was a way to allay their concerns. Merely telling them I loved Dolly, that I would marry and care for her always, would not do.

Standing on the verandah, peering into the inscrutable blackness, I decide to talk to Santos. I had casually introduced Dolly to him at a college get-together a year before he left for Tanga.

Papa will be okay but there will be trouble with Mama.

January 1953, I learn Uncle Robert will be taking a long overdue holiday to Goa, accompanied by Papa and Magda. I decide to confide in my father and join him on his daily walk before dinner.

Papa, I need to tell you something, but don't get angry. I met a girl in Bombay. In medical school. She's not Goan or Catholic. She is Parsi.

I hesitate.

We want to get married.

He is quiet for a long time.

Why have you not said anything until now?

I was nervous. I didn't know how to tell you.

Details tumble as though a floodgate has been opened. I try to be selective, hoping to make my case as persuasive as I can. But it isn't easy.

Dolly is a doctor. She graduated with me and now she works at Cama Municipal Hospital for Women. We've been writing letters to each other since I came home. Her father is an accountant. His family has lived in Bombay for years. Her mother came to Bombay from Iran when she was seven years old.

Have you told anyone?

Santos knows.

Another long silence.

This is not good. Mama will be very upset.

I'm sorry.

Ethnic customs, especially among people with a long traditional past, always acquire a greater inflexibility at the time of marriage, particularly in the period leading up to the nuptials. Customarily, marriages are arranged, and mine would have been no different. But I have elected to bypass this practice hallowed by time and sanction and done the unimaginable. I have fallen in love with someone outside my community.

As if he hears me, Papa says, It will be all right.

I ask if he and Uncle Robert can make a trip to Bombay to see Dolly. He agrees.

We'll talk to Mama after we meet Dolly.

As soon as Papa returns from Goa in April, it is crucial we let Mama know about Dolly since we plan to marry in five months.

The matter of telling Mama is extremely delicate. I shall be presenting her with a fait accompli and trust she goes along. How and when will I bring it up? What exactly do I say? Papa decides it would be easier if all of us—Santos, Magda, Papa and I—approach Mama together.

She is incensed!

What are you saying? I can't believe it! This girl . . . she's not Goan? Not even Catholic? So shameful. You should have told me! Leo, this is not right what you're doing. Aren't there any Goan girls? I can understand someone else doing this . . . but *you*?

Her eyes fill with tears. She is deeply hurt we have not confided in her.

Does she know about us, the family?

Yes.

Her parents, do they know?

Yes.

Do they approve?

I think so. I have not met them.

She will have to convert.

Yes. She's taking instructions.

You really want to marry her?

I do.

I take Mama's hand, holding it in mine for a long time. I want to admit I have dishonoured her. I need to be assured of her assent, her blessing.

6

TOGETHER AGAIN

Every day is replete with work and play, with challenges and anxieties. Not the least of which is how Dolly will acclimate after she arrives. She will be new to my family and this part of the world.

Before I left Bombay, we planned to meet and marry in Tanga in a year. Our proposed rendezvous was both thrilling and romantic. What kept us going during our separation were the weekly letters we wrote and the certainty we would see each other again. For us to marry, Dolly had to convert to Catholicism. I arranged for her to go through religious instruction with Father Angelo Innocent Fernandes, secretary to India's first cardinal, Valerian Gracias.

It is the middle of June and time for Dolly to make the journey. She will take the same route from Bombay to Tanga as my mother had taken some thirty years ago. Although leaving is difficult, she is eagerly looking forward to this moment. Tehmi comes to see her off at the dock. It is arduous for her mother and father to make the trip. They have accepted the fact that the young man she is marrying is a doctor, but know nothing about him or his family. They pray that *Ahura Mazda* protect her.

Santos and I drive to Mombasa, where the SS *Amra* berths. I am a cauldron of excitement as I spot Dolly coming down the ship's gangway. Catching sight of us among the throngs of people gathered at the quay, she beams with joy and waves. I can hardly believe she is finally here.

I don't remember much except I am suddenly holding her. We don't speak, yet we say all that needs to be said. The unbelievable has happened. Love is tangible again.

Santos is behind me waiting to give her a hug.

Welcome to Africa. How was your passage?

The first few days were rocky but it got calmer the farther we went out. My cabinmate had a baby, and with a crib, the space was too small for three of us. I

Ahura Mazda. (Persian) Highest spirit worshipped in Zoroastrianism made friends with a Mrs. De Souza and her two daughters from Uganda and stayed in their cabin most of the time. When the crew came around to deliver my meal and couldn't find me, they searched high and low thinking I'd fallen overboard!

We stop at Moa for a short break. Uncle Robert is pleased to see Dolly again. He and Papa had spent the afternoon having tea at her residence in Cama Hospital. We take some time to relax and freshen up. As we drive the last twenty miles, Dolly begins to worry.

I am scared to meet your mother.

It'll be all right.

Papa is already on the verandah waiting to greet her.

You remember Dolly?

Of course. Welcome. We are happy you are here, safe and well. I trust you had a good voyage.

Mama hurries out. She has been afraid that Dolly, coming from a well-to-do community, would be highbrow and formal. Her nervousness abates as she finds her without pretense. Dressed in a plain skirt and blouse, Dolly wears no makeup and her hairstyle is simple. Mama relaxes.

You must be tired and hungry. Come in, sit down, have something to eat. How are your parents?

They are well. Leaving them was more difficult than I imagined. Still, I am glad to be here.

It is not customary for an engaged couple to live under the same roof, so Dolly stays with Dr. Armando and Lydia Nazareth at Makorora. Dolly enjoys the company of the doctor and his wife who take to her readily and make sure she is comfortable. After the loudness of Bombay, she finds it difficult at first to get used to the quiet of the plantation. Relatives and friends drop in to say hello and pay respects. We spend our evenings visiting neighbours and having dinner with Papa, Mama and Magda. Weekends are filled with picnics, outings to Amboni and after-dinner get-togethers at the club.

Father Fred Callaran, the young Irish priest at the Church of St. Anthony, baptises Dolly and administers the sacraments of Holy Communion and Confirmation. She formally changes her name from Doulat Burjorji Irani to Dolly Marie Therese and chooses Uncle Robert as godfather and Bai as godmother.

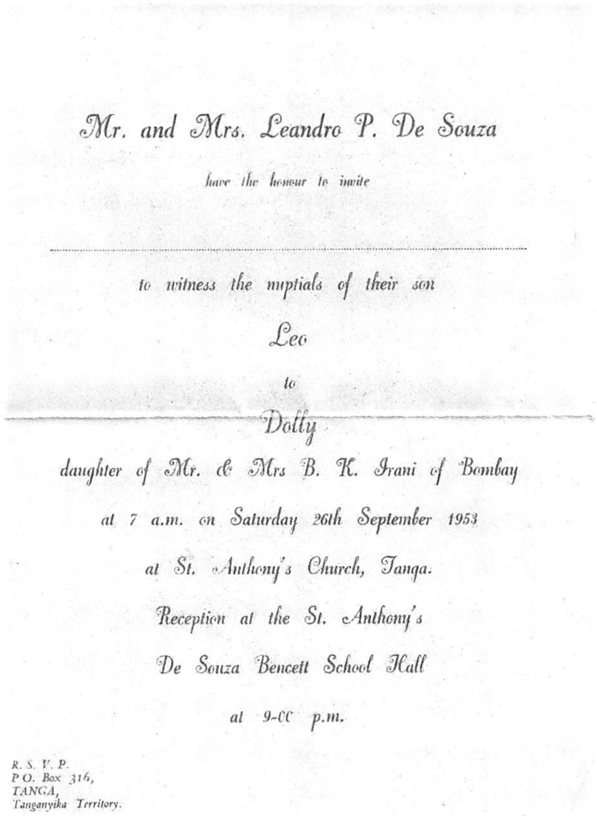

Mr. and Mrs. Leandro P. De Souza

have the honour to invite

....

to witness the nuptials of their son

Leo

to

Dolly

daughter of Mr. & Mrs B. K. Irani of Bombay

at 7 a.m. on Saturday 26th September 1953

at St. Anthony's Church, Tanga.

Reception at the St. Anthony's

De Souza Bencett School Hall

at 9-00 p.m.

R. S. V. P.
P.O. Box 316,
TANGA,
Tanganyika Territory.

Our wedding day is finally here. I dress carefully for the biggest day of my life. The occasion makes me nervous, uncertain, yet I know exactly what to do. My father hugs me, his eyes moist, his love evident. Mama gives me the traditional blessing.

God bless you, babu. You are a good son. We have looked after you all this time. From today, it will be your wife.

Dolly has been up since the early hours. Sleep was impossible thinking of her new life. The rain, falling steadily through the night, leaves her anxious. She is sure the path through the coconut grove will be washed out. My friend Manu Dias, who is charged with bringing her to the church, sets out in his sky-blue English Hillman and loses his way. Dolly paces the long verandah, eyes on the road, waiting. Manu reverses course, taking a longer route. They manage to arrive on time at the church, where the wedding party—my best man and boyhood friend from Parra, Donald Martin; maid of honour, Magda; our flower girl, Loretta, my godchild; and I are waiting.

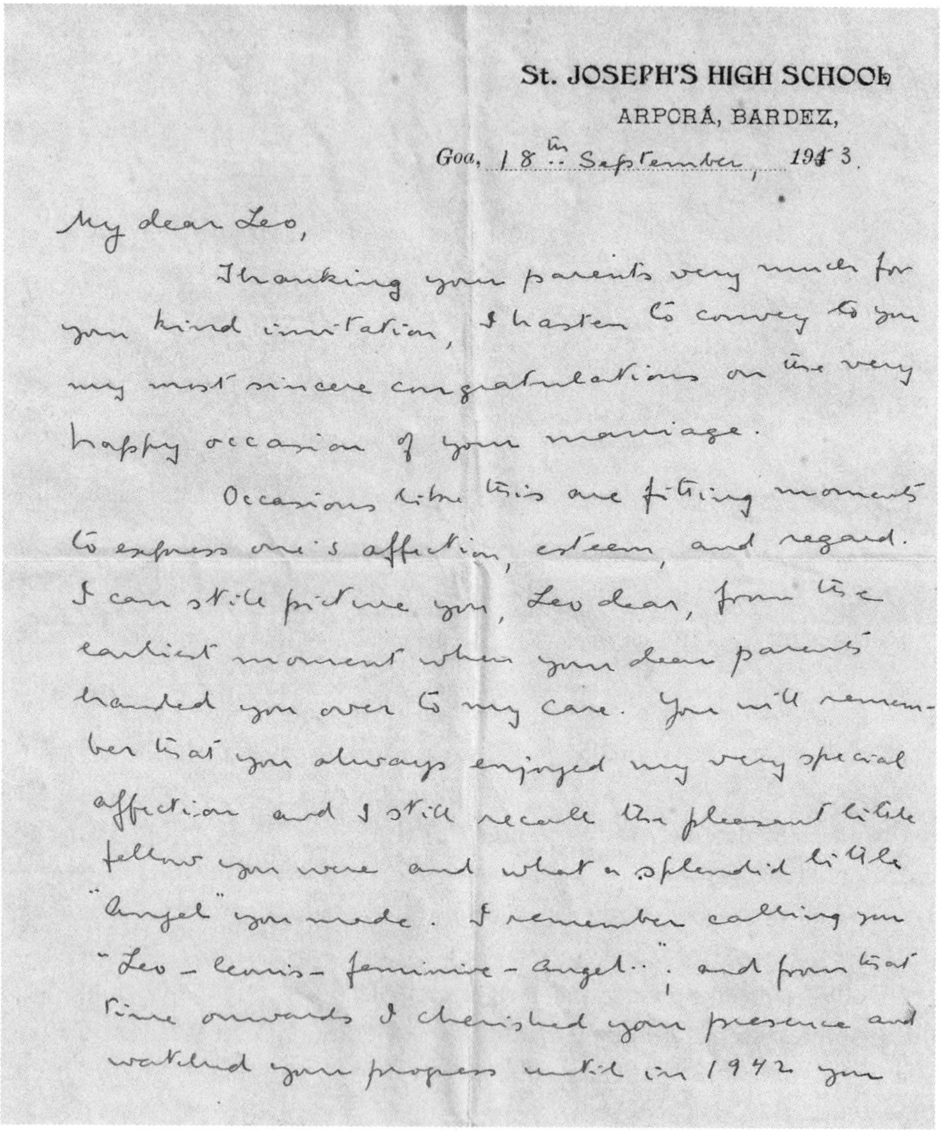

St. JOSEPH'S HIGH SCHOOL
ARPORÁ, BARDEZ,

Goa, 18th September, 1953.

My dear Leo,

Thanking your parents very much for your kind invitation, I hasten to convey to you my most sincere congratulations on the very happy occasion of your marriage.

Occasions like this are fitting moments to express one's affection, esteem, and regard. I can still picture you, Leo dear, from the earliest moment when your dear parents handed you over to my care. You will remember that you always enjoyed my very special affection and I still recall the pleasant little fellow you were and what a splendid little "Angel" you made. I remember calling you "Leo – leonis – feminine – angel..."; and from that time onwards I cherished your presence and watched your progress until in 1942 you

St. JOSEPH'S HIGH SCHOOL

ARPORÁ, BARDEZ,

Goa, ... *194*

passed your Matriculation with distinctions in Mathematics and Languages. The latter being one first in many years.

My last recollection of you was in your last year of Medicine, when you returned to Goa with Dr. D'Avoin (if memory does not play me false), and on which occasion I was able to be of some little help to you in connection with your companion.

Years have passed, and the affection I have had for you remains cemented. It is with this abundance of love and regard that I now greet you on this the most important occasion of your life. May God bless you and your young bride; may He make you both truly happy.

You have my blessings, prayers, & love

Yours ever in Xt,

Fr. Philip Mendonça

Father Callaran marries us on Saturday, September 26, at 7:00 a.m. Carrying a bouquet of arum lilies, Dolly looks lissome in a beautiful white silk embroidered sari. Her face shines with a radiance. I cannot take my eyes off her. I am overcome she would travel to a land so far away, with no parents, siblings, or relatives, to marry someone she had set her heart on. I vow to take care of her always.

For our guests, this is an unconventional union—two individuals from different worlds making their own decision to marry. Unheard of and scandalous! Yet they are here to witness the solemn ceremony. After the church ceremony, we spend the afternoon with Mr. Pinto Lobo and his wife, as it is not customary to go to my parents' home. Most of our friends and relatives return to work until noon and rejoin us at the School Hall at 9:00 p.m. for the reception—a catered event with finger foods and wedding cake made by a neighbour, Mrs. Gomes. Papa provides champagne and scotch. Everyone showers us with good wishes as we dance to the music of Jov's Blues.

For our honeymoon, we choose a tiny hill station nestled amongst the peaks of the Usambara Mountains. Once a summer resort named Wilhemstahl by German settlers, it is now called Lushoto. We find the sixty-mile drive exhilarating and the Volkswagen Beetle ideal for the two of us. Halfway up, we stop to enjoy a cascading waterfall. The rushing waters are mesmerising, and a cool white mist envelops us. We stand in awe, clinging to each other. The last ten miles are a succession of sharp twists and turns that take at least two hours.

The lone hotel in Lushoto is Indian-owned and primarily a place where Europeans stay. While the law does not prevent us from checking in at the Lawn Hotel, I am uneasy at the thought we may not be welcome. I want our days to be carefree, exuberant.

Instead, we ask Dr. Shashichandra Dalal and his wife to put us up for the week. Dr. Dalal, my associate at Tanga General Hospital was recently transferred and is in charge of the Government Hospital at Lushoto. They are generous enough to give us a room with an enclosed verandah on one side of their house, overlooking the garden.

Our days begin with morning walks, holding hands, through the verdant countryside along little streams. Dense greenery is occasionally interrupted by huts surrounded by shambas. A memorable trek leads us, after an hour along many narrow trails, to Irente Viewpoint, where spread below us is a magnificent panoramic vista of the vast Maasai Plains.

In the evenings, we enjoy Mrs. Dalal's vegetarian cooking. The doctor tells us of his ongoing tussle with Medical Headquarters regarding his official ranking in the service. He is an internist trained in Bombay with extensive clinical experience. Yet Dr. Evans at Dar es Salaam doesn't find him deserving of a medical officer's appointment. This official attitude incenses me. However, I am encouraged that here is a man unwilling to accept a lower designation and prepared to fight for his status.

We spend the second week of our honeymoon at Uncle Robert's in Moa. His modest whitewashed house sits on the edge of the plantation along the sandy Tanga-Mombasa Road. Beyond are cultivated patches of cassava and the African bush. Uncle Robert is both manager and public relations man at Moa Sisal Estate and gone all day. It is the first time Dolly and I are by ourselves.

Our world is complete with just the two of us. We reminisce about our days in medical school, our clandestine trysts, the dance at the New Year's Eve Ball, my proposal and its consequences. Now we are married. I do not want this time to end.

While the days are hot and we stay in to escape the glare and discomfort, the nights under the African sky are cool and unforgettable. The pitch-blackness of night covers everything and we cannot see each other. The sky is ablaze with a million stars like a canopy of diamonds. We hear the shrill chirps of the cicadas around us repeated endlessly. Though we remain invisible, there is closeness and touch, conversation and rapture. We are a world unto ourselves.

When it is time to return, we set out early. It rained heavily the previous day into the night. Parts of the road are washed away, requiring us to drive with caution. The Volkswagen has been sprightly enough along the mountain roads but here, with this low, road-hugging car, we are obliged to pick our way gingerly between ruts and rocks.

By midday, we cover half the distance but don't mind the slow drive. The stone bridge we crossed on our way up is covered by a voluminous sheet of gushing water. It is hard to take our gaze off the water as it rolls over the bridge with unconcealed fury. We pull to the side of the road and park alongside other vehicles. Sitting in the car becomes uncomfortable but outside is worse, unbearably hot and humid.

I'm thirsty. I'll stand by the edge of the water and scoop up some to drink.

No, no, no . . . you might slip! Let me walk to the village for oranges.

The village is a quarter mile away. I spot a young African lad of about ten, barefoot and shirtless. It is Sunday, so he does not have school. I ask if there's a place to buy oranges.

Duka yetu ina machungwa. Mimi itabidi kuleta baadhi—Our shop has oranges. I'll bring you some.

I do not have a shilling coin and give him a five-shilling note.

Buy a few and bring the change. Asante.

A grey Peugeot station wagon taxi carrying ten African passengers, instead of the regulation five, draws up. The roof is piled high with belongings tied in little bundles and some half-dead chickens held securely by their feet, a common sight on East African roads. The driver gets out. Sloppy in dirty khaki trousers and bush shirt unbuttoned at the top, he will have to wait for the water to subside. After twenty minutes, he opts to make the crossing.

The Peugeot sets off carefully in first gear. Bystanders watch with bated breath, eyes glued to the audacious cabbie. The car inches past the middle when a sudden surge of water sweeps over the bridge. The driver grapples with the flow but the force is too strong. The car is pushed to the edge and goes over. Dolly gasps. I run forward. Passengers panic and shriek. Everyone shouts instructions. No one dares jump in. The taxi is slowly dragged down giving passengers time to free themselves. All except the driver, whose door is jammed. We pray for a miracle. The station wagon slowly tilts to the right, ready to take him under any moment. This little spin helps him force open the door. We let out a thunderous roar, applauding wildly.

Emotionally drained and even thirstier, we realise the lad has not turned up with the oranges. We decide to return to Moa. At 6:00 p.m., Uncle Robert drives us to Tanga, and this time, we make it across the bridge, which is now visible. There is no telephone to inform anyone of our delayed start, to tell what has happened, and that we will be back past our expected time.

We arrive late that night to two distressed parents. Papa cries with relief as he embraces us. Mama's drawn countenance eases as she gently strokes Dolly's face and takes her by the hand. Dolly instinctively senses their reaction is one they would have towards their own daughter. She is delighted, secure in the knowledge that she is now part of a new household.

7

STORMY INTERLUDES

Our son is born on Thursday, November 11, 1954. Twenty-eight weeks and a little over four pounds. Dolly is tired and groggy from the pethidine given to ease the pain and discomfort of labour and delivery. She hasn't seen or held the baby, but hears him cry before the nurse takes him away. I stop in the nursery to see my son, a tiny baby swaddled and sleeping. Something is amiss. The baby's breathing, shallow and irregular, alarms me. I immediately rush to the rectory to speak to Father Foley about baptising the baby without delay. We name our firstborn, Martin, after St. Martin of Tours, the day's saint.

Martin dies the morning of November 12. I bring our baby home. News of his unexpected passing spreads by word of mouth from one family to the next. Papa cycles to Santos's to use the telephone, calling the church to begin funeral preparations, and Singh Sawmill to have their carpenter build a little wooden coffin. Mrs. Amboni Pereira sews the burial gown and has it ready when the women come to bathe and dress the body. Alfred Pires brings the coffin to the house, and after gently laying Martin in, we arrange flowers from the garden around it. Relatives, friends, and neighbours attend the rosary and hold an all-night vigil. Menino Rebello, professional photographer, is commissioned to preserve the memory of our son.

On Saturday, Father Foley blesses Martin's body and sprinkles the coffin with holy water while reciting prayers in Latin. Led by the crossbearer and priest, we carry the coffin, in a procession to St. Anthony's Church, singing ceremonial hymns and psalms. Dolly, recuperating at the hospital, is not present. Following the funeral Mass, we silently and mournfully fall in line behind the casket and walk the one and a half miles to Chumbageni Cemetery where Martin is buried in a corner reserved for angels. When Dolly comes home a week later, people drop by to condole. The days go by in a blur and we grieve privately, allowing our tears to flow.

Dolly and I move into a small, one-bedroom brick house in the hospital compound. I suggest she join the Medical Service to take her mind off Martin.

Dolly had done a year's internship in obstetrics and gynaecology and begins work as an assistant surgeon, taking care of pregnant women under the supervision of Dr. Currie.

I settle into an unsuspecting routine, beguiling as the weather. The climatic calendar assures long and short rains at the proper times, but it doesn't mean there are no aberrations like unseasonably arid days or incessant pouring rains. Such is the case at work. Although most days are uneventful, one day merging into another, there are times when thunder growls and storms break.

Rounds, unconventional and unvarying, start at nine o'clock. Accompanying me is Mary Mellon, the Irish nursing sister who runs the African ward. Efficient in her well-pressed white uniform and cap, she marches around giving orders and is referred to as *Mama Kubwa*—the matriarch. Shadowing Sister Mellon is an African nursing assistant in a belted red-and-white dress and smaller cap. Often a nursing student tags along. The junior nurses are young African girls, some of them daughters of chiefs. Shy and giggly, few are serious about their futures.

Jambo Bwana or *Jambo Mama*, we greet our patients. Standing at the foot of the first cot, I begin my examination, entering findings, medications and recommendations in the chart. The nursing assistant makes her own notes. The student observes. The nursing sister supervises. Sometimes, however, upheavals occur.

Doctor, you prescribed Chloromycetin for the male patient in bed six.

Yes, I did.

Why?

Because he has typhoid, Sister. His history of slow pulse, obtunded abdomen, furred tongue and fever are typical. Clinically, it is typhoid, and I don't want to wait till the tests are in.

Chloromycetin is a new drug.

Yes?

Only a medical officer like Dr. Currie can prescribe a new drug. You can write for penicillin.

I turn around to see the nursing assistant's eyes fixed on me in an enquiring gaze. As are the nursing student's. *What are you going to do?* they seem to ask.

I cannot allow myself the luxury of anger or frustration. I leave my instructions as written and replace the chart on the wall instead of giving it to the nursing assistant.

You tell Dr. Currie I prescribed Chloromycetin.

I am certain she will say something, at least to let the other two know she has the last word. But she doesn't. Her imperious face crimsons. Her anger, which should be mine, consumes her. I am not inclined to pursue the matter any further.

Dolly encounters the same resistance to her prescribing the antibiotic. Chart in hand, she strides into Dr. Currie's office and tackles him without preamble.

Are you saying I am not fit to prescribe Chloromycetin when it's indicated?

The directness of the question startles him.

Oh . . . no . . . it's all right, he stammers. You prescribe it. He cannot bring himself to insist that the rule regarding antibiotics applies to her.

On another occasion, I send an older man with arthritis for physical therapy to ensure his arms and legs remain limber. My patient is promptly returned with a note from the opinionated therapist.

Doctor, send this old man home. Don't you have younger patients with better outlooks?

I could have gone to Dr. Currie as Dolly had done. He may have reinstated my instructions, but in the existing hierarchy, no matter how frequently I protest, my orders would continue to be countermanded. I am incensed at the indignity of it all. With time, I realise I can't afford to be upset every time something happens and, in quieter moments, remind myself I am here to acquire surgical experience. It isn't easy. They are beginning to wear me down.

The surgeon I assist, Dr. Enrico Carloni, is Italian, married to an Englishwoman. He was trained in Rome and held previous surgical appointments in Italian colonies round the Horn of Africa and is offended by lack of recognition of his position as a surgeon. This subtle prejudice happens once in a while at the European Hospital, where, although white, he is not British and therefore not considered as good. He avoids open fraternisation with the Indian medical staff for fear of what the English would say.

Dr. Carloni aspires to be a Fellow of the Royal College of Surgeons of England, the highest level of surgical training. In the colonies, this rank will exalt his status in the eyes of his peers. In preparing for the first part of the fellowship exam, he encounters unexpected snags. The subject of anatomy is straightforward. Very little has altered. Physiology, on the other hand, constantly changes with new discoveries, making it a challenge to keep up with. Additionally, nuances of the English language pose obstacles for him.

Learning I plan to take the same examination, he asks if we could study Samson Wright's *Applied Physiology* together, particularly as I am more conversant with the language. I welcome the idea as being mutually helpful. We start our sessions cautiously and later settle into a comfortable routine of one or two readings a week. There is a limit to the level of comfort between us because we are not on the same social level. Nonetheless, in time, we develop a camaraderie.

I am called to the hospital one Thursday at 4:00 a.m. to see an injured labourer whose leg was caught in a sisal decorticating machine. His foot and ankle are one bloody mess.

The blackness of night is becoming streaked with grey. I am still in the operating room at six o'clock when I see my reading partner, Dr. Carloni, standing before me.

Good morning. What brings you here so early?

What brings me here? You should not be doing this case, he sputters, finding it difficult to talk through the mask. His eyes are fierce.

Why has he come in so early? I wonder. *It is not even his operating day.*

He continues mumbling angrily while pacing.

I was called in to take care of it.

But you should not be here!

What is the problem? I don't understand. I have previously treated cases of this complexity.

What *is* the problem? As if you don't know!

Mr. Starkey, who is assisting me, taps me gently and whispers in a thin and tremulous voice.

It's a work-related incident and he wanted to do it.

Ron Starkey is chief nurse in charge of the operating theatre. English, with a distinct accent different from the rest of his countrymen, he rarely associates with his compatriots. A shrewd observer, he is aware of the strengths and shortcomings of British medical officers. He has come to know me well and regularly confides in me, information that helps my dealings with the white staff.

This is work-related, Dr. Carloni blurts, and you . . . you . . . simply grabbed it!

I see the whole picture clear as day. Dr. Carloni would pocket additional remuneration since the patient was injured at work. I recall Dr. Somabhai Patel telling me medical officers get compensation and other perks for treating such injuries. Indian physicians do not. I realise instantly someone made an error in calling me instead of the medical officer on call or Dr. Carloni.

I cannot comprehend Dr. Carloni believes I stole the case from him even though I do not get an extra shilling. I am dumbfounded. After our weekly sessions together, he should know I would be the last person to do this to him. And I thought we were becoming friends.

Wait! I did not grasp the implications. I was called and came in. I did not question.

That's an excuse.

Anger builds in me, displacing astonishment at his behaviour, my disappointment, my hurt, and all my humiliations.

All right, I'm almost done. You can take over and close up.

Don't be theatrical!

I move away from the operating table, leaving the patient with his wound open, waiting to be closed and dressed. I strip off my gown and drop it unceremoniously on the floor. Pulling off my gloves, I fling them over the crumpled gown.

He's yours, Dr. Carloni, precisely as you wanted. Now, you will not lose a cent.

I shoot him an angry look and stride through the door into the changing room.

Dr. De Souza! Dr. De Souza! he yells.

I told you, you can have him, I shout back as I half run, half walk away from the operating theatre to my house, in scrubs. The distasteful incident continues to play out over and over again in my mind. I almost have to scream to halt this ongoing replay.

Whatever happens, I am certain we will not get together again for our study sessions, for that requires friendship, and that means crossing colour lines.

8

CONCEPTS TAKE TIME TO CHANGE

Can we meet today? Dr. Currie asks me one morning.

Yes, of course.

The urgency of his request takes me by surprise.

I wonder what he wants, for we do not often get together. *Have I done anything wrong? Have I said something I shouldn't? Have I upset a newly arrived nurse?* I cannot recall any such behaviour that could be described as even vaguely fractious or defiant.

He comes straight to the heart of the matter without any preamble.

Would you mind helping out and taking calls on alternate nights with Ysobel? Our children are young; they need her at home.

Ysobel Currie is the anaesthesiologist who routinely takes care of patients undergoing surgery and handles complicated cases in the African ward. A soft-spoken, gentle woman, known to put patients at ease, she covers emergencies at the European Hospital in the evenings. Surgeons stationed in East Africa need to be proficient with the use of local and spinal anaesthesia, as most hospitals do not have anaesthesiologists. We are fortunate to have her.

I am speechless.

Me? At the European Hospital?

The thought of being summoned to that sacrosanct edifice where most patients and all medical staff are white is astounding. What Dr. Currie is suggesting has never, *ever* taken place.

I truly cannot imagine myself in that white bastion. In my time here, I have been admonished, my orders rescinded. I have been made to feel inadequately trained, incapable of mature judgement. I strive to prove I am neither—a struggle without end. When Dr. Currie suddenly poses the question of helping out, it validates my belief that I have not been wrong about myself.

Do you mean you want *me* to administer anaesthesia at the European Hospital?

Yes, Donald calmly says, as if it were an everyday affair.

I am apprehensive about the actual administering of general anaesthesia, as my knowledge is rudimentary and my experience with African patients limited to local and spinal anaesthetic.

I spend time with Ysobel, who is gracious enough to go through, in painstaking detail, the essentials of my new undertaking—pharmacology of drugs, techniques of administration, and close monitoring of the patient. Ysobel is a good teacher and, in due course, declares me competent.

Our equipment is of the simplest kind, minimal and unsophisticated. It is essential the anaesthetist keeps a close watch on all indicators: breathing and state of relaxation, pulse and blood pressure, colour and reaction of pupils.

My first patient is a thirty-six-year-old Greek male from one of the sisal estates. He has a ruptured appendix and is appalled to see me as part of the surgical team.

You? You give me *anaisthitikó?* No, no, no. I don't want. I want mzungu doctor.

He probably doesn't know any nonwhite can be a doctor, much less an anaesthetist, and this is serious, a life-and-death situation. Right now, he has no choice but to submit to the services of an Indian doctor. His abdomen hurts and he is very sick. In addition to the pain etched on his face, his eyes display wild confusion and a sense of helplessness.

His relatives, a coterie of women collected in the tiled verandah, are tired, having driven along rutted roads into town the previous evening. Among them is his distraught wife, a recent arrival from the island of Crete. Her thick, wavy, dark auburn hair is loosely tied and her face without makeup. She looks young and radiates a gentle grace.

I would have put her mind at ease by telling her she needn't worry too much. Her husband's case is not unusual, his general health is good, and he will survive the surgery. The anaesthesia is straightforward and safe. However, allaying her anxiety is not my role. The surgeon is the one to explain and assure. He is never questioned; both patient and relatives repose an abiding faith in doctors' decisions and actions. Families ascribe many ills to sheer misfortune, to what destiny has in store. It is much easier and productive to pray, attend a novena, or light candles to one's favourite saint.

When the surgeon clarifies that I alternate with Dr. Currie, the patient reluctantly agrees, still worried about the outcome.

He is prepared with a shot of morphine for a calming effect, a shot of atropine to keep the mouth and air passages dry, and an intravenous drip of saline and glucose for adequate hydration. Anaesthesia is induced by having him breathe ethyl chloride sprayed onto a cloth mask placed over the nose and mouth. As soon as he is asleep, a curved mouthpiece is placed to prevent the flaccid tongue from falling back, causing choking. The anaesthesia is continued with ether.

I sit by the patient's head on a revolving metal stool and will be here for an hour or more, depending on the complexity of the surgery. My left hand holds the mask over the nose and mouth; my ring and little finger under the chin, bracing it up to extend the neck. My right hand pours ether on the mask in drops or a fine stream, enough to keep him asleep and relaxed. I check his vital signs round the minute to regulate the amount of ether. His pulse, beneath the jaw, is regular and strong. Blood pressure, stable. Pupils, large green pools, contract briskly to the slightest amount of light. His colour is a healthy pink and he sleeps like a baby.

Knife.

The nurse has it ready.

The surgeon makes a longitudinal incision an inch to the right of the midline, below the level of the navel, then splits the rectus muscle and its sheath, tying off bleeding vessels in the process. He hands the knife back and opens the abdomen. I see the moist pink, glistening bowels like strewn sausages.

Retractors.

With the wound adequately opened, he looks inside and coaxes the appendix into view.

Sponge.

The nurse dips a sponge in warm water, squeezes it lightly and hands it to the surgeon, who mops up the purulent matter. It takes him longer than usual to remove the appendix. The inflamed tissues are friable and in danger of disintegrating, and every time he attempts to disentangle the matted bowel, it comes close to ripping.

The patient does not lose ground. He is stable as I pour from the ten-ounce brown ether bottle. Strong aromatic vapours rise and, while I inhale some, my fingers curled under his chin remain steady.

Retract harder.

He removes the ruptured appendix and I smell the musty, feculent odour.

I continue pouring ether as the surgeon closes the abdomen.

Cut.

The nurse snips off the stitch ends with a pair of sharp scissors and wraps the abdomen in absorbent dressings. I decrease the ether to a few drops, then finally none. The surgeon looks at me.

Everything all right?

Yes.

I remove the patient's mask and when he is sufficiently revived, suction his throat, extract the mouthpiece, and turn him on his side until he gives one or two good coughs.

I have done my first case at the European Hospital. To the Greek patient, on his way to recovery, I am a nonentity. He does not see me as a doctor even though I help him through a difficult time in his life.

9

A REAL DARLING

Time elapses before patients at the European Hospital get used to the idea of a nonwhite doctor giving them general anaesthesia. There is no question I have to be as good as Ysobel Currie, so I conform closely to all directives and am doing well.

It comes about that Dr. Carloni is being transferred. This move makes place for the surgeon who was due in Tanga about the time I was considering my options for practice. I was informed in confidence I would find him to be an uncommonly good Englishman.

The new surgeon is John "Jack" Singleton Darling. He came to Tanganyika in 1947 as general surgeon to the groundnut scheme, a grandiose enterprise conceived by private entrepreneurs in partnership with the British Labour government. Launched in the wake of World War II, the programme planned to alleviate the international shortage of vegetable oil by growing half million tons of groundnuts annually in Nachingwea District. Pushed through in haste without a feasibility study or envisaging of machinery and terrain, the grand scheme came crashing down, was abandoned in 1951, and judged a monumental failure. Out of the ashes of this ill-thought endeavour, Jack Darling was recruited by the Tanganyika Medical Services as their surgical specialist.

I first meet Mr. Darling in the changing room of the operating theatre. His left palm cups the right elbow holding the right hand upright in a contemplative pose; I discern I am looking at a thoughtful man, an attentive listener. Standing perfectly straight comes naturally to this slim, tall gentleman as does walking with purposeful steps. His prematurely greying hair is short, wavy, and neatly parted. There is a candidness about him and utter lack of pretense, unusual in men of his position. His eyes twinkle and the corners of his mouth hold the beginning of a smile. He shakes my hand warmly.

Good morning, Leo. Very pleased to meet you. I hear you have an interest in surgery. I hope to be of some help.

I don't know whether it is genuine support or his disarming voice, but I am confident enough to respond frankly.

For one thing, sir, I wouldn't want you to lose your temper at me.

I am horrified! He, too, is startled. It is the last thing he expects. However, he quickly regains his composure and almost breaks into a laugh.

You'll find I am not given to tantrums. I'm here to assist and hope you will be part of my surgical team.

I am chastened, humbled. Here is a man who treats me as a peer, with respect. Yet what do I do? I become insufferably cocky. Mama would say I lost my manners.

I'm sorry. What I really want to say is I would welcome your teaching. I apologise for my forwardness.

It's all right.

I walk away somewhat remorseful but, at the same time, cannot repress my elation. I tell him what is uppermost on my mind and he turns out to be an understanding person.

Within a short time, I find many things I can assimilate: his sincerity and unruffled manner, his involvement in patients' problems, his clear assessment, meticulous evaluation, and thoughtful decisions. Mr. Darling becomes my mentor, my sounding board, my touchstone. I ask endless questions, and in cases where the reason for surgery is not quite so clear, he takes time to explain the pros and cons. I judge everything against what he would do in similar circumstances.

A few months later, Mr. Darling invites Dolly and me to his home for high tea. It is our first time inside a *wazungu* home. The very thought unnerves us.

This kind but unexpected invitation spawns a series of questions. Do the Darlings *really* want us over? What is his house like? We've heard that an Englishman's house is his castle. Would this be one too?

We drive to the Darlings' residence, which is not far from the hospital. The grounds are extensive with shady trees and flowering shrubs. The house is a large colonial relic from German times with broad steps leading to a wide verandah.

Mrs. Beryl Darling, gracious and welcoming, immediately puts us at ease.

Leo, Dolly, it's so nice to meet you both. Jack has been talking so much about you. By the way, you'll have to excuse him. He just got back from surgery and is

---

Wazungu. (Swahili) Plural of mzungu, white people

Grant Medical College, Bombay

Picnic at Manori Beach, 1946.
Leo is front row, third from right.

Medical class social with Max De Souza, Aziz Kazi and Leo, 1948

Leo, Mama and Magda in Mapusa, Goa, 1949

Leo Joseph De Souza, medical school graduation, June 1951

Dolly B. Irani, medical school graduation, June 1951

Leo and Dolly, Colaba, Bombay, 1952

Mombasa shoreline

Leo back in Tanganyika, 1952

Papa and Mama's house, Chumbageni, Tanga

Santos and Queenie's house, Chumbageni

The old, German-built clock tower in Tanga, erected 1901

Tanga hockey team. Leo, standing, is second from left.

Family photo, 1952

Santos and Queenie's wedding, St. Anthony's Church, Tanga, May 31, 1953

Leo and Dolly's wedding, September 26, 1953

Honeymoon in Lushoto

Uncle Robert at home in Moa

Martin De Souza, son of Leo and Dolly, born November 11, 1954

Martin's funeral, November 12, 1954

Leo, Dolly and Louella, Edinburgh, Scotland, June 1957

Willie De Souza, Alvin Ward, Leo, and Sheri Dhalla drinking whiskey at the waters of Loch Lomond, Scotland, December 1957

Peebleshire, Scotland, December 1957, with Sheri, Willie, Leo and Alvin

Amina with Mario and Louella
at the park, 1958

Papa's grave

Mr. Leo J. De Souza, F.R.C.S. Ed., Edinburgh, Scotland, 1960

having a bath. An emergency, I gather. He'll be out soon. Anyway, please come in and sit down.

She leads us into the living room. Spacious yet simple, it is adorned with conventional furniture provided to all senior government employees and tastefully decorated. The light is pleasantly lambent.

Here's Andrew, our youngest, she says, pointing to a toddler seated in a high chair. He has cerebral palsy but is a very energetic two-year-old who keeps us busy. Our three other children are away at boarding school.

Mr. Darling soon joins us. Before long, we settle into effortless conversation. Topics veer from the hospital and its inherent complexities to our schooling and families. We talk of plans at the end of our tours. The Darlings are full of encouragement for my eventual goal of pursuing surgery. They are deeply attached to their work and will remain in Africa for the foreseeable future.

The afternoon goes by rapidly. Dolly and I enjoy every moment of it. The cake, lemon tarts and finger sandwiches served with tea are in flawless English style. Yet the entire occasion has an air of unreality: that such a visit could actually come to pass seems inconceivable. Interracial get-togethers do not take place. We recognise the Darlings are a refined couple who do not give race its colonial connotation, and this defines their interactions with *all* people.

On our way home, still suspended in euphoria, we are silent for the most part. What astonishes us is the fact the Darlings see us as they do themselves. Our deep-rooted belief that whites with their inherent advantages are above everyone else, makes us forget they, too, are exposed to exigencies of life. We assume hard times and mishaps are exclusively the lot of non-Europeans. When we learn how the Darlings were displaced after the failure of the groundnut scheme, we realise crises can befall wazungus as well. The health of their youngest child also imparts that illness does not respect position or colour. We are all the same in the face of adversity.

The year goes by swiftly. I notice Mr. Darling tires easily. His colour, never ruddy, has paled. He is losing weight. The medical specialist in Dar es Salaam confirms Mr. Darling has contracted tuberculosis, requiring he immediately return home to England for treatment. This is a grievous blow. On one hand, I want him to begin specialised care; on the other, I am disconsolate, filled with a deepening sense of hopelessness. Despite his affliction, he puts on a brave face.

You'll be fine, Leo. We will meet again.

Mr. George Johnstone, Scottish with a strong Glaswegian accent, replaces Mr. Darling. Mid- forties with a balding head and round face, he has a charming smile and dimpled cheeks. He is good at surgery, decisive and swift, but is quick to anger, with a fierce temper. His eyes become hard and icy as he explodes. At the first shout, the African staff scuttle away, then return cautiously to the operating theatre. The daktari is deemed to be *kali sana!*

I watch him closely and reflect on Jack Darling's character and temperament. I know in whose footsteps I will follow. I stand with my left hand cupping the right elbow, my right hand in the thinking position. I sit in listening mode, my chin resting in the comfortable curve between my right index and thumb.

Kali sana. (Swahili) Very strict, severe

10

A CONTRARY POINT OF VIEW

The colonel wants you to come over for drinks, Uncle Robert tells us. Dolly and I are in Moa, our retreat on occasional weekends. The village is far removed from town and we enjoy its seclusion.

Lieutenant-Colonel the Honourable Mildmay Thomas "Tommy" Boscawen, youngest child of the seventh Viscount of Falmouth, came to Tanganyika after World War I. Being a student of history at Eton and Trinity Colleges, Cambridge, and specialising in Arabic studies, he was euphoric to be on the very coast where Arabs plied their trade for centuries and vowed to spend the rest of his life in East Africa. He owns several large sisal enterprises and lives on his plantation, Moa Sisal Estates. His sister, Honourable Kathleen Pamela Sherek, takes care of his holdings in England.

In the midst of the wild African bush, Moa Sisal Estate, symmetrical in geometry, looks like an accomplished work of an architect. Uncle Robert, in khaki trousers, cream shirt, and felt hat protecting his bronzed face and thinning hair, chugs along in his old sputtering *box-body* checking in on workers every day.

The drive to the colonel's house raises a cloud of dust on the narrow road between rectangular sections of crops. In spite of the breeze, humidity hangs heavily in the air. The only sound, other than the rumbling of the lorry, is machinery in the distance.

Uncle Robert opens the door and we follow him into the house. I notice the tiled floor, white walls, high ceiling and an impressive art collection: Persian rug in sensuous rose and porcelain blue, English landscape painting, silken portrait of Rama and Sita, and an ancient map of the Middle East. When the colonel comes in, Dolly and I are startled by his unusual attire. He is barefoot, wearing an ivory-coloured *shuka* like the Arabs and short-sleeved chequered shirt.

Box-body. Pickup truck
Shuka. (Swahili) Loincloth

Make yourselves comfortable. It is very hot. When you plant sisal, you clear all the trees and the sun bakes the land. Instead of complaining, which would do me no good, I adopted the local dress.

Very practical, Dolly comments.

An enigmatic smile plays on his face.

I am glad you see it that way. For some, there is an element of oddity in all this. My compatriots believe I have gone native, which is terrible in their estimation, considering my upbringing. The natives cannot comprehend it. How can a mzungu become a Swahili? But I can afford the freedom to be unconventional. Robert, could you please do the honours?

Though the colonel is Uncle Robert's employer, they are good friends. My uncle is obviously familiar with the house. He brings fruit juice for Dolly and the colonel, scotch and soda for me, and beer for himself. We munch on Dutch cheese and biscuits, Basra dates and roasted peanuts.

I am interested to hear what you have to say about Tanga. You've been here for a while.

Yes, almost three years! It's nice to be home, although Dolly, coming from Bombay, had to leave her family.

It was a new experience for me. I didn't know what to expect, Dolly says.

New place, different culture. Must be quite a change.

It was at first. I came here to get married and work at the hospital. Tanga is a small town and I notice people are treated differently according to colour. In Bombay, working at Cama Hospital, we were used to treating everyone the same.

What about you, Leo?

Well . . . I agree. Right now, in Africa, we live in an unequally divided society. This is unacceptable. It is very important for me to be part of an unbiased whole.

Colonel Boscawen's interest deepens.

You are prevented from being part of a whole. Why is that?

The current situation polarises people. At the hospital, our three wards separate patients solely by race, not cultural differences . . . and therein lies the inequity. Whites get the best medical care based on assumed superiority. This bias is replicated in the town every day.

You are referring to the *colonial policy*. The fact that you live in a British colony puts you in an unenviable position and there is nothing you can do. You

---

Colonial policy. A policy by the British or any country that has invaded another country, giving them the right to enslave and exploit people through military, political and economic coercion.

may rail against it but you can't change it. I sense your discomfiture.

I am somewhat surprised at the colonel's bluntness.

You know, the British were forced to leave India, and the beginning of their end was brought about by Mahatma Gandhi and his nonviolent resistance, *satyagraha*.

That's true, but this country was mandated to the British by the United Nations until she is capable of ruling herself.

In the meantime, Tanganyika functions for the benefit of the coloniser. It's discouraging.

Can I get you another drink? I think I'll join you. I enjoy an occasional scotch when the conversation promises to be interesting. The houseboy was going to fry some shrimp. Robert, could you check on him? Mrs. De Souza, would you care for some wine, a sherry, perhaps?

I'd love a sherry.

The houseboy brings in the shrimp. Fresh from the sea into the frying pan, they bring the saltiness of the ocean into the room. The meat, crisp outside, is soft and flavourful as we bite into it.

It helps if you look at things historically. This may be difficult, since you are the aggrieved one. Colonies are founded on economic need. We took raw materials from our protectorates and manufactured goods for sale. Then, when we ended slavery, we hired indentured Indian labourers. After their contracts ended, these Indians stayed on as *dukawallahs*, traders and clerks. A generation later, they spawned a few professionals like yourself. The rulers did not expect this. According to their plan, doctors were to come from Britain, not India. No provisions were made for people like you. That is truly your tragedy.

I am nonplussed.

Let's look at it this way . . . suppose the British never ventured out. There would be no British Empire for the sun to shine on. No colonies. Your parents and Robert would not have come to Africa. I wouldn't be here either. You would not have been educated at the prestigious university founded by the British. Go even further back in time. Let's suppose the Portuguese navigators were weak, feeble sailors who never put out to the big seas, who never conquered places. There would be no Goa, no you . . . or put another way, you'd be a completely different person!

Dukawallahs. (Hindi) Shopkeepers

An interesting concept, but you cannot change history. After their experience in India, I think the British could use history to be more like the Portuguese. As Goans became educated, the Portuguese considered them equals, at least in theory.

It is too late for the British to do anything. We are more insular than haughty and less racialist than wanting to be with our own kind.

Your words dishearten me.

Forgive me. I was merely saying change cannot come from the British. Change will come after we leave in fifteen, twenty years. There will probably be an intense struggle for independence by the Africans. The question is, how will it affect you and me?

I haven't thought that far yet. My struggle is with the present inhabitants.

Uncle Robert rises. It is getting late. We thank the colonel.

Sunday afternoon, Omari and Salimu, friends of Uncle Robert, host a luncheon at which the colonel, Dolly and I are special guests. The brothers from Yemen run the plantation workshop, taking care of the machinery and fleet of lorries. They greatly admire the colonel, for he understands their Islamic ways.

We are comfortably seated while the young men anxiously wait by the door. The colonel's jeep approaches and they go out to receive him.

Salaam alaikum—Peace upon you.

Alaikum salaam.

They clasp his hands in turn and escort him in.

Omari's and Salimu's wives in voluminous, flowing buibuis of fetching pale pink and sky blue whisk in and out, shy as new brides. Banana leaves are spread and layered on the ground, and a mound of steaming *biryani* set in the centre. The mixed fragrance of cinnamon, cardamom and cloves is intoxicating, and saffron adds an alluring yellow colour.

We sit on the floor, eating with our fingers. The lamb in the rice is succulent, and yoghurt provides a contrasting flavour. I watch as Colonel Boscawen puts a small morsel of rice in his mouth and recall a story I read in college by W. Somerset Maugham. In *The Letter,* an Englishman on a remote Malayan rubber plantation tries to hold on to his lifestyle. He insists on having a formal dinner every evening, dressed in a stiff high-collared shirt, tie and tails while two Malaysian boys wave palm fronds to keep him cool and two more wait at table.

Biryani. Dish made with highly seasoned rice and meat, fish, or vegetables originating among the Muslims of the Indian subcontinent

Colonel Boscawen, in contrast, comfortably sits on the floor, relaxed in a shuka, relishing his meal and enjoying the company of the people who work for him. What I like most is he is an honourable man who treats us as equals. I wish there were more like him.

11

A MOTHER'S DILEMMA

In our four years at Medical Services of Tanganyika, we have not been on holiday, only short weekend trips. Ordinarily, we do not venture too far outside Tanga, as distances to places of any significance are long, the roads dreadful, and services nonexistent.

I request three weeks' local leave to go to Dar es Salaam. We plan to visit Magda who is expecting her first child. Our daughter, Louella, born in January 1956, is eight months old, and a change of scenery would do Dolly a world of good.

Mama has always been loath to accompany us, making all sorts of excuses: *Who will look after the house? The road is too rough, the drive too long, the car might break down, what would we do so far from everything? What if we are robbed or attacked by a lion?* It is different this time. Excited at the thought of being with Magda, who got married in February, Mama decides to come along.

The question of lodging looms up. Major hotels are white owned-and-operated. Staying with relatives is not without its attendant feeling of imposing on their generosity.

We'll stop at Morogoro and spend the night with my friend Dr. Robertson.

Mama pricks up her ears as I spell out details of the journey.

He's mzungu, yes?

I nod.

Who is this doctor chap? Papa asks.

A medical officer. He was transferred to Morogoro because he was friendly with all of us and the bwana mkubwas didn't like it. He's a great fellow.

I am *not* coming, Mama states with finality.

An awkward silence ensues. It won't help to discuss the subject any further, let alone persuade Mama to change her mind. In her understanding of the world, it is difficult in a matter of a day to alter course from deference to the European to commingling. To appease Mama, I try to commiserate with her.

You know, Dolly and I have only been to a mzungu's house twice and we've never stayed overnight!

You haven't and you want me to?

But Charles is my friend. I would not agree to this if I thought you'd be uncomfortable.

Babu, Father Callaran is the only mzungu I give my hand to shake. And just like that, you want me to sleep at a mzungu's house?

I realise I am pushing my mother more than I should, more than she can endure. Holding Charles' friendship in high esteem, I don't consider the fact he is white and take for granted Mama's experience will be the same as mine. But Charles is not *her* friend. All she knows is he is mzungu.

Let's postpone the safari. We can go another time.

By the end of the week, the steely determination in her demeanour evaporates.

I want to see Magda. You want to stay with the mzungu. If we don't go now, it will be the same later on.

Are you sure? We can find some other way for you to get to Dar.

No, we'll go.

Over the next few days, Mama has a constant barrage of questions for Dolly: *How old is Dr. Robertson? How long was he in Tanga? Is he married? Do you know him well? Will I be all right in his house?*

We leave at the crack of dawn. The route is long and bumpy, sometimes hazardous. I aim on driving most of the way. Dolly sits in front and functions as navigator, which entails watching for animals crossing, vehicles hurtling by and boulders in our path. Mama is in the back seat, Louella on her lap.

The road, wide enough for two vehicles, is paved for the first twenty miles. Then it continues as a murram strip with stones and potholes followed by mile upon mile of corrugated sections. Every passing car leaves a long funnel of dust and between Dolly and me, we are constantly rolling windows up to keep it out or down to let in fresh air. I'm not sure what is worse, being rattled by the rough road or smothered by the red dust.

We have little time to take in the fleeting scenery. Glimpses of green clumps and waves of golden grass, black rock and nameless trees rush by. We break to change from driver to navigator, for sandwiches and refreshments, or when Mama and Louella need to stretch a little.

As we approach Morogoro, the vegetation turns dense and green. *What a beautiful, lush place! No sea like Tanga. No ocean breeze. No smell of salt in the air.* We arrive tired and dusty. Mama is exceptionally quiet. Dr. Robertson, still at the hospital, left instructions for Yousufu, the houseboy, to take care of us. We bathe and rest. Mama has a chance to slowly get accustomed to the place. The house is neat, comfortable, and practically furnished. Three big bedrooms and two bathrooms on one side, dining room and kitchen on the other, living room and study in between. Its many windows let in abundant natural light. Mama takes it all in.

Are you all right, Mama?

Why do you ask? You know.

Dr. Robertson has not changed. Of British origin, Charles is from South Africa, having left the country due to the inhumanity of apartheid. In Tanga, he could not find any place where all races integrate and socialise. His superiors politely asked him to desist from being too familiar with Indians and Africans. Charles paid no attention and was subsequently relocated.

Welcome, he greets Mama. Please make yourself at home.

Thank you, she replies nervously.

Tea is served on the verandah. Yousufu brings out scones and slices of sponge cake. Mama appears a little settled and whispers that the tea is good quality, probably Brooke Bond. She likes the pastries. I can tell she is comparing what is served to what she usually prepares.

You make much better tea, I whisper.

You're simply saying that.

Charles takes us on a drive to show us the hospital and town.

Morogoro is at the foot of the Uluguru Mountains, he explains. Behind us, on the slopes, they cleared the forests to grow coffee and harvest timber. Here, in the valley, all our shops and markets are near the bus and railway stations. It's a very busy area.

As we drive away from town, Charles points out a new sports facility recently built for cricket and football matches.

I don't come here very much. I enjoy the quieter game of golf at the European Club.

The *mpishi* has dinner ready when we return: consommé, roast beef, mashed potatoes and green beans. Rice pudding, cheese and biscuits round off the meal.

I ask Mama how she liked the food.

Meat needs masala. Maybe I teach the cook how to make doctor's meals more tasty.

Mpishi. (Swahili) Cook

After dinner, Mama and Dolly stroll through the rooms again. Look! she exclaims, eyes wide with disbelief. I am in a mzungu house!

I join Charles in the living room. We have coffee and sip Drambuie.

Is your mother all right?

I think so. She was quite unnerved when we talked about stopping at your home. To her, even though you are my friend, this house belongs to a mzungu.

Oh . . . that never crossed my mind. How dreadful. Perhaps, on your way back, you could stay for the weekend? It'll give her an opportunity to know me better. One night is enough for formalities only.

I am apologetic for making Charles responsible for my mother's unease.

No, no. If you hadn't said anything, I wouldn't have known.

We are in Dar for a fortnight. Mama revels being around Magda. They while away the hours reminiscing and making plans for the new baby. When I mention we will stop at Dr. Robertson's for two nights, she does not raise any objections. Her reservations seem to have been put to rest.

We arrive late Friday afternoon. Charles has arranged to show us the Mikumi Game Reserve, seventy miles southwest, but it rains the entire evening. The roads are submerged and impassable in the morning. Mama is disappointed.

So much trouble, no? All for nothing. Such a nice man.

When the sun finally shows up, Charles insists on taking us to Market Morogoro. He believes it would be of interest to Mama.

It is the biggest *soko* in all of Tanganyika, he tells her.

They chat animatedly about the fruits and vegetables, compare prices, and bargain with vendors.

We leave for Tanga in the morning. Charles acknowledges Mama's graciousness.

It was my great pleasure to open up my home to your family. I still have to show you the lions. You must come again.

Mama holds his hand and says, Thank you. God bless you.

A letter from Charles arrives in reply to the one I sent in gratitude for his hospitality. In it he writes: *And please give my love to your mother. I enjoyed her company. It was as if my own mother were here.* I read it to Mama. She does not quite believe me and thinks, perhaps, I am making it up. I show her the letter. A smile spreads across her face.

Soko. (Swahili) Bazaar, marketplace

12

INTO THE LAND OF THE MZUNGU

I go ahead with plans for surgical training in Great Britain, something I have wanted to do since my first year at St. Xavier's College, when I stumbled upon the compelling biography of the most acclaimed English surgeon, Sir Astley Paston Cooper. Smitten by the romance of surgery, I would return to the quiet of the college library every day at noon to find out more about this man who was a great anatomist and surgeon. A man of simple beginnings, he worked with indefatigable zeal, striving to make a correct diagnosis and using the knife promptly and deftly. I select Edinburgh because its graduate programme starts when my contract in Tanga ends. This is a momentous step.

For nonwhites in East Africa, the British Isles are the centre of the world. All decisions affecting our lives and welfare originate there: power and policy, trade and tariffs, staffing and compensation. None of us have gone abroad to Great Britain, yet we pay obeisance to, even idolise, that hub of the vast empire. It is the land of cricket and The Championships, Wimbledon, of Prime Minister Harold Macmillan, and the BBC. It is also land of the mzungu.

The British Council goes out of its way to help and, as part of our long leave remuneration, proffers to pay airfare and provide a three-day stay in London before proceeding to Edinburgh. In July 1957, Dolly, Louella, and I fly to Nairobi and, after an overnight stopover, embark on an eighteen-hour British Overseas Airways Corporation (BOAC) flight to London. We are weary from endless travel.

The Knightsbridge Hotel, in an elegant, quiet area bordering Hyde Park, is a welcome respite. Nestled amidst shade trees lining a busy avenue, the place has an air of muted sophistication. Rooms are comfortable and plush. To our astonishment, baggage handlers, waiters and maids are white. We aren't used to that! Back home, jobs of this nature were the preserve of the African or Asian. We are both conflicted and in awe.

Hyde Park, one of eight royal parks, is an unexpected blessing. Its proximity allows an easy getaway, giving us time to enjoy the soothing green and revitalise. But it is our daughter who delights in it most and for a different reason.

Horsey, is her constant chant.

The horsey she has taken a fancy to is one of the immaculately groomed horses ridden by the mounted guards at Buckingham Palace. Clad in flaming red tunics, white breeches tucked into knee-high black leather boots, and plumed silver helmets, the guards move in unison during the solemn Changing of the Guard ceremony. Their horses' hindquarters shimmer as sweat steams off their beautiful brown bodies.

A British Council representative escorts us on a tour of the city. The red double-decker bus we board is exactly as we have seen in pictures. Streets are crowded—buskers, nannies pushing prams, bankers in tailored coats and bowler hats. Our guide provides commentary of facts and anecdotes, pointing out stately Houses of Parliament by the Thames, Big Ben, Westminster Cathedral, palaces, theatres and museums. Grandeur, opulence and a sense of history surround us. We get off at Oxford Street and stroll alongside throngs of sharply dressed shoppers through enormous shopping houses offering a plethora of merchandise. It is exhilarating.

New to England, we do not wish to be on the wrong side of prevailing etiquette. In East Africa, when meeting Europeans, we are reflexively deferential—tipping our hats, murmuring greetings, then going our way. Now, we face a dilemma. How do we respond when encountering them here? Like in Tanga? Tip our hats, mumble greetings, and move on? It takes some time to clear our confusion, and we find, free from contagion of colonialism and unaware of what their colour stands for, Londoners are pleasant.

We ride the train to Edinburgh and stay a fortnight at a private home recommended and paid for by the British Council. Having a white woman cook and serve us at table, scrub, wipe and clean causes much angst. However, Mrs. Macleod is a warm, affable person in her late forties who immediately puts us at ease. She is surprised we come from East Africa.

Whatna you do thaere? I thocht all Indians cam frae India. Eniewey, you've come to the right place. Oor Royal College and Surgeons' Hall are best in the warld. You havenae seen oor city yit. Take a walk along Princes Street an' relax in the Gardens. Don't miss oor Festival and Tattoo next month. Naethin' like it.

Princes Street Gardens is breathtaking, a gorgeous find in the heart of the city, with the immaculately tended floral clock and stunning view of Edinburgh

Castle. Age-old statues stand by silently, unable to protest the endless droppings of pigeons. In the distance, melancholy drones of bagpipes drift through the air.

What a bonnie wee gerrl? What do they call you? we overhear as Louella wanders into a group of Edinburghians at the bandstand. The music catches her attention and she stops to watch dancers, whose high leaps and intricate arm and footwork are captivating!

Meandering through knots of tourists and picnicking families, we come upon what looks like an amorphous mass of people about to engage in fisticuffs. *Thugs*, I think. But they aren't. In the centre, a man perched on a platform is orating in a stentorian voice. From the waist up, he is dressed normally with shirt and tie. From the waist down, he wears a skirt—short, pleated, chequered green. A leather pouch like a woman's handbag hangs in front. His knees are bare and his strong calves covered in white stockings. This is the first time we see a Scotsman in traditional garb.

The speaker, we learn, is with the Scottish National Party, which represents over half the Scots in the country. We have never heard a white man run down another, yet here is an impassioned Scot roaring against the English. To us, they are all mzungus, the English and Scots, Welsh and Irish.

We have been shackled too long. Prisoners o' these damn Sassanachs. We want independence noo! We canna wait.

Sassanachs? Who are they? I ask the man next to me.

Oh, them English, he spits out the word. We are Scots. Highlanders . . . Lowlanders . . . bit Scots, nae Sassanachs!

They've taken our whisky! Noo they want our ouil from the North Sea. What is it tha' we should fight for?

Independence!

And when, I ask ye?

Noo!

I begin to see the Scots in a different light. Incognisant of the fact they sought secession from Great Britain, we appear to share a common adversary.

Mrs. Macleod's is a temporary residence for students outside the British Isles. Besides the three of us, there are husband-and-wife physicians from India and two young male teachers from New Zealand.

Does it bother you taking in nonwhite guests? Dolly asks.

I hadnae thought aboot that. Mostly, I have students from the colonies. I canna say I have problems with them.

In Tanga, you serving us would be unthinkable.

An amused look comes over Mrs. Macleod's face.

Of course, it makes nae difference if you are Indian or Chinese. None at all. Well, maybe yes. If it was the English I have to serve!

She bursts into laughter.

We can't afford to stay at Mrs. McLeod's and move into less expensive and more convenient digs. We are no sooner in when the landlady makes it clear, since another child is on the way, she will not have us after the end of the month.

We rent a flat near the university but the move turns out to be unmanageable. Dolly is past her seventh month and tires easily. Her time, after taking Louella to the neighbourhood day care, is consumed with an inexorable list of chores—walking to the shops for groceries; preparing breakfast, lunch, and dinner; washing pots, pans, dishes; laundering nappies and fine washables, hanging them to dry on the line outside; ironing, dusting, tidying . . . *If only we had help like at home.* More distressing is a lack of companionship, the barrenness of not knowing anyone in a strange land. Not a person to talk to. No one from whom to seek advice. Nobody to share anxieties or banter with. Dolly is in a place where formality and reservedness prevail. We cannot fault Edinburgh for this. Nor can we love it.

I am absolutely no help. Gone the whole day, I leave early and return late. My evenings are spent studying for the next day's extensive assignments. Louella wonders why I don't play with her. She has had her mother since noon; now she wants me. Pulling on my trouser leg, I hear a persistent "Daddy . . . Daddy." Sensing I am in no rush to separate myself from my books and give in to her pleas, she sidles up to me and, in a voice you cannot choose to disregard, says, Carry me.

Unable to resolve the arduous situation we are in, I decide it best to send Dolly and Louella home to Tanga. As the day nears, we find it more difficult than imagined. Dolly and I will be separated for the first time since our marriage. Our little girl will soon wonder where her daddy is. Our next child will be born within a few months. I will miss them all. But our love is strong, our faith, too. At the airport, in the departure lounge, we cling to each other. For these few moments, time stands still.

13

A ROLLER COASTER OF A YEAR

My first winter. Mornings are bitterly cold. I wrap a woollen scarf round my neck and slip into a heavy coat. My boots crunch on pristine white snow. I am awestruck as only a man from the tropics can be. Evenings are shivery. If lucky, I toast myself in front of a crackling fire. More often, it is an inadequate single-coil electric heater which merely warms one side of my body and promptly switches off when shillings in the meter run out. I miss Dolly, Louella and Mario, our new baby, but am relieved they are spared the cold.

Chill and gloom aside, I look forward to the soiree arranged by the British Council. It is an attempt to bring students from Africa together. One of the hosts, Mr. Harry Gill, was provincial commissioner of northeastern Tanga Province.

A slight man sporting a broad moustache, Mr. Gill had a reputation for being approachable. Prior to his retirement in March 1956, the Indian community threw a spate of lavish send-off parties. We met him at the Goan Gymkhana farewell reception, where he mingled without pretense, an unusual trait for a man in his position. The Gymkhana spared no expense, serving the choicest scotch whisky, Goan appetisers and English hors d'oeuvres. As a token of appreciation, its president presented him with a silver tea service.

Learning that Dolly and I were leaving for Britain, he gave his calling card and suggested we look him up in case he may be of assistance. The address listed was that of his bank. I was surprised. I always envisioned a man of his rank owning a mansion but subsequently discovered few colonials possessed homes since they lived most of their years abroad.

The reception begins at five and I arrive a little after. A buzz of earnest conversation emanates from a crowd of mostly Africans with a sprinkling of mzungus. Curly wisps of cigarette smoke rise slowly against the muted light. As I look around, I feel a hand on my shoulder.

This way, please, Dr. De Souza. Mr. Gill is waiting to see you.

We shake hands warmly and greet each other cordially. His quizzical smile and manner of speaking haven't changed. The conversation eventually turns to Tanga. It is a common bond and we dwell on it as if we had been next-door neighbours. I marvel at how time and distance can change perception. I begin to understand why it was important for him to meet me. No one at this gathering knows of him and, although our worlds would never converge in a thousand years, he is eager to find someone to whom he can relate. An unexpected conviviality is born between us even though we met just once. We cleverly skirt issues of colonial inequities that create the fabric of life in Tanganyika and gloss over matters that were invidious, waxing instead on its pleasanter side—the sunshine, easygoing pace of the people, how things are with us, and what the future might be.

Mr. Gill is drinking coffee instead of the preprandial scotch. Early evening is prime time for scotch and soda, and his predilection for that libation in Tanganyika was undisguised. But this is Edinburgh, and Mr. Gill has a cup in his hand instead of a glass. He gives a subtle nod.

I'm not used to coffee at this hour. Tastes like something a medicine man would dish out. Life here is different and difficult. I'm a foreigner in my own land. Does it surprise you?

I shrug, not knowing what to say.

I firmly believe you belong where you've lived rather than where you were born. Of course, believing is one thing, and being accepted is another. This is the dilemma for people like me—and, I would imagine, for you, too, Leo.

I have to agree.

The party is going well. Sherry is served in the spirit of the season. And cake. Mr. Gill, on the dais, thanks us for coming in his hesitant voice. Suddenly, a big, beefy English fellow jumps up and starts enumerating benefits of the colonial system.

Africa is backward. It is a dark continent. Rhodesia had nothing before we came. We brought and we built everything in that country!

Shock and fury paralyse the group. As he continues his denigration, the African physician next to me, a Southern Rhodesian, goes rigid. His jaws clench, nostrils flare and veins bulge. Anguish envelops his face. He rushes to an open vantage spot and rage explodes in his voice.

Take your damned penicillin. And your hospitals and schools and whatever else you built. Take it all! Leave my country alone. You are not there for our benefit. Better for us to die in rags as free men than continue as lackeys in three-piece suits. Take everything and go! Please, go!

A hush descends. Mr. Gill ushers the man off the platform. Had this occurred in Tanga, his staff would have taken care of it. The mzungu would have been counseled to be discreet, the African reprimanded and kept under surveillance. Gill is no longer the powerful man he once was and can simply mumble an apology. The world he knew in Tanganyika is passing him by. And he knows it.

I am fortunate to obtain a position of demonstrator in the Department of Anatomy tutoring medical students as they dissect human body parts. For a brief period of four weeks, each team of two is allocated one part—upper or lower limb, abdomen, pelvis, chest, or head and neck. Gowned, gloved, knives and forceps in hand, these young men and women cut into preserved human flesh quite undeterred by the stinging formalin vapour. At the end of the session, they sprinkle generous amounts of additional formalin on the diminishing part, wrap it snugly in a plastic sheet, bid it good night and return the next day.

December 25. Christmas has always been a time for kith and kin, a day of joy and merriment. Today, there is nothing. Dolly and the children aren't here, and in Scotland, it is an ordinary working day. Into this emptiness, Harry Belafonte's song 'Mary's Boy Child' cascades from the radio like a yuletide gift. Its distinctive Caribbean melody adds poignancy to my nostalgia.

I survive winter, pass my primary fellowship examination in spring, and decide to go home for a brief holiday. Drained, I cannot stay any longer in Edinburgh. I miss my family too much. I catch a train to Naples, Italy, and board a cargo ship that takes me through the Suez Canal and Red Sea. While not the quickest way, it is the least expensive. Twenty-one days later, after stopping at every single port en route and conducting routine assignments of unloading and loading goods in Mogadishu, the HMS *Diana* drops me off at Mombasa.

Dolly, Louella, Mario and Santos receive me at the dock. It is a joyous reunion. I fold Dolly in my arms and hug her a long time. She looks pale and has lost weight. Santos is holding Mario, and as I reach for him, realise he is a sickly child. *By God, my son is light as air! His face is haggard, his skin loose; he lacks the energy of a ten-month-old.* It tears at my heart and my excitement is swept aside.

At my parents' house, Santos's wife, Queenie, and their three children, Susan, Stanley and Safira, join us for dinner. Running up and down the verandah alongside her cousins, Louella pauses every so often with a confused expression, looking back and forth between Santos and me, as my brother and I look a lot alike. Mama and Papa are overjoyed the house is full.

It is close to midnight when we are finally alone and Dolly tells me Mario began having frequent bouts of diarrhoea soon after he was born and was always hungry despite nursing every two hours. Appointments with different doctors resulted in negative lab tests and ineffective medications. The baby's condition remained unchanged. She refrained from sending me details as she didn't want me to worry. Tears fill her eyes. I stroke her hair, caress her face; she relaxes, falling asleep, but not for long. Our son wakes, needing to be fed.

Mario's unabated appetite gives me reason to believe his ailment is not serious. I recall an immunology lecture in Edinburgh where it was postulated that protein from cow's milk ingested by lactating mothers could pass virtually unchanged into their own, causing sensitivity in a small percentage of babies. Mama has been insisting Dolly drink a glass every evening to keep up her flow. Could Mario be allergic? Papa's Arab friend from Moa arranges to get us goat's milk. Dolly stops breastfeeding and switches Mario to the new milk. In a few days, he is better and in two weeks, brimming with mischief.

In early September 1958, Magda takes the boat from Dar es Salaam, bringing Owen, my godson, along. The whole family is together, children and grandchildren, and life continues at a leisurely pace. Every morning, after a quick cup of coffee, Papa rides his bicycle to Mass. Mama prepares lavish breakfasts of eggs, sausages, toast, cheese and liver pâté. Saidi, our mpishi, washes the previous night's crockery and cutlery, then goes over the daily menu with Mama. *Kidogo* Mosi, the houseboy, diligently dusts and sweeps each room. Amina, the children's *ayah,* bathes, dresses and takes them to the park to play, meeting other ayahs and their wards. She gives them an early lunch before the rest of us sit down to a substantial, unhurried meal of soup, vegetable, fish or meat curry, and rice. The midday heat makes afternoon lie-downs a must and all is quiet for a few hours. Santos brings the daily newspaper after collecting his mail from the post office. Reading the *Tanganyika Standard* is the highlight of the day. At four o'clock, we enjoy tea and biscuits. Later, Papa walks to church for devotions while Magda, Dolly and Queenie take long strolls. We all meet at Santos's for drinks and gather round the radio to hear the BBC news. On weekends, the *dhobi* from Kissosora delivers our clean, freshly starched and neatly ironed clothes and bedding and gathers the pile of dirty washing. Friends drop in, unannounced. *Hodi, hodi. Karibu.* I offer the menfolk cigarettes and pour beer while the ladies

---

Kidogo. (Swahili) Small

Ayah. (Hindi) Domestic, nanny

Dhobi. (Hindi) Laundryman

Hodi, hodi. (Swahili) May I come in, may I enter

sip Cinzano. Ashtrays and lighters are conveniently placed around the sitting room. Frank Sinatra croons on the radio. These are carefree, happy days.

Papa dies on September 12. His heart gives out. He is seventy-five.

Mama is up early making coffee. The children are asleep. Dolly, returning from the WC, tiptoes past my parents' adjoining bedroom and sees Papa awkwardly propped in bed, his leg dangling over the side. She hurries to get me.

Come, come, Leo! Something is wrong with Papa!

I get to my father's side in an instant. Grasping his hands, still warm, I notice his breathing is shallow and am afraid we are losing him. *Do something! What good are you if you cannot save your father?* I give a frenzied cry. *Please! Please don't leave us. Please, God, don't let this happen!* I run to Santos's house and telephone Dr. Torquato, who arrives in haste and administers a Coramine injection. But Papa is already gone. I break down sobbing.

The men from St. Francis Tailor Society arrive to bathe, dress and prepare Papa's body. They owe a debt of gratitude for his invaluable advice and ongoing support. The funeral is held that evening.

In the aching quietness that follows the burial, a pall settles on the family. These are long, drawn-out, sorrowful days. The immensity of what has taken place gradually sinks in and overwhelms us. Papa was soft-spoken, sympathetic, tolerant. He made time for people from all stations of life who sought him as friend, advisor, elder. He was the kind of father I would wish for everyone. It saddens me I will not sit beside my father anymore, listening to stories of his past.

Tradition dictates widows wear black for the rest of their lives. Men don the conventional black armband and women wear black attire for a year. No jewellery. However, a month into the mourning period, Mama tells Dolly, Queenie and Magda they are too young to continue wearing black.

My bereaved mother needs help and solace. I postpone my return to Edinburgh, certain I can obtain a temporary appointment since the hospital is in need of staff, but I presume wrong. Displeased at my leaving somewhat peremptorily to further my interests, Medical Headquarters isn't willing to give me a position merely because I need one.

Dolly and I decide to start our own private practice. We rent two rooms from Dr. Dias and open our dispensary on Mombasa Road, a five-minute walk from home. Patients are predominantly African, and the reciprocal arrangement is simple enough. We take care of their ailments and they compensate us whatever and whenever they can, including fruits and vegetables from their little plots of land, eggs and chickens, and cash when they can spare it. Dolly keeps the office organised, maintaining the ledger and ordering clinical supplies, anaesthesia, and morphine from Khanbhai Pharmacy while I perform minor surgeries—hydrocele repair, treatment of varicose veins, and suturing of wounds. I enjoy the work immensely, but for Dolly, being away from the children is difficult. She is concerned that, in spite of having Amina, we are expecting too much of Mama.

Our second daughter, born a year later on September 1, 1959, is a gift who fills the void my father, Leandro, left. We call her Lea. The joy she brings is tempered by the fact I will soon have to rejoin the programme in Edinburgh. There isn't money available for all of us to relocate. So the decision is made that I should go alone.

My heart goes out to Dolly, saddled with three young children, each a demanding claimant on her time. Louella doesn't understand why I have to leave and becomes quite upset. At two, Mario is his playful self and doesn't see beyond his world. Lea is blissfully unaware of what is going on. I feel I am deserting my family and can't hold back the tears.

14

FROM ROYAL COLLEGE TO BUCKINGHAM PALACE

Returning to Edinburgh is not easy. I am reminded of boarding school when the first few weeks are miserable. It is difficult to think of home without missing everyone terribly.

Alvin and Arlene Ward, a semi-retired Scottish couple, are delighted to take me and my four associates—Sheri, Willie, Marwa and Singh, graduate students from India—as paying guests in their terraced house on 14 Rosebery Crescent, off Haymarket. Knowing our families are far away, they make our stay as congenial as possible.

Mr. Ward, in his sixties, wears a kilt. I imagine him to be a retired diplomat but discover he is in the marketing business for Scott's Porage Oats. His wife, wearing red lipstick and a touch of rouge, cooks us breakfast and dinner. On weekends, she is not averse to letting Marwa and Singh, who love to cook North Indian food, use her kitchen. An aroma of hot, pungent masala wafts through, trapping the lingering odour of cooking oil and spices in a house sealed against winter.

Mr. Ward buoys our spirits recounting stories of Scottish valour while Mrs. Ward, comfortable in bedroom slippers with blue pompoms and white stockings, graciously listens to our daily anecdotes with motherly interest. He rents a Vauxhall and drives us through the picturesque countryside, along rugged coastlines, around a myriad of lochs. We learn Scots are descendants of the Irish and single-malt whiskies are the real thing. Stopping at Loch Lomond, Mr. Ward brings out a flask and pours a jigger of his favourite single-malt whisky into a glass for each of us.

For a perfect nose, it tastes best with water. Even better when it's from the loch!

He adds just the right amount. We clink glasses and become part of a Scottish ritual.

A letter from Lord Chamberlain, Earl of Scarbrough, Lawrence Roger Lumley, asks to confirm my status as a graduate student from Tanganyika and if

I would be in London during the spring. I am on a list of possible invitees to Her Majesty The Queen's Garden Party and will be contacted in three months' time.

I read the letter twice, thrice, and once again. *Am I being invited to Buckingham Palace? To this exclusive event? Me? The Queen? There must be a mistake!*

Elated, I want to share my excitement with Dolly but cannot telephone because logistics are difficult, connections poor. I pour out myself in a letter and send it post haste. Meanwhile, although the potential invite has no connection with the forthcoming final examinations, it bolsters my self-assurance.

The college informs us the oral exam will be a test not only of knowledge and skill but also maturity and poise as surgeons in the making. We are expected to be suitably dressed, which means a sober three-piece suit. This sends me frantically from one men's clothing shop to another. I reckon I have to look older than my years, experienced, composed and exuding confidence. I buy a charcoal-grey suit with a claret-and-black striped tie. As the date draws closer, I become nervous one moment, confident the next, deprecatory one day, assertive the next.

On April 4, 1960, I take the Royal College of Surgeons final examination, composed of both written and oral tests. It lasts two days, with the written portion consisting of multiple short-answer questions on general surgery, orthopaedics and allied fields. The oral component conducted the subsequent day is quite daunting. A team of two interviews me on diagnostics, judgement and problem-solving. My heart beats wildly. As soon as we start, I collect myself and my apprehension abates. I am presented with a case study and asked how I would manage breast cancer. Thinking it might impress the examiners, my response is to select the London method of radical mastectomy over the more conservative Edinburgh approach of lumpectomy. Questions come quickly as I discuss my rationale for doing so. The long, stomach-tied-in-a-knot day finally comes to a close.

As is custom, a silver-haired woman stands on the landing above a flight of stairs, majestically reading the names of those who are successful. *Will she read the names alphabetically? Will my name be with the D's or the S's?* I try to calm my thumping heart. *Is that my name? Yes, it is!* The image of those examiners flashes through my mind. *They accepted my contrarian response to the breast cancer question. They were open to another point of view. They were magnanimous! They made me a Fellow of the Royal College!*

I can't believe it. All tension leaves and a curious peace descends. The enormity of the moment envelops me. *Thank God it is over.* A smile spreads across my face. If Dolly were with me, I would have jumped for joy, hugged her. This victory belongs to both of us.

It slowly starts to sink in. I am a surgeon by British standards. I have been upbraiding the British all along for inequities experienced in their colonies, but to be honest, they are well advanced in the field of medicine. It makes me extremely proud to be a product of British education bequeathed to India.

As if to pat me on my back, I receive an invitation to The Queen's Garden Party:

1

EIIR

The Lord Chamberlain is
commanded by Her Majesty to invite

Doctor L. J. De Souza

to an Afternoon Party in the Garden of Buckingham Palace
on Monday the 9th May 1960, from 4 to 6 o'clock p.m.,
(Weather Permitting.)

Morning Dress or Uniform or Lounge Suit.

I smile as I imagine myself in morning dress: a heather-grey tailcoat, vest, and matching top hat. A pretentious mzungu! The image of the African doctor at the British Council reception comes to mind. *Better to die in rags as free men than continue as lackeys in three-piece suits.* No, the morning dress won't do. I settle on the suit I picked for the exam and set off from the Midlands in central England, where I have begun my practice as surgical registrar at Peterborough Memorial Hospital. Full of excitement, I motor down the hundred miles to London in my sporty two-door, orange-and-cream Auto Union DKW (Dampf-Kraft-

Wagen). At Buckingham Gate, the parking badge allows me in. The invitation and admittance card bring me into the palace through the regal white-and-gold Bow Room, where I make my entrance into the garden.

It is a fairyland. Enchanting. Magnificent blooms of roses and rhododendrons, immaculately pruned shrubs and hedges. Guests slowly trickle in, ambling in pairs, many holding hands. Top hat and tails, dignified military uniforms, and staid grey suits contrast with colourful day dresses and hats. Canary yellow, Nile blue, lively tangerine pop against the lawn's emerald green—a scene far removed from the bustle of the city. Few people know each other but high tea on royal grounds brings us together under a large white tent. Mutual introductions lead to polite conversation. *Oohs* and *aahs* are preludes to surprisingly detailed observations: how exquisite the cups, how lovely the tea, how delicious the finger sandwiches, Victoria sponge and lemon tarts. The air is electric with anticipation.

At precisely four o'clock, the military band strikes up 'God Save The Queen,' the national anthem. Queen Elizabeth II and the Royal Family—Duke of Edinburgh Prince Philip, her sister Princess Margaret, and the Queen Mum step out and slowly make their way between the two rows of guests. Her Majesty stops intermittently, making eye contact, smiling, chatting. Her subjects curtsy and bow, clapping softly as she goes by. All too soon, she is in front of me, raising a hand in greeting. I take it all in—her poise, her grace, her youthful face, her simple, elegant spring dress. I clap louder as she slowly moves away and there, in the Queen's cortege, like gossamer, is the fair princess.

My thoughts go back to October 10, 1956, when Princess Margaret, in the midst of her East African safari, stopped to visit the new wing at Tanga General Hospital. About the time her plane was due to land, I was sitting in a small boat at sea accompanied by an African male nurse, with first-aid equipment. Should anything catastrophic happen to the plane bearing the princess, I was to render emergency treatment.

Uncomfortable in the bobbing boat, I remember thinking how ineffectual it would be should anything untoward take place. In that unlikely event, there was hardly anything we could do. However, the significance of the princess's visit and the awe and respect she commanded required the British colonial administration to make certain all corners were covered. Seeing Princess Margaret now, I feel a connection somehow, for having been in that boat for her sake, a long time ago.

The band plays softly. Guests mingle, taking more tea and refreshments as commonwealth dignitaries and the royal party join in. At 6:00 p.m., the national anthem is played once more, signaling the end of festivities. The Queen and family return to the palace. It is an afternoon I will always remember.

Dolly and the children arrive after a two-month holiday in India on the following afternoon. Our three-bedroom, semi-detached brick home at 8 Atherstone Avenue, provided by the hospital, is in a brand-new housing development. It is wonderful to be together again. Louella begins kindergarten at the local nursery school. Dolly is busy with Mario and Lea and, twice a week, takes the car to go shopping.

In August 1961, I am appointed to the post of registrar in thoracic surgery at Papworth Hospital in Cambridge. Thinking about my return to Tanganyika, I make time to drive to the colonial office in London and submit an application for a surgical appointment. Their delay in responding to my request leaves me uneasy about our future. I go back twice more to expedite matters, with no success. Having put everything into my career, I can't imagine what I will do if denied a position. Whenever colonial politics exasperate me, I find myself dwelling on the gentility of sipping tea on a spring afternoon in a royal garden.

PART III

1

TANGANYIKA HAS A NATIONAL ANTHEM

I receive a letter from the colonial office regarding my enquiry for a surgical post. *Tanganyika is scheduled to be independent in the very immediate future. You will understand where our priorities lie with regard to time. We would enjoin you to be patient.* This official foot-dragging worries and perplexes me. Obtaining an appointment in the Colonial Medical Service is not in my hands. How can they deny me a place, considering there are only a handful of surgeons in the whole country?

Dolly and I receive an invitation to the Tanganyika Independence celebration in London set for the evening of the ninth of December 1961. I am exhilarated independence is coming at a time when I can be part of the festivities, albeit from afar. We are fortunate to have a good leader, a thoughtful, charismatic man, *Mwalimu* Julius Kambarage Nyerere. Thirty-nine years old and thin as a wisp, the former primary school teacher has a master's degree in history and economics from the University of Edinburgh. His timid look belies a sharp mind, inner strength, and selfless commitment to liberation. President of the first nationalist political party, TANU, Tanganyika African National Union, since its founding in 1954, Nyerere often said, *Independence will follow as surely as the tick birds follow the rhino.*

While I wonder if the timing for the British departure is appropriate, I know changes are imminent. Britain's skepticism that the country was not ready for self-government has led to widespread restlessness, discourse and negotiations, and politically, events moved quickly. Uppermost in my thoughts now is whether the new government is adequately prepared to run the country so its people can benefit. Do we have enough trained administrators? Experienced professionals?

Mwalimu. (Swahili) Teacher

A sound economy? The die has been cast and the task at hand is for us to put our shoulders to the wheel and work towards a prosperous future.

I go to London alone because Dolly, unfortunately, is ill. She is expecting our fifth child and immensely disappointed to be missing out on yet another party. Dressed in my best—*the* charcoal-grey suit—my mood is one of elation. I am soon lost in thought, contemplating the exciting future devoid of restrictions synonymous with the British. *Tanganyika is my land too!* The passport I carry says *British Protected Person of Tanganyika Territory,* although the designation *Territory* was dropped after World War II. I will cease to be protected by the British, whatever that means. After they leave, I will be Tanganyikan. Not being native, I must apply to be a citizen, which should be no problem. As I drive, relaxed yet soaring with anticipation of the evening's festivities, I am awed by the significance of the event.

The function opens with 'God Save the Queen.' Invitees are predominantly African, many of whom are students in the United Kingdom; others include Tanganyikan embassy staff and guests from various African countries. There are a few Indian businessmen and a sizeable number of Europeans. I join former Tanga Provincial Commissioner Harry Gill standing at attention and it dawns on me—this anthem with its implied national greatness proclaimed in all solemnity has sustained this man during his post in Tanganyika. It's been a year since we last met at the British Council reception in Edinburgh.

Nice to see you again, Leo. An odd moment for you and me, isn't it? Neither of us African.

It is. But Nyerere's cabinet will include some Brits and Indians.

Ah, you're being naive. TANU members, particularly Bibi Titi Mohammed and Oscar Kambona, vociferously believe Indians and Europeans should not be granted citizenship. The majority of Indians did not support their campaign for autonomy. They eschewed politics and relied on us for stability. And now that we'll be gone, they remain suspect.

I agree, Indians will be in for a rough patch. You mustn't look on them as pro-British or anti-African. They will serve the new country just as they did the old one.

What about the rest of you Goans?

Most Goans, as you know, are in the civil service. They may retire and return to Goa.

He lights a cigarette, inhales deeply, and blows out a shaft of pale smoke.

What about you?

I should be all right. I'm actually looking forward to a position with Medical Services. I applied and am waiting to hear of an opening.

Ever so slow, aren't they? Perhaps they'd rather the Africans make the appointments.

The band plays stirring pieces before settling into a string of conventional compositions. I move on, circulating, meeting people. Lazarus Njonjo, from the province of Iringa in the southern highlands, is studying education at Loughborough University. He is apprehensive, yet filled with euphoria.

I am really nervous today. I don't know if we are ready. Look at England, so efficiently run. Like a clock. Their institutions are old, their government stable. We are starting from nowhere, with nothing.

I'm with you. We may not be fully prepared to run the country but the country has plenty of natural resources.

And we are the first of the three East African countries to gain freedom!

A wiry young Indian joins us. He introduces himself.

Ramesh Shah from Dar es Salaam, doing accountancy in Bradford.

Shah's father and older brother have an accountancy firm. He plans to join them.

I don't know if the new Tanganyika will want us Indians. I'm worried.

Of course we do. Mwalimu wants us to develop a self-sustaining economy. You helped the mzungu. Now, you can teach us how to run a business. But you need to be part of us. Here in Leicestershire, I have Indian friends. At home, I did not have any. In my school, we were all Africans.

It is true even if Njonjo and Shah had lived in the same town, they would have gone to different schools, resided in separate areas, and their social circles would have revolved quite unconnected to each other. Partially due to the hierarchical colonial system and largely the result of Indians' adherence to their own customs, they are separated not only from the African but also from those Indians not of their caste. The Africans resent them for their clannishness, which adds to the uncertainty of their future in the newly independent nation.

Our British hosts are pleasant, sociable and gentlemanly in their comments. They congratulate the young country for its achievement and their monarchy for its understanding, and toast the future. *It is going to be a glorious period*, they predict, *one of mutual cooperation and advancement*. I am thrilled by the oratory: words befitting this great occasion even though the sentiments seem studiously vague. The past, I notice, is not alluded to at all. It is forgotten. Colonial history written off. Everything assumed to be harmonious between the two countries.

A fresh troupe of performers replaces the band. The music is primarily Congolese, played with a frolicsome beat. In addition to dainty English sandwiches and cocktail sausages, hors d'oeuvres include Indian tidbits, shish kabobs and samosas. The bar is stocked with the popular Tusker beer. While the gathering was unmistakably formal in the beginning, guests are slowly unwinding. There is laughter and relaxed conversation. Everyone is aware of the significance of this historical event. Tanganyikans are a free people, able to call the future their own.

From radio reports of the celebrations back home, jubilation sweeps across the land. *Uhuru*—Freedom. Ngomas in every village. Singing and dancing. Drums come out, bodies sway, feet shuffle, pombe flows.

In Dar es Salaam, the capital, following the banquet, ceremonies and speeches, the Union Jack is slowly lowered at midnight. Lights go out and darkness settles on the hushed crowd. A lone spotlight shines on the flagpole. The flag of Tanganyika—a tricolour of green, yellow, and black—is raised. Close to a hundred thousand people, nearly all Africans, packed in the stands of National Stadium, break into a roar, cheering wildly. Thunderous fireworks go off. *So this is what freedom is!*

It is getting late. I look for Mr. Gill to say goodbye.

It has been a grand evening, sir.

An evening when hopes for the future are born. An evening to read auguries. Better times ahead for the new country? I hope so, Leo.

The band begins to play Tanganyika's national anthem, 'Mungu Ibariki Afrika'—'God Bless Africa.' We rise. Its strains are melodic, not martial. It is solemn and has an element of calmness.

Hekima umoja na amani, hizi ni ngao zetu—Wisdom, unity and peace, these are our shields.

Tubariki watoto wa Afrika—Bless us, the children of Africa.

The anthem ends. We remain where we are.

It's a pity I won't hear it again, Gill laments.

You would if you came to Tanga. I shall be there.

2

NOMADS LIKE THE MAASAI

My place is with the new Tanganyika and we decide to return home in February, even though I have not been offered a job. Filled with high hopes, we board a BOAC flight for Nairobi, ready to start afresh, but not without reservation.

Our local flight to Tanga shudders to a stop on the runway, a good fifty yards from the long single-storied building that is passenger terminus, immigration check and skeleton fire brigade. We climb down shaky aluminium air stairs to firm ground. The tarmac, softened by the midafternoon sun, yields to our eager returning steps. The sultry air is a warm embrace and the brightness makes us squint. A soft breeze plays on our faces.

Here we are, home again! The five of us, Dolly holding Mario's hand, me carrying Lea, and Louella trailing behind. Triumph exudes through me. A Fellow of the Royal College of Surgeons of Edinburgh. I am proud. I am humble. I am grateful. This success is not mine alone. It is my brother's, my mother's, my friends'. It is my father's too. Emotion fills me as I remember him and still grieve, *I am back. I wish you were here.*

Early Sunday morning, the first of April, Dolly is in labour. After admitting her to the hospital, I drive to Santos's, where I can use his telephone to keep in touch with the delivery ward. Queenie is surprised; she's certain I'm playing an April Fools' trick.

I'm sure I saw Dolly in church this morning! When did she go to the hospital?

A few hours ago. She had pains all night.

When I talk to the nurse at noon, she tells me we have a healthy seven-pound baby girl.

Before the end of the week, I receive a call from Medical Headquarters asking me to leave for Arusha, in the northern province, to replace a surgeon who fractured his leg and left for England. It is urgent; the sizeable British farmer population in the region is increasingly restive without access to surgical treatment. This is not a formal post, only one of caretaker. When the English surgeon comes back, my appointment at Arusha will obviously end. Santos thinks it's a good idea. Arusha is a beautiful part of the country, he says, and something may come of it. After some consideration, I decide to accept. My plan is to see how the offer works out: remain in Arusha for the better part of a fortnight, return to Tanga at Easter for Maria Joanna Stella's christening, then finalise the position.

Dolly and Mama worry about the long drive. The distance does not particularly bother me. I drive the 250 miles along a road that closely follows the railway line. It ascends gradually from Tanga at sea level to Arusha at 4,600 feet. After the first thirty miles, the safety of asphalt switches to irregularly graded rough murram. I switch my mind from dwelling on the lively household I leave behind to dealing with the constant demands of the mutating road, keeping an eye out for potholes and large stones. This is the very same road Dolly and I had taken on our honeymoon. The Usambara Mountain range on my right stretches mile after mile, keeping me company until I reach the South Pare Mountains. Migratory herds of elephants and buffalo in the distance let me know the Mkomazi Game Reserve is near. Approaching the town of Moshi, I am not prepared for what comes next.

A towering wonder! Breathtaking. Mesmerising. Majestic. Mount Kilimanjaro, the tallest mountain in Africa. Clouds swiftly move in, covering its peak, but the image of its shimmering snow-capped summit, distinctly etched against the clear sky, stays with me. I marvel at its solidity as it stands, dominating and dwarfing the scene. Its supreme endurance reveals my insecurities as I rush to fill a spot in an unknown part of the country.

Arusha, nestled at the foot of Mount Meru, is positioned at the very centre of East Africa as well as the halfway mark of the continent, north to south. From my room at the New Arusha Hotel, I see both mountains. Mount Kilimanjaro a little distant, often covered in clouds, full, rounded, soft. Mount Meru, equally beautiful, leaner with a craggy peak. I gain immediate comfort from their permanence as I ponder my future.

The next day, I present myself at the hospital. The staff are relieved to have a surgeon, and I find the layout and routine similar to Tanga, however, on a smaller scale. The only difference is I am now in charge. I take over my predecessor's clinic, his operating schedule, and make myself available should the doctor on call need me. Kathleen McPhillips, an Irish medical officer whose friendship I come to rely on, counsels me on matters relating to the hospital,

British farmers, tourist patients and local tribes—Maasai, Arusha, Meru, and Chagga. The Maasai and Arusha are *Nilotics*, the other two *Bantus*. Nilotics tend cattle. Bantus till the soil and grow food. They are minorities like me and part of the grand mosaic.

Dolly joins me for a week, with Mario and Joanna. Louella and Lea stay with Santos and Queenie. Arusha enchants Dolly. Broad avenues of orange, lavender and red radiate from the central clock tower, colours coming from large flowering trees, bougainvillea, jacaranda, and flame tree. Its vegetation is lush; the air, rarified and bracing.

Arusha National Park teems with wildlife. Entering the park's west end, we drive along the foot of Mount Meru towards Ngurdoto Crater on the east, amidst banana groves, scattered fields of wheat and maize, and flourishing, rich, dark green coffee plantations. At the crater of this small, extinct volcano, we watch animals roam the four square miles of its floor through telescopes mounted at vantage points on the rim.

Over the weekend, strolling the colourful open-air market, we see Maasai women dressed in ochre and red shukas with big beaded collars, selling brilliantly coloured trinkets worn on wrists, ankles, waists and necks by their menfolk. The women paw at Dolly, speaking a language of smiles and gestures interspersed with snatches of Swahili as they entice her to buy.

The Maasai, in spite of a reputation as fierce warriors, are pastoral nomads who wander the land in search of food and water for their herd. They live in semi-permanent *bomas* built by their womenfolk using mud, grass, wood, and cow dung, and their existence revolves around cattle, the main source of livelihood.

Our week draws to an end. The uncertainty of my tenure in Arusha remains unresolved. On the last evening, Dolly voices her concern at dinner.

Leo, it's really hard being apart. I go home tomorrow; you stay here. The girls are in Tanga. We need to settle down and have our own house. I'm tired of all this moving. We are just like the Maasai . . . nomads.

Her voice cracks, her words trail off. I am at a loss. Our separations become more difficult each time.

Nilotics. Northern Ugandan peoples living along the Nile Valley region

Bantu. Individual ethnic groups including the Zulu of South Africa, Kikuyu, Kamba, and Luhya of Kenya, Buganda of Uganda, Shona of Zimbabwe, Luba of Democratic Republic of Congo, and Hutu of Rwanda

Bomas. (Swahili) Enclosures

A month into my stay, I receive instructions from Medical Headquarters to move south to Lindi on another assignment. This unexpected directive angers Arusha farmers and townspeople, who request the minister of health rescind the order. His response is crisp: *De Souza belongs to Tanganyika, not exclusively to Arusha.* The Chamber of Commerce and persons of influence continue to press the ministry, yet the order stands. I don't know why I am being sent a thousand miles away; the English surgeon is not expected any time soon.

Resentment pervades my entire being but I can do nothing. All that can be done has been done, to no avail. At least I know Arushans stood up for me, which makes me feel good. I conscript my constant companion, the sprightly ivory-and-orange DKW, for the return safari. It will be the first leg of yet another move in keeping with the life of a nomad.

My focus has always been on completing my training and being professionally acceptable to the British, except they have left. *Have my problems ended, or do I face new ones? Will my life be spent in uncertainty, moving from town to town? Will I be granted a permanent position, or will our lifestyle be peripatetic? What is my future in this country? Will I be accepted as a citizen? I belong here. I want to spend my life here as a doctor.*

No more than half an hour into my trip, I notice a giraffe crossing the road at his own unchanging pace. Certain to crash into this lofty interloper, I tense up and press down on the clutch and brake with all my strength, bringing the car to a screeching stop, mere feet from the graceful animal. The startled giraffe skitters out of the way and gallops off. Everything is a blur. My taut body goes into an unstoppable shiver. I cautiously steer onto the verge, switch the engine off, and lean back to take ahold of myself.

Driving along, my eyes alight on a lone ostrich, and I recall the carefully wrapped ostrich egg in my suitcase given to me by an Italian nun, whom I operated on six weeks ago. She painted an African landscape covering the egg—wooded grassland with homesteads, open plains with acacia trees, and an ostrich. And here it is . . . all around me!

I also carry with me a watercolour by the French artist Maurice Fiévet. His photographer wife, Jeannette, very appreciative of the medical care provided, requested her husband gift both Dr. McPhillips and I a piece of his work. Done in glowing shades of pink, green and orange pastels, my print depicts a startled herd of five elephants in a thicket.

Now, on my way out, I have two pieces of art, made more precious by a personal connection to their creators.

3

MY BONDS ARE SEVERED

Why are you going away again, Daddy? Louella asks.

I'm headed to Lindi, once more without Dolly and the children. I hug them and promise to be back soon with a big present for each. The East African Airways Dakota DC-3 flies south to Dar es Salaam, then onwards to Lindi, an old administrative coastal town in the southern province, sixty-five miles from the Ruvuma River.

I find myself in an aging hotel, with dull, weather-beaten colours and a general air of dilapidation. Provincial Medical Officer Dr. Robert Halahan welcomes me to Lindi Hospital. A warm, affable Irishman in his mid-forties, he suggests we meet for dinner at his residence so we can talk in more relaxed surroundings about my role as the new surgeon.

The hospital loans me a jeep. It is old but the motor runs well. Filled with a sense of adventure, I speed to the foot of the hill, snap the stick shift into first gear and accelerate to Dr. Halahan's home at the top. I am astonished! The house, surrounded by extensive grounds, is huge, the largest I have seen! As we sit on the verandah with our scotch and sodas, my eyes feast on the sweeping view of Lindi Bay—wide, curved shore; white sands; calm bottle-green sea.

Dr. Halahan is due to return to Ireland for good, joining his family, who left several weeks earlier. He could have accepted the position of deputy chief medical officer at Dar es Salaam but wishes to enter the profession in Ireland.

I don't want to go home a day late, else I will be a first-class misfit, good only to talk of old times in Africa and drink myself to death.

I had not considered life would be difficult for him back home and am reminded of Mr. Gill's plight in Edinburgh, following his return to the British Isles after a lifetime in Tanganyika.

At dinner, Dr. Halahan brings up the true reason for inviting me.

Leo, I want you to move into this house after I leave. All government housing comes under the authority of the Ministry of Works. They allocate lodging to applicants based on occupation and seniority. Many politicians are angling for this one but I believe it is best suited for your family. Put in your papers tomorrow.

Wouldn't it be nice to live in this house?

What I have to say next will disturb you. Here it is. I strongly suggest you consider leaving this country. The earlier the better.

Shocked, the fork in my left hand impaling a wedge of potato, reverts to the plate.

My connections in Dar report you are a fine doctor, but presumptuous. You resigned from service in Tanga, left for Britain, and, as soon as you earned your fellowship, expected a specialist appointment.

I am amazed the man is so well informed.

Although your gumption is impressive, this is not the right way to do it, no matter how wronged you feel. There's a reason your application has been held up. Independent Tanganyika is in the throes of change. Politicians are vociferous in their contempt for the Indian. You have no place in this new country.

I stare at him, a loss for words. We are silent for a while.

My mind is reeling. I need time to weigh Dr. Halahan's words. I go over his startling statement that there is no future for me in Tanganyika. While I appreciate his candour and desire to rescue me from my own trusting optimism, to realise at the end of it all I am not wanted in this country is a bitter pill to swallow.

Jack Darling is in Kampala; he may be able to get you a post in Uganda.

I had written to him in March letting him know I was looking for a permanent position and had not received any offers. Jack forwarded my letter to Chief Medical Officer Dr. Davis, who now wishes to interview me. The Uganda Ministry of Health plans on recruiting enough surgeons to meet their needs. My dilemma is I prefer to remain in Tanganyika. I was born here. My mother, brother, sister, and their families live here.

Dolly flies to Lindi with the children for a month's holiday. She inspects the house thoroughly and is impressed by the five large bedrooms, polished mahogany hardwood flooring, and that it is fully furnished. Stepping onto the verandah, the view is intoxicating.

Such a lovely place. Why would we ever leave? She looks at me, aware the decision is not ours to make.

Dolly and I stroll along the edge of the water. Protected from unruly winds, the beach is isolated enough; we feel it belongs to us. We can walk forever, our feet bathed by the playful surf. Between the swooshing breakers, the children's voices are carried on the breeze. A retreating wave, stronger than usual, plucks

Dolly's red plimsoll off her right foot and sweeps it out to sea. We stand, watching in amazement, as the receding shoe gets smaller and smaller until it disappears. Holding the other lone tackie, we laugh all the way to the jeep.

At breakfast, Dolly tells us she dreamed of her plimsoll floating away. And we laugh again. Returning to the beach that afternoon, Louella, Mario and Lea run ahead of us. Before long, we hear shouts of glee.

Mummy, Mummy, look, look, your shoe!

Her soggy red plimsoll, lying on its side, has washed up above the watermark.

Summer holidays over, Dolly and the children return to Tanga. The large house is empty again. Every morning, I stand on the verandah sipping coffee and watching the sun rise over the sea. It is never the same, one day to the next.

A week later, I fly into Uganda's Entebbe Airport. A little over two hours, it is emotionally tiring. The interview goes well. They offer an appointment that would place me at a major hospital, but can't tell me yet where it will be.

On the twenty-fifth of September 1962, a letter arrives from R. J. Onyango, on behalf of the chief medical officer.

TELEGRAMS: "MEDMIN."
TELEPHONES: GENERAL OFFICE 666.
ACCOUNTS OFFICE 666.

UGANDA PROTECTORATE

MINISTRY OF HEALTH,
P.O. BOX 8,
ENTEBBE, UGANDA.

IN ANY CORRESPONDENCE ON THIS SUBJECT PLEASE QUOTE NO. P.5887

25th September, 1962.

AIR MAIL

Mr. Leo de Souza, F.R.C.S.,
P.O. Box 316,
TANGA.
Tanganyika.

Dear Sir,

I thank you for your letter dated 21st September, 1962, addressed to Dr. Davies who has passed it on to me to reply. We are very pleased that you have accepted our offer of appointment and that you will be able to take up this appointment in a fortnight's time.

I presume you know that Uganda will celebrate the attainment of its Independence on October 9th. People here are awaiting anxiously the arrival of this day and for a few days before and after our offices will be closed. Also due to a large number of visitors coming to attend the celebrations, accommodation in hotels, hostels, and even in private houses are all taken up. In the circumstances it will not be possible to attend to you if you came during this period and even to find accommodation for you in any of the hotels. It would, therefore, be convenient if you made arrangements to arrive in Kampala by rail from Tanga on or about the 16th October, 1962. If you inform this office in good time the exact date on which you expect to arrive, accommodation could be arranged for you beforehand.

... As regards posting, you will see from the enclosed that after your visit to this office you will be required to report to your new station which is Lira in the Northern Region.

Yours faithfully,

R. J. Onyango

(R.J. Onyango)
for CHIEF MEDICAL OFFICER

Enc.

At last, my dread of uncertain days ahead diminish. We have a contingency plan in case our future in Tanganyika is taken away from us.

My days fall into a placid routine. Once a week, I drive to Mtwara, another coastal town farther south. Accompanied by a theatre nurse who brings along surgical instruments, the treacherous, fifty-mile stretch sometimes takes close to two hours. A typical day of surgery can include setting fractures or clubfeet, performing caesarean sections, managing intestinal obstructions, or hernia repairs.

A government circular at Lindi Hospital informs us the minister of health is scheduled to visit in a week. He will meet with staff in the afternoon, inspect the hospital, make an appearance at a public rally organised by TANU and be the guest of honour at a social evening hosted by District Medical Officer, Dr. Chimanbhai Jiwabhai Patel. We doctors are requested to attend all three events.

The Honourable Austin Shaba enters wearing a Chinese Mao jacket—no collar and buttoned all the way up to the neck, standard dress officials have recently adopted. Its popularity is visible demonstration of the leaders' desire to move away from influences of the West. The simple dark brown suit securely contains his stout frame. After the physicians line up to meet him, Dr. Patel introduces me as the long-awaited surgeon, recently arrived from Arusha and already put to good use. Mr. Shaba shakes my hand and moves on, leaving me deeply disappointed. I had been eagerly waiting to discuss Arusha, as I assumed he decreed my transfer, and am left with the impression he has more important things to do.

I drive to the rally held at a football pitch. A simple platform with three lone chairs and microphone has been hastily erected at its north end in front of the goalposts. The field is rapidly filling up.

The stern-looking secretary in shuka and grey jacket addresses the people, reminding them of the party's strength and condition of their coffers; one is high, the other low. He exhorts them to pay their dues, as much remains to be done.

Next, the local TANU president bellows into the microphone, *Jambo! Uhuru!* The crowd cheers *Uhuru na TANU*—Freedom with TANU—with increasing exuberance. He stirs them to an impassioned intensity before introducing Minister Shaba. An astute politician with practical knowledge of medical affairs, Shaba has quickly gained an important position in the cabinet. His brown suit has been shed for a collarless, loose-fitting cotton shirt, open at the neck with a bold symmetrical pattern on a cream-coloured background. This is evolving as the official informal dress code. He speaks in Swahili, softly, gradually becoming louder, using his hands to forcefully make a point. He beseeches, demands, praises, and promises more amenities, even those outside the ministry's jurisdiction. He has done this many a time and is skilled at playing to the crowd. He stokes the fires of resentment when touching on the subject of Indians. Since independence, this nationalistic rhetoric surfaces at political meetings, brewing and seeping slowly through the fabric of the body politic.

The mzungus are gone because of Mwalimu! But the wily wahindi remains. These Indians still own dukas, taking money from us. Taking, taking, taking. Always taking. Never giving. What should we do? Let's throw them into the sea!

A thunderous roar erupts.

Ndiyo, Ndiyo, tupa yote wahindi barini!—Yes, yes, throw all Indians into the sea!

I cannot stand it any longer. My faith in the country now battles the spoken will of the people. Bewildered, I get up to leave. With not a whit of nervousness, I stride to the jeep, holding my head high through the agitated horde, looking neither right nor left. Fury propels me. *How dare the minister say what he did! How could he say he wanted to throw me out?*

I know I am not of African origin, but I was born here, for heaven's sake! I work hard every day and see myself as Tanganyikan. This is everyone's country and belongs to anybody willing to work for its betterment. I gather this from President Nyerere himself. The problems between the Indian and African need to be resolved, and the first step in that direction is for Indians to reconcile themselves to the new reality and for Africans to give them that chance. Instead, the minister chooses to escalate tensions, encouraging resentment and distrust.

Dr. Halahan's ominous words came to mind: There is no place for me here. This land has disowned me.

Dr. Patel telephones.

I saw you leave and know what you're thinking. Remember, it was a political rally to get money and members, so they do anything and say anything. You cannot miss our party in the evening. If you don't come, it won't help, least of all yourself.

Nursing a drink, I circulate among guests, a mix of Indians, Africans, and some Europeans, none of whom I recognise. When the minister and his entourage turn up, everyone lines up to shake hands. Sociable and relaxed, this is not the same person I saw at the football ground. Regardless, I look to avoid him. He spots me and freeing himself, greets me effusively, then gently veers me away so we are by ourselves. He is not smiling.

Mr. De Souza, you from Tanga, yes? You born there, worked at Tanga Hospital, yes? You have mother there and brother, yes?

I nod.

You see, I know all about you. You one of us. Yes? Then why you leaving and going to Uganda?

I swallow hard, my mouth bone-dry. He is waiting for an answer, and I am dumb struck.

He notices my discomfiture.

I tell you something. Tomorrow, I go to Mtwara. I like you to meet me at my hotel. Twelve o'clock. You tell me what you need. I will give it to you. Salary, terms, anything. Don't forget, I look for you at twelve.

I have no answers for the barrage of questions that plague me: *How did he find out about my arrangement with Uganda? Does he really mean I am one of them? Then why did he want to throw me into the sea? Can he possibly give me everything I ask for? Why is he trying to buy my services?*

There is nobody I can confide in. No one to seek advice from. I review the pros and cons many times over and cannot get the minister's derisive tone and manipulative gestures out of my mind.

I do not go to Mtwara.

I know I have severed my bonds with Tanganyika, forfeiting the only opportunity of resuscitating my dormant application, the only chance I have of being officially accepted as a surgeon.

The days that follow are shrouded in a haze. I go about my work with no emotion. Uganda is open to me; however, I cannot bear the thought of leaving Tanganyika.

The hospital receives a circular from Medical Headquarters stating those doctors who have not signed contracts yet, if not in compliance by month's end, will be terminated. Oddly enough, I had never signed a contract since my appointments have always been verbal requests. I use this technicality to take the matter out of my hands, to make my exit less painful. When the month is up, I fly to Tanga, en route to distant Uganda, my next destination.

4

THE PEARL OF AFRICA

Leaving Tanga and bidding family and friends goodbye is heart-wrenching. However, I have great expectations of finally beginning a more permanent position in a country, though far from home, reputed to be beautiful. Jack Darling puts me up while I await ministry transportation to my new post in Lira, the main town in Lango District, 150 miles from the capital city of Kampala as the crow flies. Dolly and the children will join me once I settle in.

With time on my hands, Jack takes me to the teaching hospital, named after the hill it was built on, one of seven celebrated hills that make up the city of Kampala. I imagine it to be like any other medical facility in Africa—an odd collection of single-storied buildings, peeling paint, the odour of disinfectant—only bigger. It turns out to be nothing of the sort. The new Mulago National Referral Hospital, constructed by the British before Uganda's independence, is grand!

Built into the side of a hill, the hospital is cleverly tiered to accommodate the slope. Its slate-blue colour blends well into the surrounding green and red. Spotless offices and glistening corridors hint at its relative newness. Patients, unused to such size and grandeur, are overwhelmed as they queue up like docile children, waiting their turn to see the doctor.

Jack introduces me to his Chief of Surgery, Professor Ian McAdam. I can't help but observe his spruce appearance, and even in his white coat, he looks athletic. Born in South Africa, of British descent, he is an all-round sportsman and devoted to teaching.

Welcome to Uganda.

Following initial pleasantries, Professor McAdam presents an ardent commentary on his desire to liaise major hospitals in the country with Mulago, thereby providing cases for research and learning to medical students. He does not endorse the misguided modus operandi of segregating hospitals according to race. He is referring to the kind of facility I will soon be a part of.

Stay in touch after you get to Lira. I haven't been there but Denis Burkitt was district medical officer for eighteen months prior to joining us.

The next afternoon, Jack arranges for us to have tea with world-renowned Mr. Burkitt, famed for his unique and extensive studies of a rare jawbone cancer afflicting children in East Africa.

Remarkably observant, he discovered a distinct connection between their tumours and the virus carried by the mosquito.

Lira was my first posting. It wasn't much of a town; neither was the hospital. I was busy instantly. So many medical problems waiting to be resolved. You'll find your work cut out for you. Keep meticulous notes and buy a quality camera. You'll need good photographic records of your patients. I return every three months to examine children with lymphoma. I'll see you then.

Mr. Burkitt moves his head often as he speaks—like an observant bird. He has a distant look on his face and appears to be looking at me, but isn't. Subsequently, I learn he wears a glass eye, the result of a childhood injury.

I envy you going to Lira. Good luck.

Chief Medical Officer Davis in charge of government medical personnel calls from Entebbe, the administrative capital, to inform me Lira is the hometown of Prime Minister Apollo Milton Obote. Davis, too, wishes me luck. That makes two of them. I have a hunch I am heading into something unknown but don't let it bother me.

A chauffeured station wagon is sent by the ministry. Leaving this city built on seven hills, heading down Acacia Avenue, we drive past old graceful residences half hidden by hedges. Making our way around the outdoor market at Nakasero, I get a glimpse of the imposing St. Mary's Catholic and St. Paul's Anglican Cathedrals and Kibuli Mosque before passing by modern shops along Kampala Road. At the outskirts, the road broadens and winds comfortably over the rolling countryside. Vegetation is plentiful and the banana tree, heavy with large clusters of fruit, ubiquitous. When the driver stops outside a tiny village, children materialise like moths to light, as do pushcart peddlers selling bananas.

Matoke, he says, pointing to the large green bunches. You cook, eat like potato.

I spot the small yellow *ndizi,* for which I have a fondness. On impulse, I buy a few.

The road enters a swampy stretch before reaching a rotting wooden landing by a lake.

Matoke. (Luganda) Plantains

Ndizi. (Swahili) Bananas

This Lake Kyoga. We cross ferry.

Midstream, we come abreast dense islands of papyrus with gently swaying green-and-gold crowns. The slow-moving body of water is a tributary of the big river, baffling early explorers looking for the source of the Nile. We get into the car after stepping off the ferry and the driver's easy demeanour vanishes.

This bad country. I no like Lango. They bad people. Not clever.

Are you *Muganda?* His light brown skin, broad nose and thick lips are characteristic of his tribe.

Yes.

He smiles, acknowledging the recognition. He speaks no Swahili, so I cannot get him to tell me why he mistrusts the Lango.

More than halfway through our journey, the papyrus swamp gives way to dry savanna, coarse brush interspersed with scattered solitary trees. No signs of houses or cultivated land, only the occasional wildlife. The driver points out mongooses and, in the distance, hyenas tearing a carcass. I see acres upon acres of bronzed grass trodden upon and broken, stunted trees, squat dusty brown shrubs and termite mounds.

Dismay and shock pervade my being. *Where is the car speeding to? How did I get here? I should never have left Tanganyika. What a mistake! How could I have allowed myself to be led all this way?* Right into the bush. Mr. Burkitt and the chief medical officer implied I was going to a favoured place. I made what appeared to be a good decision, good on paper, of course. Unfortunately, Jack has never been out here. He would have warned me. I can't turn back.

I wonder how much worse it will get. I close my eyes to shut out the world and doze off. Almost immediately, the driver wakes me up.

Sah, we in Lira.

A few mud-and-wattle homesteads come into view, small plots of beans, millet, and cotton, and welcome signs of human habitation, chickens and dogs. We arrive at a roundabout made of large painted white stones, from the middle of which the new Ugandan flag flies. Buntings flutter, remnants of independence celebrations. The town of Lira is rural with large trees, tall grass at the periphery and unpaved roads. A right turn and we are at the hospital.

Muganda. Singular of Baganda, a person from the kingdom of Buganda

The one-room office of the medical superintendent is cluttered, disorderly and poorly lit. Files are strewn haphazardly against the wall. A white man emerges from behind the desk.

John Skinner, Medical Officer and Superintendent. So you're the new man?

He is wearing khaki shorts, a rumpled cream shirt, and brown socks that disappear into the back of his shoes. I am used to British doctors in white well-pressed shorts, white shirts, and white stockings folded below the knees. This doctor's dress brings home to me the already well-known fact the heyday of the British Empire has passed and this man is on his way out. It is too late for him to impress anyone and he doesn't care.

We walk to his old, mud-caked Land Rover, and he points to the passenger side, a scuffed wooden seat covered in dog fur and a generous sprinkling of dried road dirt. I hesitate.

It's all right. My dog usually sits there.

Loath to do so, since I have on a suit and tie, I have no option but to take the seat.

John speaks rapidly in a low voice, often necessitating an audible deep breath.

The hospital has one hundred beds and three doctors, myself included. I'll be leaving for England in six months. Thank God for that! You'd be surprised I took the London Primary Fellowship exam once. Didn't pass. So what? You don't need it here. I've got along well without it. He chuckles defiantly.

The Primary Fellowship is the first of two examinations surgical residents in Britain take in the course of their training.

I don't know why they sent you. I do all the surgery. The politicians have been touting the arrival of a new surgeon. It's you, I suppose. I reckon they want to please their people. Just another show of politics. Like I said, we don't need another doctor. No offense intended.

I remain silent. It is obviously difficult for him to accept me. He is doing his best not to appear any more bald-faced than he is. We are certain to clash in the months ahead.

Lira does not have a hotel. Government personnel are put up at the guesthouse until housing is available. Fortunately for me, there shouldn't be a long wait, as many British expatriates are in the process of leaving.

The house, painted white, is of simple construction, three rooms on either side of a central corridor. The dining room and kitchen are at one end, bath and toilet at the other. There is no sign of any staff. I am dusty and hungry. A telephone stands in a corner, however, I'm not sure whom to call.

Eventually, I hear a rickety bicycle that squeaks at each turn of the pedal. Okello speaks little English and Swahili of sorts but is eloquent with gestures and facial expressions. Face flushed, eyes red, he smells of *waragi*. A bath and meal, he lets me know, are out of the question. Nobody has informed him of my coming, and since more expats are leaving than checking in, the staff has been whittled down to himself and the clerk who comes in the mornings to make arrangements for the day. Aware he is mellow from drink, I try to soften him up, hoping he might relent. I ask about the celebrations and offer congratulations on his country's freedom and the new prime minister, his *ndugu*.

You good man. No worry. I heat water for *baaf*—bath. I make *chakula*.

At this late hour, though, he can only cook chicken and rice but first has to go into town to buy a live fowl.

I settle in one of the two bedrooms. As I bathe, Okello lights kerosene lamps for my room and the bare dining room. The guesthouse has no electricity. I leisurely eat the freshly prepared meal, adding the ndizi I had fortuitously purchased, while he waits on me and plies tidbits of information about the people and place.

When he leaves, I am struck by how unusual the entire day has been, one disheartening circumstance leading to another.

The hospital is drab, dirty, and depressing. The exterior of every ward—men, women, children, maternity, and isolation for tuberculosis—has been painted the colour of mud halfway up and orange-yellow to the eaves. These structures, in the midst of the rough greenery on the grounds, look like termite mounds commonly seen in the open countryside. The facelift in honour of recent independence promotes a sense of complacency that all is well. A mere facade. The core is rotting.

Rusting iron cots line the walls. The dreary dark grey cement, unchanged despite mopping and polishing, is dismaying. Half the beds are empty. The remaining patients, listless, curl on their sides on sagging mattresses covered with sheets that look as if they have been washed in muddy river waters. A small number of patients have died in past weeks from infection following surgery. This sends a shiver through me. I can't visualise myself doing any surgeries in this present state except for emergency cases. The hospital does not conform

---

Waragi. Locally distilled gin from all parts of Uganda

Ndugu. (Swahili) Brother

Chakula. (Swahili) Food

to the definition of a major hospital, even though it is accredited as one. Its problems are phenomenal.

A week after my arrival, although the jubilation has not diminished, the entire country is undertaking extensive renovations of unpaved roads and public buildings demanding repair. At the hospital, Skinner does not take me into his confidence as to what type of surgery he routinely performs. I let it stand.

The foreman of the repair crew, Harbinder Singh, a tall, bearded Sikh, slips from the scaffolding and breaks his wrist. I review his X-rays and advise the fracture be set quickly using local anaesthetic. Oddly enough, in spite of not wanting to miss time at work, he asks it be done later. I wrap his wrist, rest it in a sling, recommend an ice pack and arrange to have it reduced first thing next morning.

At eight o'clock, we are ready and waiting in the cast room. No sign of Mr. Singh. We wait another half an hour and then proceed with the caseload for the day.

At the end of the day, he approaches me to check if I will set his wrist. By this time, I realise he has sought Dr. Skinner's opinion to confirm what I had advised. I struggle to keep my composure and, as nonchalantly as I can, make it clear he should follow up with the mzungu doctor.

Why you not do it?

Because you will be happier with Dr. Skinner.

He professes artlessness. Doctor *saab*, I went there, just simply.

I know he values a white man's opinion more than mine and believes a white doctor would do a better job. It is not enough to be a Fellow of the Royal College of Surgeons. I am neither British nor white.

Damn. I am mortified. How could Mr. Singh think I was less than John Skinner? How could an Indian think so little of his own countrymen?

I grasp now why Skinner said there was no use for me here.

In my quiet evenings at the guesthouse, the children are constantly on my mind. I really miss Dolly and long to get her impression of this dead-end place. My road trip terminated at what I had been told was an up-and-coming town. It isn't busy or bustling. It isn't big enough to get lost and have to ask for directions. You will not find a restaurant, hotel or cinema here. It isn't lit at night. There isn't even a school to take your child to. Lira is a tiny dot on the map.

The town itself comprises two parts. The administrative sector by the stony roundabout includes the police station, post and telegraph run by Postmaster Monteiro, and the Public Works Department. The shopping area consists of a single paved street lined with Indian and local shops. The British live in a residential area jutting up to the golf course. Around this core, indigenes live in scattered dwellings, working the land. Men, using *pangas* and hoes, clear and prepare their plots. The ground ready, women sow millet and plant beans, spinach and cotton. They sell eggs and termites at the Lira market.

After striving all these years, it rankles me I should end up in Lira. Now I see why I was wished luck at the very outset. As Denis Burkitt predicted, my work is cut out for me.

Pangas. (Swahili) Machetes

5

WHEELS SET IN MOTION

The Lango shun the hospital. They cannot forget their people go in alive and come out dead. They don't want a woman in labour with a ruptured uterus or a child comatose with fever or a young man whose leg is crushed by a falling tree to die. Desperately seeking ways to keep well, they go to the local dispensary, a government first-aid station run by a medical assistant, for the magical sindano. With little faith in tablets and mixtures, they also seek out the traditional medicine man whose ritual ministrations do little to help or harm, but bring solace.

I am profoundly disappointed with Lira Hospital. It has not been functioning the way it should for some time now.

In the operating room, dust filters through fine wire-mesh screens. Shutting windows makes the room unbearably hot. A Petromax lantern, the sole source of illumination, hangs from the middle of the ceiling, drawing all insects, till then flying invisibly in the closed, confined room. As I stand beneath this incandescent light issuing from the bulbous kerosene-fed wick, my capped head and gowned shoulders come close to being singed, even though, shining sideways, it does little to illuminate the exposed anatomy beneath where the lamp is suspended. For this, I need another person armed with a torch to shine into the dark recesses of the open body. Bottle-green flies, drawn to putrid matter, buzz everywhere. As night falls, mosquitoes start their whine. Even if I shoo insects away, I discover instruments, perfunctorily brought to a boil, have not been effectively sterilised. Patients' skin at point of incision, I find to my horror, is not cleansed nearly enough, so when wiped with an alcohol sponge still picks up grime.

In all my years, I have never encountered anything as deficient or slipshod. *Who do I turn to for help?* Nurses and aides assume it doesn't matter much what they do. British expatriate doctors, preparing to leave, show little interest. Ugandan doctors, those not Lango, are biding time, hoping to be transferred elsewhere, preferably close to home.

John Skinner leaves. His place is taken by another Brit, John Harding-Cox, a smallish man full of his own importance and lacking qualities of leadership. Fortunately, before he can believe he is a man of consequence, a transfer comes through. Dr. Eddy Moné, a soft-spoken gentleman from the Dutch Peace Corps, takes over as medical superintendent. Having spent some years in West Africa, he is familiar with needs and demands of the African patient without being affected by the customary colonial arrogance.

It dawns on me nothing will happen unless I, in my role as surgeon in charge, initiate change. A workable plan is required to renovate the entire place, change the attitude of staff and make it a hospital worthy of the district. I have the backing of Professor McAdam and Dr. Ivan Kadama, Chief Medical Officer and Permanent Secretary at the Ministry of Health in Entebbe, who will not let me forget Lira is Prime Minister Obote's town. Nevertheless, the enormity of this challenge daunts me.

I recruit Margaret Bradley, a nursing sister from Ireland, who has the zeal of a missionary and an iron will. Her husky voice captivates people; no one can refuse her. Drastic measures are necessary. We talk it over with Eddy and his wife Annie, our resident child psychiatrist, and obtain their professional blessing.

All old and soiled mattresses from the female ward are placed in a pile in the centre of the grounds and torched. The burning pyre continues to be fed by mattresses from other wards. Margaret tells the excited throng of patients and staff gathered around we are exorcising the devil and eliminating all disease. It is a ritual of fire everyone understands.

Next, we speak to every person in the operating theatre, singly, stressing how instrumental each is to our success.

Your participation is extremely important in helping us improve. Patients come here scared, in pain, looking for relief and instead receive poor care. One of the first things we must do is control all traffic in and out of operating rooms. Equally critical is following aseptic procedures, sterilising instruments in boiling water for at least ten minutes and practising proper pre-op procedures when we bathe and clean patients. Safety must be our number-one priority. Together, we can restore people's trust in this hospital.

Everyone performs with diligence, and slowly, an awareness that something is happening for the better fills the place. Word spreads. People turn up from remote villages, trudging distances to connect with bus routes, sometimes in overfilled taxis. Mothers bring babies sick with diarrhoea, women check in with obstructed labour, men with blocked bowels. There are children with broken arms who climbed trees to pluck mangoes and lovers seeking protection from a spell their spouses cast on them. The grounds are dotted with families cooking meals on small open fires under the shade of spreading trees. As more patients recover from surgeries, the theatre staff get immense satisfaction and are proud of their role in the success of the hospital. To our good fortune, within a few months, electricity arrives.

Meanwhile, Dolly is asked to join the clinic. They want her to care for pregnant women who, by nature, are reticent to share more than the bare minimum with male doctors. Eyes averted, a slight shake of the head, they often give monosyllabic answers. Pregnancy, they believe, is a token gift from the spirits and the born child, the ultimate offering to their men. It is the unequivocal reason for being wives. Someone who can comprehend femaleness—like a woman doctor—would be showered with ancestral blessings. Dolly becomes their medicine woman and many name their baby girls after her. She is thrilled with her work and begins to pick up *Lwo*, as she wants to communicate without an interpreter. I speak Swahili, and between the two of us, there is little we can't decipher.

Every three months, Mr. Denis Burkitt makes the three-hundred-mile dusty drive to Lira to check on his young cancer patients. I help him keep accurate records and use my Minolta SR-7 to take photographs of the affected children at the time of diagnosis and, subsequently, after treatment. He is gifted with extraordinary powers of observation, seeing things clearly and able to put two and two together, so I am pleased whenever he comments favourably on my work.

As time goes by, he becomes comfortable being with us. On one occasion, when there is no accommodation available at the guesthouse, he consents to stay at our home for the two days he is in Lira. Dolly bakes a cake for afternoon tea.

I was planning to serve cake but it hasn't risen. I'm sorry, I wanted everything perfect!

Just bring it out and we'll eat it. As long as it's good, it doesn't have to be fancy.

That is the way he is—down to earth, always getting to the heart of the matter. Externals aren't all that important.

It is almost two years since our arrival, and a distinct change is clearly evident. I have put in a lot of work and Lira Hospital is making noticeable headway.

Lwo. (Also called *Lwoo, Lango or Leb-Lango*) A Southern Luo dialect spoken by the Lango people of Uganda

In April 1964, the *Uganda Gazette,* the official government journal, advertises three consultant surgeon posts, seeking applications from across the country. In Great Britain and its erstwhile possessions, Tanganyika and Uganda, consultants are the most senior grade of hospital doctors specialising in a particular area of medicine and responsible for leading a team. It is a role to which I have always aspired. *I should apply. Why not? It would be a fitting reward for all the years spent in the study and practice of surgery.*

Professor McAdam is a man I trust, and I ask his advice. He enjoys the confidence of both the minister of health and chief medical officer. At this point, in the country's second year of independence, there is no better person to guide the destinies of the surgical department. I drive to Kampala.

When I put the question to him, his puckish smile disappears. Silent for a moment, his clear blue eyes look steadily at me.

You'd be a fool to apply, Leo. These placements are meant for the local lads. Not for you. There's no question you should be considered for a consultant's appointment, but these are political times, and it needs to be a Ugandan. You know that, don't you?

The professor is utterly frank, and he is right. He presumes I had known. It is time Ugandans take precedence in their own land. They have been denied opportunities all these years. More than a few Ugandan doctors have trained as surgeons in Britain, and it seems right these assignments should be reserved for them. A sense of dejection stays with me all the way back.

Two months later, on a Saturday afternoon, I receive a telephone call from Dr. Kadama. A man of high standing, he has worked at many institutions and is cognisant of his status, a doctor first, then a politician.

Leo, we have not received your application for the consultant's post!

I'm sorry, it escaped my attention, I lie. I can't tell him the professor informed me these were for the locals.

You are the only surgeon in the country who has not applied. Fill the forms and send them to me first thing Monday morning.

Yes, sir. But today is the last day.

I know. I want you to complete those forms and make sure they get to me, he repeats, his authoritative voice thinly veiled with impatience.

Quite perplexed, I stand, telephone in hand long after Dr. Kadama is done talking. The call is most unexpected. Why would he ask me to apply? Maybe the ministry wants every eligible surgeon to apply so an appearance of impartiality is maintained.

I get the application from Dr. Moné, complete it with care, and drop it in the post.

Three months go by with no word. Then, one day, a familiar-looking, long brown envelope from the Ministry of Health arrives. The letter reads:

September 1, 1964

Sir,
I am directed by the President acting on the advise [sic] of the Prime Minister, and the Public Service Commission to offer you appointment as a Consultant Surgeon with effect from the 1st of July, 1964.
2. Salary terms . . .
Would you please indicate in writing whether or not you wish to accept the appointment on the above terms?

I am, Sir,
Your obedient servant,
Permanent Secretary for Establishments

I remain glued to the chair, letter in my hands as I read it over and over again, not believing what it says. I take a deep breath and impulsively run towards the obstetric ward to Dolly. She is holding a primipara's hand, encouraging the frightened woman to push. One look tells me she knows.

Who are the other surgeons selected? The government gazette will list the names, but I have to wait. It arrives three weeks later. As I leaf through the ten-page publication, I only find my name. Three positions had been advertised, just one filled. What happened to the other two? It is most unusual and I can't fathom what led to my selection. Can it be a political designation to keep me in Lira?

I go to Entebbe, then Kampala. It is a trip I undertake every quarter. Dr. Kadama at Medical Headquarters is warm, effusive.

Our prime minister is very happy with you, and we are too. This is the first time in a long while good news has come out of Lango. Mr. Obote listens to his people when he is home. He hears of all the favourable changes at the hospital and never forgets good done to his people. He telephoned me to make sure you applied.

The wheels were thus set in motion that went on to make me a consultant.

At Mulago, I meet Professor McAdam.

Congratulations, Leo. You proved me wrong! The challenge you faced was immense and you dealt with it in the only way there was, a complete overhaul. Well done. You deserve this opportunity.

His comments and those of Dr. Kadama make me proud of all the effort put in by Margaret, the Monés and our staff.

I do not expect to see Mr. Burkitt, who is on a visit to an outlying hospital collecting valuable data. I am about to leave when his recognisable, mud-splattered station wagon drives up. I greet him as he gets out of his car. He looks tired but doesn't slow his pace as I walk with him back to the hospital. This is not unusual for him. He always walks fast, and social niceties come after work.

Nice to see you, Leo. How are things in Lira?

Very well. You're looking at the new consultant!

He stops abruptly, then turns to look at me.

What? They promoted you! What about Arthur Pendleton from Jinja? A fine fellow. Absolutely first-rate. Has been doing surgery for five years. So they didn't make him consultant? A real shame.

I am astonished and, after an awkward pause, faintly remark, I have to be getting back, sir.

Yes, yes, he mutters and keeps walking.

It is impossible to get Mr. Burkitt's reaction out of my mind. Perhaps he supposes I have not been here long enough or am not good enough. How can that be? He always said I was a top-class surgeon doing sterling work, that the hospital is functioning better than he has ever seen it, that his lymphoma cases are meticulously documented. He even told Professor McAdam the surgical ward was well run, I was of academic calibre and my request for any research assistance should be heeded. Then why does he not take delight in my promotion? I think I know why, but to admit it would destroy my faith in his sense of fairness.

At the hospital we continue to receive more patients than there are beds, the operating theatre runs full-time and the maternity ward is filled with lusty cries. The Lango are content until they learn we will be gone from Lira on our next tour. We are being transferred to Gulu, eighty miles away, a larger town and headquarters of the northern region, which includes Lira and its district of Lango. This distancing of our relationship upsets them. Wringing their hands, the women gather around Dolly, touching her white coat, pleading, weeping.

The men shake their heads, decide they will take the matter to party elders to have our transfer rescinded. We, too, are saddened.

Obote, in making me consultant, has inadvertently removed us from his people.

6

THE GATEKEEPERS OF MURCHISON

Chobe Safari Lodge, on the eastern end of Murchison Falls National Park, is fifty-seven miles from Lira. Untouched by man and uncontaminated by progress, its wilderness has always appealed to Dolly and me, and we frequent it whenever we need to get away. On this particular occasion, Park Ranger Okello Otim invites us to spend a few days. Two years earlier, Dolly played a critical part in his wife's difficult first delivery of twins. In Lango tradition, boys are preferred, and to have two at one time is heaven-sent, an event certainly mediated by the ancestors. A graduate of Makerere University in biology, Okello is shaped not only by old confining tribal customs but also by contemporary thinking kindled at a modern university. With his short, stocky frame, thick spectacles, and sensitive face, he looks the part of a postgraduate student in serious pursuit of his doctorate instead of a fieldman responsible for a large slice of wilderness that abounds with untamed animals in the hundreds of thousands. He understands his charge well—the vegetation, how it nurtures animals and birds, how it affects their movement each day—and is eager to show us his domain.

The morning is cool and fresh. Salimu, at the wheel of a Land Rover, is an excellent driver familiar with the terrain. Okello is seated by his side. Dolly and I are in the back.

Elephants, whispers Salimu. Nine, he continues.

Tails whisking, ears flapping, trunks swaying, the elephants walk at an unhurried pace, stately, and in single file to a watering hole. Their large frames move forward evenly, placidly, ceremoniously. Occasionally, the line bunches, then straightens.

You see three generations, Okello adds, looking excitedly at Dolly and me. We stand at full height through the roll bars.

Magnificent, Dolly murmurs. I have never seen anything so majestic!

The littlest member of the herd, trying to do the best he can, has difficulty curbing his exuberance. Impulsively, he bounces to the front of the line, rubs heads, then retreats to do the same with those in the rear. The second calf, slightly older, goes on a similar social round.

In the elephant world, the matriarch is in charge. When memsaab leads, all follow. When she stops, they stand still. When *mama tembo* rumbles, everyone listens. They talk back to her.

Elephants are like you and me, very human. Okello takes innocent pleasure in relating these facts.

We follow the herd, trying to remain inconspicuous.

After a long, leisurely drink at the watering hole, they enjoy a mud bath. High-pitched trumpeting fills the air as they douse themselves, spraying muddy water on each other. Calves cavort and splash. Lying on their sides, rolling around completely covered in mud, they cool off.

Off they go foraging—picking fruit, uprooting grass, ripping out shrubs. Acacia trees with leaves stripped, branches and bark torn, end up broken, twisted and forlorn ghosts of former selves. The few left whole keep lone sentry in the valley.

Difficult to believe elephants can do so much damage, Okello mentions sadly.

It is close to noon. Lumbering slowly towards the mottled shade, the elephants stop to take a siesta. Time has slowed. Hardly anything moves.

Okello gives us a solicitous look.

Let us return for lunch. You can rest, then we go out later.

On our afternoon expedition, Salimu drives into a large herd of hartebeest. He gets clear, yet remains in the vicinity, following them closely. A type of antelope, this animal looks comical with its long face, white beard, high shoulders and sloping hindquarters.

It's the season of the rut, Okello informs us. Mating time. After the rains, they will migrate, hundreds of them, to feed on new grass. Now, it's all excitement.

A young bull, having fought off contending males, stakes out his territory. He rounds up his female entourage, all intensely aroused, singles out his choice, and nudges her aside. Their urge is primeval, their ardour close to effervescing. He climbs on her and joins. For that brief instant, he is blinded to the ever-present threat of a predator nearby.

Salimu points to a lioness. Cunningly camouflaged in the thick, dry brush, she bides her time.

Mama tembo. (Swahili) Mother elephant

Watoto—little ones, need food. I think we see a kill.

The dazzling moment over, the hartebeest senses danger. Disengaging reluctantly, he looks in the direction of the lioness but does not see her. Instinct tells him imminent danger lurks. The lioness flicks her tail once, twice. In a flash, her crouched, muscular body springs loose with ferocious force into the air. The chase is on. Head down, bushy tail up, the rufous-coloured buck takes flight. Straining every muscle, he zigzags at tremendous speed, attempting to increase the distance between himself and his enemy.

Not wanting to miss anything, we follow as best we can, oblivious to the dangers of driving so fast. Hearts racing, we hold tightly to the steel supports.

The powerful lioness gains on her prey perceptibly. Soon she is abreast with him. A single swipe of her paw knocks him down, and in a trice, she sinks her teeth into his mouth and nose, crunching them shut. Only when he is lifeless does she let go. Grabbing the underside of his neck, she drags him off.

No one speaks on the way back to the lodge.

We wake refreshed to a leisurely breakfast—porridge, bacon, eggs, toast with marmalade—topped off with Ugandan coffee. Okello arrives promptly at nine.

The morning is unusually hot. We espy half a dozen giraffes, a pair of startled Uganda kob, impalas nibbling, dik-diks prancing and monkeys chattering in the trees. The Land Rover begins to overheat. Salimu searches for a place to pull over, winding his way slowly to a denser, greener area, similar to the daily haunt of varied denizens who seek the shade to rest. Today there are only a few of them. Equally surprising, they are on their feet, tense and watchful. Okello immediately notices fright in their faces.

Something is not right . . . something terrible has happened. Go to that small clearing, Salimu. *Haraka, haraka.*

Accelerating hard, Salimu brings the jeep to a shuddering stop.

A horrific sight.

Nine dead elephants. Tusks hacked out, roughly, savagely, hurriedly. Blood oozing from gaping holes. Severed trunks grotesquely bent, misshapen. Eyes glazed, unseeing. An entire family annihilated. Slaughter. Carnage. There is no sound, no movement, no living creature anywhere. A shiver runs up my spine.

Okello jumps out, hand on his gun.

Haraka. (Swahili) Hurry

Oh God . . .

Face contorted with pain, he kneels by the matriarch and gently strokes her side. Salimu cannot take his eyes off the felled elephants. Never has he imagined this is what poachers do routinely. We hear shots and shrieks.

Poachers making off with tusks! Bloody bastards! Let's go!

Goading the aging vehicle, carefully at first, Salimu quickly grows reckless as he sees no sign of the poachers.

Easy, easy, I think they got away. *Basha!* Fuckers! Let's go back to the elephants.

Okello looks at the mutilated bodies, yowls, curses, and weeps.

What did he say? Dolly asks.

Oh, very bad. Salimu translates. *May their testicles shrivel, their stomachs never fill. May they be disowned by their wives, thrown out by whores. May their money run out like sand. May they die a thousand painful deaths.*

I take you to lodge. Okello want to be alone. Talk to spirit of elephants, say sorry.

In the animal world, the small and weak are preyed upon by the strong and fleet of foot. A natural order prevails, not too dissimilar from the human world where, in spite of being civilised, the frail are at the mercy of the powerful. It is another matter when seemingly upright men wantonly mow down defenceless, trusting animals, and infinitely worse when done for shameful gain.

Our friend MacIlwain, recently arrived from Scotland, on staff at Lira Teachers' Training College, has never been to a game park and joins us on the last day of our excursion. We take his white Volkswagen Beetle and reach the entrance at almost three, the hottest part of a sweltering day. The little car rasps along at fifteen miles an hour. In the shimmering haze, a big black rhino suddenly emerges. The massive animal turns around awkwardly, as if not built for that kind of manoeuver, and takes off for a larger thicket. Mac stops.

Solid as a tank, he whispers, and, by God, how swift!

Watching its receding rear, the rustle of another rhino appearing from the same shrubbery startles me.

His mate, Dolly tells Mac, following her bwana, to keep an eye on him!

Dolly is not a forward person; nevertheless, she engages in friendly banter with Mac. What a change from Britishers I had known in Tanga. I am struck by how different this new generation of post-independent mzungu is. How I wish this change had come a decade ago. I wonder, though, if l would have achieved what I had, pushed as I was to prove myself.

Look, another one! Mac exclaims as he spots a solitary male trundling along not too far from us.

We drive by two more, a mother and calf.

They are all coming to greet you, Mac, Dolly teases.

A few more stroll out from their hiding places. Mac is thrilled.

Tea comes just at the right moment. We look for an open area to picnic. Dolly opens the thermos flask and slices the cake she baked. The sounds of the evening are all around: twittering birds, continuous chirp of crickets, an occasional low grunt.

The unusual outline of a tree silhouetted against the sky draws my attention. Branches, bare of leaves, tapered like fingers of a corpse. Seven vultures perch, motionless, soundless, clearly profiled. Scavengers on a dead tree at this time of day bode no good. *Are they digesting recently fed carrion? Or biding their time for the tail end of another kill?*

The sun is setting and the western sky glows. Shortly past seven, we head home, Mac happily chanting, What a day, what a day, by God, what a day! Thirteen rhinos in an afternoon!

The park gates close at eight. Guiding Mac, I keep an eye on the road and, to my left, notice a black smudge on the horizon, gradually growing larger as it moves rapidly in our direction.

S-T-O-P! I scream.

Mac jerks straight up, white knuckles on the steering wheel. Gripping my seat, I push hard on the imaginary clutch and brake. Dolly wedges herself between our two seats.

Waves of buffalo wash across the road. Hooves pounding, nostrils flaring, loud snorting. Two, three hundred of them! A formidable force. Thick clouds of sand envelop us; we can barely make them out. The smell of dung fills the air. Eventually, their pace slows to a stop, making the road impassable. The dust settles and they begin to graze. The group of buffalo in front of us stare. I notice how hefty they are and how frail and insignificant our tiny car seems. Buffalo stories flash through my mind, how these placid creatures turn dangerous when threatened, prone to attack and gore.

I steal a glance at Mac and Dolly. Neither have moved. The air, charged with a sharp smell of foreboding and sweat, is distinctly unpleasant.

Mac, can you roll your window down a little?

I do the same.

Minutes tick by as we wane. I tell myself they'll soon be gone on their way and we'll be gone on ours, except there is no sign of movement. Almost dark, we dare not put the lights on for fear of risking a stampede. They are peacefully grazing, with no sign of agitation. I hear lowing and grunting and the splash of dung as it hits the ground. It appears they are settling in for the night.

What can we do, Leo?

Nothing.

What if they don't go away? Mac sounds despondent.

I have already thought about that. The park closes at eight; no one is supposed to remain after that hour. It is seven forty-five and pitch black.

I want to get out, Mac declares, a crack in his voice. He is afraid. So am I.

You can't do that. It's too dangerous.

At seven fifty-five nothing has changed, except for the whine of mosquitoes. No one makes an attempt to thwack or shoo them away. In another five minutes, the gates will close. I am not sure how to deal with this situation. Not at this moment.

My thoughts are interrupted by loud bellows, one after the other. The earth resounds under the impact of a thousand thundering hooves. I smell dust. An eerie silence follows.

Mac gingerly turns on the lights. The road is clear.

I exhale in one long breath all my unrevealed terror. Dolly leans back, eyes closed, arms lax. Mac is quiet too, chin on his chest.

Let's go.

We arrive at the gate fifteen minutes after eight. The gates are locked but Okello and Salimu are still there.

We know Dr. Souza went in but didn't see the car return. What happened?

Mac recounts our adventure. There is a sense of indescribable relief, a feeling of immense exhaustion.

I was really scared, Mac says after a while. I need a beer!

I agree.

7

THE LOVE OF A WOMAN

The town of Gulu is like a frontier post, open and growing. Its inhabitants, the *Acholi,* are kin to the Lango but taller and darker with martial traditions. Since hostilities between tribes are a thing of the past, the Acholi keep their prowess alive by regularly staging awe-inspiring war dances. Adorned with leopard skin, spear and shield, headdress of long, colourful feathers, they shuffle and thump their bare feet, letting off whoops of victory.

Gulu Hospital, constructed in 1934, is capably operated by the Ministry of Health. Unlike the Lango in Lira, the Acholi have no reason to stay away. In fact, within a week of our arrival, we are treating chronic ailments, poliomyelitis, skeletal tuberculosis of bone and joint and a large share of fractures.

It is exceptional for a town to have two hospitals within a five-mile radius when for hundreds of miles there are none. St. Mary's, a private hospital in Lacor, was founded by the Italian Comboni Missionary Sisters as a dispensary in 1959. Conditions were basic, with unreliable electricity, irregular clean water and scarcity of drugs.

The rough road leading to Lacor runs north, a red streak through green flatland. Up close, this is a wide mud path where dust swirls constantly except when it rains. There is continuous activity at all hours as villagers brave sizable distances all heading to St. Mary's Mission, the location marked by a large white signpost with a red cross, its name boldly written beneath. These are not carefree, happy travellers, for everyone accompanies a whimpering child or ailing adult. Some walk bicycles carrying their sick, meager belongings, and food. Others catch the unreliable bus, and a few arrive in speeding, overfilled taxis.

The small building with forty beds has an unusual open setting, allowing patients' families to camp on the grounds and assist in their care. Unobtrusive shelters available for domestic use house separate cooking and washing facilities,

---

Acholi. Part of Luo-speaking Nilotic people of East Africa who live predominantly in Northern Uganda making the hospital less forbidding and more of a home away from home. At first sight, it resembles a marketplace. No sellers, buyers, or mounds of produce; only ceaseless activity from anxious relatives, cooking meals, washing clothes, bathing children. The nuns ensure they follow regulations and settle in as best they can.

The mission's first physicians, Pietro "Piero" Corti from Italy and Lucille Teasdale from Canada, arrive in 1961, a year before Dolly and I come to Lira. We meet the husband-and-wife team when we begin referring patients to St. Mary's, as Gulu Hospital does not have an X-ray machine. Intensely dedicated, Lucille examines an endless stream of outpatients in the mornings and performs surgery three afternoons a week on a makeshift table with a single light bulb. Cases often spill over into the weekend. We decide to combine our surgical expertise, routinely operating at both hospitals. Piero cares for those walking in with a variety of conditions—diarrhoeal disease, pulmonary tuberculosis, or chronic fever. The Cortis, a charming couple, live on campus with their baby daughter, Dominique. *Thank God for the nuns who tend to the hospital and Dominique Atim!*

The fledgling institution receives more cases than it can hold and survives on donations from benefactors. Piero recruits doctors from abroad to work for little or nothing beyond living expenses. His planning mind constantly thinks of expansion, adding a new paediatric ward and operating theatre, another surgeon to help his wife, and additional nurses. All is dependent on the availability of money and how to obtain it is the pressing question. Piero—doctor, administrator, director, planner, builder, teacher, father and dreamer—takes it upon himself to raise funds to fulfill his vision of building a world-class hospital for sick Ugandans.

The ebullient doctor from Besana, I discover, is an avid hunter. He is an excellent shot and loves his guns. Every few months, at the crack of dawn, he drives to the northwest end of Murchison Falls National Park, finding tranquility tramping the wilderness of the savannah. Brother Rafael accompanies him.

I mention to Piero I would like to go on a hunt, something I have never done. So it happens one early December morning, Brother Rafael and Piero invite me along. It isn't quite night; it isn't quite morning. Insects buzz incessantly, interrupted by alternating booms of a different pitch. Brother Rafael tells me

---

Atim. (Acholi) Dominique's middle name meaning 'born in a foreign land'

they are ground hornbills, large black birds trying to mate. Shrill, agitated chirps, *weep-weep-weep-weep-weep,* come from long-legged plovers flying abreast of the Land Rover. In the distance, we hear the high-pitched giggle of hyenas.

We pick up our guide ten miles from Pachwach. Okech has worked for the game park ranger since he was a little boy. We leave our vehicle outside the mud enclosure of his family homestead and, with Okech leading the way, follow single file on a sinuous foot track not much broader than the back of a large snake. Brother Rafael is behind him and I bring up the rear. The elephant grass, six feet tall on either side, shuts the world out. Piero, in front, constantly admonishes me to be attentive: We don't want to lose you.

No talk, Okech whispers, only listen. Listen for noise. And look.

Soon, we are on open ground. The earth is potted with shallow holes dug by pigs, and animal droppings are plentiful. We remain on the edge of the thicket, searching for tracks and checking the freshness of large piles of dung. I move slowly and am cautious where I put my feet.

You find mark of elephant. It tell you which way they go. Look at *cet,* tell you what time they pass.

A sudden loud snort, a rumble, and a large rhino storms out from one side of the copse, then disappears.

White rhino. White rhino, Okech whispers excitedly.

I catch a glimpse of its massive mud-caked rear end and don't want it hurtling my way!

The excitement of the rhino's charge subsides and we continue a quarter mile over rough terrain to the top of the rise. From our vantage point, the sweeping expanse of the park in the dewy haze spreads below us. It is almost daybreak. The land is slowly shaking off its dark shroud and putting on its forest-green mantle. Peaceful. Herds of grazing zebras resemble broken geometric patterns. A gang of buffalo by the water hole, amble onwards. One tarries, turning in our direction, the light easterly wind carrying our scent. He raises his head, surveying the rise. Piero quietly hands me his binoculars. The beast is over 1,500 pounds, magnificent, his hide dark and glossy, horns impressively swept back. Raising his head, his wet, glistening nose senses danger lurking nearby.

Brother Rafael passes me the rifle, and remembering instructions, I put my left foot forward, press the stock underneath my collarbone, peer down

---

Cet. (Acholi) Dung

the scope, bringing the target within the reticle till the crosshairs line up just a little above his neck. Emptying my mind of thought, my heart of feeling, I pull the trigger.

Nothing happens. I am pleased. A shot goes off. The buffalo crumples slowly, his hind feet folding first. He strives to keep his head up, shudders, and collapses. Rafael has a shy smile of elation and a glint of victory in his eyes. He brought it down with one shot through the head.

Okech points to a deep red streak over the animal's left shoulder. Look! This . . . your shot. Not enough to kill *jowi*.

The buffalo's large eyes do not see, do not close. A sweet grassy breath still lingers. I lay my hand on the body. It is still warm.

I get jowi with spear or arrow. No use gun, Okech explains. I have *akili*—brain. Be clever. He fall in hole I make. I kill for food. Need meat for my children, my wives. Not enough food.

Brother Rafael agrees. I hunt for the same reason. Meat is good for our patients, especially children who have been hungry a long time.

That same evening, Dolly and I are invited to the Cortis' for dinner. Comfortably seated on the verandah, we sip chilled tamarind juice, its tartness softened with sugar.

I hear you almost got a buffalo, Lucille teases in her French-accented English, a playful look on her face.

She is relaxed, leaning back on the reclining sofa, her long legs crossed, fruit juice glass on her lap. Slim, with a sharp-featured, sensitive face, Lucille wears her hair short and uses no makeup.

It was a large target and, fortunately, stationary.

This is your first time, yes?

Yes and no. I used to go hunting with my father in Tanga. Not to bag big game. Only guinea fowl or green pigeon.

Piero loves big game, yes? Lucille gazes at him fondly.

Y-e-s, always. In school, pheasants, quail, hare, mountain goat, chamois. But nothing like the wildlife here. I think, maybe, I can get a lion or elephant sometime. So, yes, I came to Africa to work, but opportunities for big-game hunting also influenced me. It is a long story.

He glances at Lucille, love in his eyes.

Jowi. (Acholi) Buffalo

If Lucille had not agreed to come here and stay, there would be no story.

Dolly and I are all ears. Who can pass up a love story? Besides, Piero is telling us how it all began.

In 1958, we were at Hôpital Sainte-Justine in Montreal for our postgraduate studies. I was completing my internship in paediatrics. Lucille was busy doing surgical residency. She was *molto bella*! Of course, she had no time for me!

Lucille smiles indulgently, shaking her head.

When Lucille finished, she need further training outside Canada to practise as a surgeon. Can you believe it? She could not get a single appointment anywhere in the United States, Piero continues.

They did not want a woman surgeon, see? Lucille explains.

So she decides to apply for a job in France—because she speaks French—and gets two offers. In the meantime, I work in Africa with my brother and from there to a hospital in India. I think of her often and we write letters back and forth a few times. Lucille, she was working in Marseilles and when I return to Italy, I go to meet her. I tell her about my trip to Uganda, such a beautiful country . . . and about a small hospital my friend wanted me to visit. Right away, I know this is where I want to be. I know I can make it great. I ask Lucille to come with me. I offer to buy her plane ticket. I offer to buy her cigarettes . . . even toothpaste!

Lucille laughs. He was so persistent!

The . . . the thing is, I was serious from the beginning, the first time I met her. At Christmas, I invite her to join my family and she agreed.

It was my chance to get to know Piero better before I make up my mind. You can see what was my decision!

We flew to Uganda in May of '61, and Lucille was so happy doing surgery, she stayed two extra months. The day before leaving for Marseilles, I ask her to marry me. She said no. But then she telephoned me a few weeks later and told me yes, because she loves me and cannot live without me. It was a good answer, yes?

I think dinner is ready. Shall we go in? Lucille leads Dolly inside.

Piero and I follow. We say grace. Piero pours Chianti and we clink glasses.

Ravioli is served, then pork scaloppini, and what looks like tiny shrimp. I know so little of Italian cuisine, I will not risk exposing my ignorance by asking what it is. They are crunchy, with a soft, oily core. Lucille, Piero and Dolly watch

---

Molto bella. (Italian) Very beautiful

me take a second helping. Mischief plays on their faces and they explode with laughter. The Chianti has unwound them.

Do you like what you are eating? Lucille asks.

It's delightful!

It is *ngwen*—termites! Flying ants. The Acholi love them. They remove their wings and roast them on a flat pan. You see, if I *told* you I was going to serve you termites, you would say, No, no. Now, you will eat it again. Yes?

Of course. They are an absolute treat.

We have a good laugh. And drink more Chianti. The Italians love their red wine. I am learning to like it.

It was the same with me, Lucille continues. I did not know what Africa was like until I came here. Now, it is my home.

For me, too, Piero adds. After you stay for some time, it becomes a part of you.

Piero is right. Africa grows on you like the love of a woman. The British discovered this when it was time to leave. A few even returned. For Lucille, Piero, Dolly and me, the immense vastness and grandeur of Africa is in our blood. Its challenges draw us in, and in due course, we identify with its needs and fall into rhythm with its pace.

8

UNCERTAINTIES OF A SURGEON'S CALLING

Gulu Hospital is efficiently managed by Dr. N. O. Edyegu, Medical Superintendent and Senior Medical Officer for the northern region that includes Lira and Lango. Endowed with a large frame, which suits his position, Dr. Edyegu is the first *Itesot* to qualify in medicine. Modest and reserved, he has a profound dislike for politics. We talk of ordinary things, share an occasional joke, and get along well. I like him.

Oddly enough, there is no other Ugandan doctor on staff. The roster is made up of an English gynaecologist, Russian paediatrician, South Korean ophthalmologist, two Polish doctors, a surgeon, an internist, Dolly and me. This multinational conglomerate is a lucky happenstance, for the presence of an indigenous doctor from another tribe might complicate the situation. Dr. Edyegu trusts me and is comfortable leaving town when he needs to, knowing I will take good care of the hospital. I fill a role for him that is useful. In addition to my customary work, I am occasionally called on to do something out of the ordinary. This is an aspect of involvement almost every surgeon encounters at one time or another.

Dr. Edyegu's secretary calls me frantically one morning.

There are some gentlemen to see Dr. Edyegu, but he's not here.

A four-man pharmaceutical delegation from the Soviet Union is here to familiarise senior doctors with their products. Used to protocol, the Russians are expecting to be welcomed by the hierarch.

Dr. Edyegu not here? they ask, faces falling.

Unfortunately, he was called away. Please make yourselves comfortable.

The secretary serves coffee and biscuits. Sitting around the conference table, they enquire about the nature of medical problems we face and, awed by the

---

Itesot. People of Teso, from eastern Uganda and western Kenya immensity of our tasks, are impressed with what is currently being done.

I send for our paediatrician, Varya Karakozova, to meet her compatriots. Her face lights up as she speaks Russian with her countrymen. The remaining doctors who are also free, join us.

The visitors bring out medical samples from three bulging leather cases, leaving the fourth one unopened. Spreading vials of antibiotics, tiny bottles of vitamin tablets and small round tins of food and mineral supplements, we hear brief dissertations on their uses. Although familiar with these medications, we listen to the presentation. If the prices are competitive, the ministry will buy them; however, that is not a decision for me to make. My responsibility is to be a good host.

I compliment them on being involved with the progress of this young country. It is thoughtful of their nation to send physicians like Dr. Karakozova, and I thank them.

They stand up and clap. The last leather case is laid open with the ease of previous practice. It holds three bottles of Moskovskaya vodka, two bottles of Hennessy, and one Gordon's London Dry Gin.

Glasses, yes?

Vodka is poured. I lift my glass nearly half-filled. We clink.

Zastorovia.

The police receive information of a suspicious death. A twenty-eight-year-old Lango man, probably killed by his *rafiki* who was drinking with him, has been buried four weeks, thirty miles outside Gulu. A postmortem examination is necessary.

Would you do it, Doctor? It is important.

Taking the morgue attendant, we drive to the outskirts of the village. The last five miles are impassable and we are forced to take bicycles provided by the police. I haven't ridden in years. Precariously perched on a seat uncomfortably slanted, I follow my assistant, who carries the box of instruments. The meandering path, a foot wide, is trodden earth closed in on either side by tall elephant grass. Eyes riveted on the narrow trail, I pedal nervously, filled with dread I will fall off and disappear into the grass.

Zastorovia. (Russian) To your health

Rafiki. (Swahili) Friend

We arrive at the burial spot marked by the police. Two young men, bodies glistening with copious sweat, dig steadily with *jembes.* A kind villager fetches a chair for me. Small thatched huts huddle together, bony curs yelp, naked children chase each other and knots of villagers collect at a respectable distance solemnly watching the digging. There isn't the slightest stirring of breeze.

The body is exhumed and laid some distance from the excavation site. The fetid smell makes my stomach turn somersaults. I try to beat back waves of nausea and break into a sweat. The attendant sprays bursts of paraffin-smelling antiseptic to dislodge flies asserting their rights to the decomposing body. Donning face masks; thick, long rubber gloves; and rubber aprons, we set about investigating how this man died. I desperately hope it is something obvious. My spectacles fog repeatedly from the humid air trapped in my mask and it is impossible to wipe them clean.

Beginning systematically with the limbs, then the trunk, I look at everything. All soft parts are in various stages of decomposition. I observe a large wound on the side of the skull where it has caved in, most likely, from the impact of a blunt instrument. This turns out to be the cause of death.

Always woman, sah, the attendant says.

What about the *kwete* they were drinking together?

No, sah. He crazy for that woman. She belong to his friend. He plan long before to enter her. His friend catch him. Kwete give courage.

A young man walks in with the ponderous gait of a woman far along in pregnancy. His face pales, and he avoids my eyes as he bares the source of embarrassment. His scrotum, large and swollen, hangs down to his knees. His penis is lost somewhere in the scrotal skin, which has thickened many times over. When I look at him, he does not say anything, though his eyes are eloquent. *Is there any hope? Can you do something?*

He has elephantiasis, a tropical disease resulting from deposition of larvae in the blood through the bite of a mosquito. The larvae subsequently grow into slender filarial worms, which at first irritate, then block the network of lymph channels that empty into the bloodstream. So the blockage of lymph flow in a leg makes it look like that of an elephant. In this man's case, it enlarged his

---

Jembes. (Swahili) Hoes

Kwete. (Acholi) Alcoholic beverage brewed, particularly by the Lugbara people of Uganda, by fermenting millet scrotum to elephantoid size. I have never seen anything so large. It actually weighs seventy pounds and stakes him to the ground!

I know I can help him but the immediate problem is size: How do I perform the operation in a clean, surgical way? After days of planning, rehearsal and use of a sterilised butcher's hook to hoist the scrotum, I am able to take away nine-tenths of the mass, leaving behind slightly enlarged testicles, one on either side of his penis, which he is delighted to see again. His eyes widen at its unexpected appearance and he coos like a child. Patients around him giggle uncontrollably.

The superintendent of police calls me at home, close to ten at night on February 22.

We have five ministers here who have been shaken up by the rough ride and would like to see a doctor.

These are not ordinary prisoners. You should get Dr. Edyegu.

I know, but we cannot find him. The ministers are all right. Can you see them in the morning?

Senior cabinet ministers Grace Stuart K. Ibingira, George B. K. Magezi, Dr. Emmanuel B. S. Lumu, Balaki Kebba Kirya, and Mathias Mbalule Ngobi are detained in Patiko Prison after being arrested during a cabinet meeting in Entebbe at the prime minister's directive. The ministers had accused Obote and his Army Commander Colonel, Idi Amin, of looting gold, coffee and ivory from Congo and were seeking Obote's impeachment.

Three years into independence, the prime minister has become increasingly authoritarian. People begin to fear him. Being part of the ruling clique means power, glory, adulation. Being on the other side invites constant harassment—party headquarters ransacked, meetings broken up, members beaten, spurious charges filed. If you are with the establishment and have fallen out, you run the risk of jail, banishment, possible death.

The superintendent picks me up at eight. There is a note from the senior medical officer explaining he had to leave urgently for his hometown of Soroti.

Shards of glass protrude from the top of Patiko Prison's high, forbidding walls. Inside, everything is bleak—no grass, no shrubs, no greenery. The quadrangle has three white buildings, each surrounded by a wall, also white, the better to spot prisoners attempting to escape. A guard stands at every corner, his weapon on the draw.

We walk to the middle building. The sergeant on duty barks an order, a heavy black door opens, and we go through a corridor to a third set of securely locked steel gates. *There isn't the slightest chance of escape for anyone foolhardy enough to contemplate an attempt!*

Each minister is confined to his own cell. Tired and dejected, they complain bitterly: haven't slept well, are stiff and sore, find it difficult to squat on the hole in the corner. One has mild back pain, but no significant problems requiring a doctor's services. Their main concern is what lies ahead.

The last man I see is Dr. Lumu. He is the minister of health and, subsequently, my boss. Wearing blue striped pajamas, courtesy of the prison, he smiles wanly when I greet him.

You remember me?

A year ago, I attended a meeting in Entebbe presided by Dr. Lumu. He was addressing senior staff to acquaint them with his vision for the country. His face lights up when I remind him of the occasion. The furrow in his forehead eases.

Yes, that meeting. A great conference. I remember Dr. Kadama introducing you to me, Mr. De Souza.

I see them every day for the better part of a week. They do not need medications, only solace of human interaction, a window from which to look out. I ask if they would like some reading materials. Their spirits rise at the prospect of connecting with the outside world. Concerned about political implications, the police request I stop bringing in newspapers and books after a few days.

In a week's time, the ministers are removed to an unknown destination.

Dr. Edyegu is at home with his family, grieving for his daughter, who died suddenly after an unexpected three-day illness.

The news jolts us, for we had not known she was ill. I decide to visit him in the middle of my workday, a spontaneous response to a colleague's grief. Nurses and assistants, instead of being at work, are seated on the floor in the living room, sipping *ajono* from earthenware pots through long, slender *epi.* Communal drinking is a custom that bonds people together, making them resilient during adversity, enhancing their joy in good times.

I find a cushion and sit with other mourners around a pot, sucking on the tepid homemade brew, freshly fermented from millet. It is sour and bubbly, nowhere near the bottled beer I drink. A warmth slowly builds up in my stomach,

---

Ajono. Ugandan local brew

Epi. (Acholi) Slender hollowed-out reed used as a straw

then spreads to my limbs, and I relax. With little need for conversation, the act of drinking from the same vessel links me to the mourners in their tradition.

Dr. Edyegu comes in, disheveled, with reddened eyes. I rise to condole with him.

Leo, my daughter . . . my family . . . I . . . we are very shocked. My poor little girl. Her entire body burning like hot coal. A fever . . . malaria. She was shivering so much, we gave her a mixture of medicinal leaves boiled in water to drink and began sponging her to bring the fever down. It did not help. Neither did aspirin. I thought, maybe, she has cerebral malaria, so I gave a chloroquine injection. She complained her neck was stiff, so I could not rule out meningitis and administered penicillin as well. We tried everything . . . I was hoping she would recover . . . but it was no use.

Did you have her blood checked, her spinal fluid examined?

Only a thick blood smear for malarial parasite. I did not draw spinal fluid because I don't trust the lab.

Dr. Edyegu could have taken his ten-year-old daughter to the paediatric unit at St. Mary's Lacor Hospital, yet was reluctant to do so out of concern it may reflect badly on Gulu Hospital, where he is chief. Besides, there would be political ramifications.

A woman, head covered in black cloth and wearing a blue-and-black loosely gathered *gomesi*, enters the room. It is his sister. She lets out a high-pitched, ululating cry that is taken up by the women in the house. I leave quietly for the hospital.

After the loss of the chief's daughter, it is clear our tranquil frontier post is not geared to take care of anything beyond daily routine. Dolly and I are aware anything can go wrong at any time and we worry about our children. It is imperative we have a sense of adventure to live by and an abiding faith all will be well.

Gomesi. (Luganda) Traditional colourful full-length garment worn by women in Uganda

9

CONFLUENCES OF OLD AND NEW

As soon as I get to the hospital, my patients are there to greet me. On the cement floor, an active, inquisitive five-year-old lad crawls, feet dragging, as best he can around his mother while she advances slowly in the long line. His little body, covered in an oversized faded blue shirt, recently washed but already dirty, sags off his shoulder. Afraid of the doctor in the white coat, he clutches at her as they approach me sitting solemnly behind my desk, my nurse and translator waiting by the examination table. As he looks up, the whimpering child lets out a howl. Tears streaming, snot bubbling, he does not trust me and, now, isn't sure if he should trust his mother, who has difficulty prying him off. He smells of *mandazi,* the sweet roll she just fed him.

Her little boy fell ill one day. Nothing serious, a runny nose, mild malaise and low fever. Insidiously, his legs weaken. First, he refuses to walk, then he cannot stand. Bustling energy that had powered his legs vanishes. He only crawls. To see him go through tortuous attempts to get around breaks her heart. She tries all customary treatments. They fail. She takes him to the medicine man, who tells her, You have been cursed by the woman who lost her man to you and is the father of your child. This child will not get any better, but I can cast a spell so that your next one will be healthy.

She hears of a doctor who can straighten her son's bent legs and enable him to walk with aids. She is intrigued.

Daktar, you help him, please? she implores. *Caro*—village—say you got *timo tango*—magic. A glimmer of hope eases tension in her face. I wish, if only for a brief moment, to possess the powers she ascribes to me. I could then heal her child the way she wants and her heart that weeps for him.

I make a quick assessment. His legs, curled beneath, frail, birdlike, shriveled. His hips stiff, knees permanently bound in a flexed position as he sits on top of clubbed feet that grow callosities. The boy has polio, a common affliction among children and youth, probably triggered when the virus settled in the spinal cord, killing anterior horn cells. There isn't any way to bring those cells to life again.

Yes, I can straighten his legs but they will always remain paralysed. We can fit them into metal uprights and wooden clogs and train him to walk with a pair of crutches.

Aniang—I understand. You do good for my son. I bring you *gweno*. She smiles.

What would you like to do after we take care of your legs?

Head thrown back, face brimming with mischief, eyes full of sparkle, his answer comes, swift as an arrow.

Mupiira—Football! Shoot goal!

Making tiny incisions in the groin, inner sides and backs of knees, I straighten out the boy's hips and knees, then divide tight tendons and tissues causing contractures. His heels, in a position of equinus, require additional incisions. After obtaining the corrections, I hold his fully flexed legs in plaster of paris casts from groin to toes, which, though heavy, don't slow him down. He merely tugs them behind him. Following a series of casts, I place his legs in metal braces attached to wooden clogs, specially ordered from Kampala. He learns to walk using crutches, and in a manner of another few weeks, begins to show off to his mother. She is ecstatic! Seeing other children crippled with polio who crawl and drag themselves on calloused palms, buttocks grazing the floor, she does not ask for anything more.

We are fortunate to be visited by Professor Ronald Huckstep, senior lecturer in orthopaedic surgery at Makerere University and specialist with a consuming interest in poliomyelitis. There is no question in the Professor's mind that polio is the foremost health issue facing the country, crying to be addressed. His observant eyes noticed cases of polio at hospitals, local markets, the city and farther afield, which led to his decision to expand the small clinic started by the Kampala Round Table in 1957. He presented his suggestions to Professor Ian McAdam, sought assistance from the National Fund for Research into Poliomyelitis and Other Crippling Diseases and Royal College of Surgeons of England, and then set out to create an appropriate clinic at Old Mulago Hospital. It was ideally suited for what the Professor had in mind, with rooms for patients, offices for doctors, nurses, staff, and volunteers, storage areas for medical records and supplies—crutches, clogs and calipers, and a workshop to produce them.

Gweno. (Luo) Hen

On our part, we are always delighted to host someone who has ideas to share. His trip, a fact-finding mission, is to acquaint himself with the magnitude of problems we encounter. Astonished by our accomplishments, he promises to send us a larger supply of calipers, crutches, and a few wheelchairs.

The work you do here is brilliant. I will designate Gulu as a satellite polio clinic of Mulago. When this is finalised, I'll send a physiotherapist and technician to take care of your appliances.

I am most pleased. The designation will give us access to many more resources, allowing us to treat the majority of patients afflicted with polio. These tragedies could have been averted had they sought treatment earlier, but poor, uneducated families in rural areas are unaware of what can be done.

The government's energies, however, are deflected in other directions. The air is rife with news of unrest. Army Commander in Chief Brigadier General Shaban Opolot, an Itesot, is demoted from service to make room for Idi Amin, next in command. The five ministers are still in jail, and there is an increasing restlessness among the Baganda, the nation's largest ethnic group in the south.

The Professor returns to Gulu for a second look around. Since his last visit more than three months ago, he has travelled the length and breadth of the country and is astounded by the staggering number of those disabled by polio, which runs in the thousands.

Leo, imagine what we could achieve if we made every polio child able to walk and become self-sufficient? So full of life, even though many are ostracised. Makes me want to help as much as possible.

Ron's altruism and optimistic disposition lend excitement to his conversation regarding what he has already begun in Kampala and what can be implemented countrywide. Even so, I am startled when, out of the blue, he asks if I would consider coming to Kampala to be part of their orthopaedic team. Subsequent to extensive training under his tutelage, the Ministry of Health would designate me surgeon in charge of the polio clinic.

The invitation is appealing. I take a few days to think over his offer. Experience alone, I find, is a good teacher but isn't quite enough. It has taught me to be self-reliant, make quick assessments and follow through with appropriate measures. But it does not provide a second opinion. I am the only surgeon here, and even if I consider alternative diagnoses in complex cases, I am still likely to fall back on my own biases. At Mulago, on the other hand, there would be cumulative knowledge from other surgeons, and different perspectives would enhance my learning, sharpen my skills. Besides, Dolly can continue her hospital attachment and the children will attend an established school. There are, of course, advantages to moving. Sadly for us, they come at the expense of people we leave behind—Piero and Lucille Corti at Lacor Hospital, our patients with whom we have close rapport and our many friends in town.

Among the latter is Okot p'Bitek, an Acholi writer and poet, articulate about the customs of his people. Sitting on the floor, sipping beer from an earthenware pot with friends, he tells us of tribal legends and lore, how he believes the peoples of Uganda are defined by them, going into some detail on how missionaries and, later, the British encouraged Acholi to drop age-old customs. He has a soft manner of speaking, and as he gets more involved in a topic, his sensitive face acquires added intensity.

He is incensed that meaningful, colourful traditions are in danger of being cast aside by the younger generation.

Our young men and women look askance at their past. In fact, I'm presently working on a poem about an Acholi character who is doing just that.

Can you read it to us?

Not ready yet. Needs more revisions, some modifications, he protests, but agrees after some persuasion.

I will read what I have put together so far. Tomorrow, the verse may change or be moved. *Wer pa Lawino.* The character is Lawino, a wife complaining about her husband, Ocol, who is being seduced by Western ways.

The reading puts us in a pensive mood as we relate to the young couple's plight. The theme of eroding traditions leaves us saddened. How true what he says, how disappointing the early fruits of freedom.

Across Uganda, its people struggle between traditional ways and encroaching Westernisation. They adapt to their vicissitudes, albeit slowly. It is the beginning of new times and with it comes choices. Western medicine prevails over tribal cures. Diseases such as polio, tuberculosis, and Burkitt's lymphoma are being managed effectively. However, not all changes are for the better. Instead of claiming what is truly their own, youth are mesmerised by the glitter of the white man's culture. A smattering of English and taste for whisky among men and preference for high heels, short dresses and lipstick among women pass for liberation and progress. For many, independence is not taking the country in the direction it should go.

p'Bitek sucks deeply on the slender reed to get a large swig of beer. During a lull, I tell him Dolly and I are leaving Gulu.

We will miss you. Almost everyone eventually goes to Kampala. But I am pleased we could make your acquaintance. You've always been interested in our people, our culture and our politics.

As a parting gift, p'Bitek gives Dolly and me an earthenware beer pot to remember the ways of the north.

Toast Given to the Staff at Gulu Hospital

I would like to tell you how much my wife and I have appreciated this fine warm-hearted party, this fine gesture of continuing friendship. My wife and I thank you from the bottom of our hearts.

One and a half years is too short a period to spend among friends. All the same, it has been for us a pleasure to be in your midst; and a privilege to be in the land of Acholi, the land of the Nanga and the Bull; the Bwola and the Dingi-Dingi; the Otole and the Apiti; in the land of the Keyo [mountain] and its five rivers, where in the hoary distant past Labongo and Kipir fought amongst themselves and founded the great Luo people from one end to the other.

While we have derived great pleasure here, we hope that at the same time we have been of some service to you.

Long, long ago, it used to be said that "Doctors pour drugs of which they know little, to cure diseases of which they know less, into human beings of whom they know nothing." I hope your verdict will be that my wife and I have been better.

For our part we would like to thank you for two things—professionally for trust and confidence in us, and socially for your understanding and friendship . . . and whichever place we may be, I'd like you to remember that in that place you'd have two friends in us.

Apoyo matek. Dong wu bedi. Rubanga ogwok won ducu. Thank you very much. Be well. God bless all of you.

10

AN ILL-CONCEIVED PLAN COMES UNDONE

Kampala is the showpiece of the Ganda. This is their city, ruled for the past two hundred years by a succession of *kabakas*—kings.

The powerful Bugandan kingdom was slowly stripped of its autonomy as Britain acquired contiguous portions of land in 1893 and, a year later, cobbled a country, Uganda, by incorporating peoples who would never elect to live side by side—in this instance, Luos of the north; Lango, Acholi and Bantus of the south; and the four tribal kingdoms of Buganda, Bunyoro-Kitara, Busoga and Toro. The tribes had little in common; they spoke different languages, and food, dress and customs were dissimilar. Yet Britain, the avid coloniser, paying no heed to ethnic rivalries, placed all within boundaries conveniently drawn in Europe.

When the British departed in 1962, they made Kampala the new capital and left behind a duly elected national government. Uganda became an independent state with the four kingdoms in a loose federal arrangement and a single, all-powerful national assembly. The victorious party, Uganda People's Congress, predominantly northerners, with Apollo Milton Obote as prime minister, formed an alliance with Kabaka Yekka, King's Party. The kabaka was reluctantly recognised and made ceremonial president in November 1963.

The Ganda, an advanced people who dominated the entire lake region for as long as they could remember, could not forget their past. It intruded into the present, a persistent reminder of previous achievements. The tenuous relationship with Uganda People's Congress disintegrated, and tribal animosities once again prevailed.

In February 1966, Obote suspended the constitution, putting an end to Kabaka Edward Frederick William David Walugembe Mutebi Luwangula Mutesa II's position of nonexecutive president. Obote then proclaimed himself executive president. Three months later, the *Lukiiko*—Parliament of the Kingdom of Buganda—promptly withdrew recognition of Obote's government and ordered it off Buganda soil. May 24, on orders from Obote, Idi Amin stormed the *Lubiri*—kabaka's palace—in Mengo, setting it ablaze. A violent confrontation ensued, killing many and forcing "King Freddie" to flee to Rwanda and eventually to England, where he lived in exile.

The city was rife with insecurity. Deep hostilities simmered. A lack of normalcy rolled from one day to the next. Pedestrians did not loiter, instead glancing one way, then the other, and darting in the direction of safety. There was undeniable resentment of Obote troops by the Ganda.

July 1966. Driving to Kampala, we notice how different Buganda is from the north. Vibrant green foliage, red loam and low golden hills give the undulating countryside a natural richness. Like the Ganda, I believe this is God's country, a land abundantly blessed.

Government employees are allocated housing, which is considered part of the remuneration. When we arrive in Kampala, there is no housing available, so the ministry puts us up at the modern, five-star Grand Hotel on Speke Road situated on Nakasero Hill, an old residential area, home to many established families, Ganda, British and Indian, who live comfortably as neighbours. Colourful blossoms adorn these expansive dwellings, filling the air with distinctive scents.

By seven in the evening, curfew shuts down the city. Intense bursts of heavy artillery pound at odd hours. Gunfire, miles away, sounds harrowingly close in the quiet of night. We are cocooned in the hotel, enough that it is not terrorising. In the daylight, fragmented wisps of black smoke float aimlessly in the sky, often screening the sun. Grim soldiers toting unwieldy weapons pace at major intersections.

Hotels are comfortable the first few days. The children discover this early on. Initial excitement diminishes and feelings of confinement set in. They miss running around, being free to devise their own games. Dinner hour for children is six o'clock. Dolly takes them to the hotel restaurant, where they pick meals from the limited menu. At the next table, a boy and girl eat alone while teasing each other. Kevin and Janine Brown, ages seven and three, tell her their dad is sitting outside the dining room. Dolly meets Larry Brown and that evening, at the bar, introduces him to me. Larry's wife, Jo, joins us for a drink. Theirs is an interracial marriage. Larry is black, Jo is white. They met through Jo's classmate who was dating Larry's cousin. Like us, their union is unique.

On a two-year contract with the United States Agency for International Development (USAID), Larry is here to train Ugandans in the Pay As You Earn system of taxation prevalent in the United States, where the money estimated as tax is deducted from income before employees receive it, as opposed to the British system, where the earner declares income at year-end, then proceeds to pay the tax. The latter system is ineffectual, as it brings in little cash to a government increasingly strapped for monies. Living at the Grand Hotel is akin to being on a holiday cruise—you happen upon the same people regularly. And so we see a lot of the Browns, and a close friendship develops.

We enroll Louella, Mario and Lea in Norman Godinho Primary School founded in 1933 by Goan philanthropist and entrepreneur Norman Godinho, because Goan and Indian children were not allowed to study alongside the Europeans. Dolly drives them to school and then takes Joanna to the park and shops with Jo and Janine. Weekend mornings, we frequent the Uganda Bookshop, where the siblings happily pore over comic books like *Princess, Tina, Jack and Jill*, and *Treasure*. Louella and Mario routinely voice doubts about my classics selection. I dispel their disgruntlement by suggesting they choose on our next visit. By good fortune, we discover Cristos, a popular Greek confectionery and bakery, well known for delectable pastries. Smiling contentedly, radiance emanates from the children's faces as cream horns fill their cheeks, leaving little time for conversation.

Within a month, we relocate to 4 Upper Kololo Terrace on Kololo Hill. A sprawling three-bedroom, one-bathroom brick bungalow with clay-tiled roof, two-tone whitewash and chalk-red paint on a terraced plot. Detached garage and servants' quarters match the house. The Public Works Department furnishes beds, basic furniture, stove and fridge. Clean and spacious, there is plenty of room for all six of us.

The garden, enclosed by a tall, sparse hedge, is coarse lawn, a scattering of bushes, and few trees. Colour truly spills from the flora. Deep yellow flowers issue like trumpets from dark green foliage. Tiny creamy amber florets with borders of pink dance to earth. An eight-foot shrub gives rise to three distinctly coloured flowers, all blooming at the same time: white, light and dark purple, oddly enough, named Yesterday, Today, and Tomorrow. The tall slender jacaranda tree in the centre of the roundabout is ablaze with clusters of lavender-blue flowers. Two leafy mango trees, one in the front left corner and the other diametrically opposite, produce fruit not of the best quality but still edible. In the back, a solitary papaya tree like a capacious green umbrella imparts cover for its fruits.

One weekend, I give the push mower several quick runs. *Ideal physical exercise.* Later, I receive a concerned telephone call from my neighbour.

Wouldn't advise you to cut your own grass. You'll be seen as tight-fisted, taking a job from some willing African.

Quite disconcerted, I ask Otiri, our Lango houseboy, to arrange for a *shamba boy*.

No, Bwana. Is okay. I do it. *Shilingi yango.*

Otiri, who worked for us in Gulu, is familiar with the city's social attractions. Saturday nights, looking handsome and poised, dressed in his best white shirt, long, narrow, black trousers and pointed Italian shoes, he ventures to a local bar, his female friends' quarters, or out with his own people. On occasion, he returns in the early hours quite intoxicated, sometimes surprisingly stoned on *bhang.* One Sunday, Otiri is loath to enter the house. His badly beaten face says it all. Swollen tongue and lips, unable to articulate, he is embarrassed and full of regret. Without delving into his private life, I suggest he be more careful, for fear of coming to serious harm. He is aware of rivalries that exist among tribes who gravitate to the city and of prevailing hierarchy, the Ganda being at the elite level.

Quite unknown to Dolly and me, Louella and Lea have a mutual monetary alliance with Otiri. Having already drawn an advance on the following month's salary, they regularly bail him out, lending a shilling or two from their meagre pocket money, which he always pays back. For the favour rendered, Otiri turns a blind eye whenever the girls forage the pantry for *njugus*, biscuits and fudge.

Pennina, our ayah in Lira, sends word she will join us after delivering her third child, but hasn't said when. Her two sons are in Lango with their respective fathers. Close to four one afternoon, as I prepare to leave Mulago Hospital, I notice her in the hospital parking square near my white Fiat station wagon. Dropping to her knees in deference and respect, she greets me. Uncomfortable by her traditional obeisance, I look about furtively, then quickly raise her to her feet. A shy smile spreads over her wan and tired face. From her *kikapu,* she takes out a gift, a drooping white hen.

How did you get here? I ask, with a hint of surprise.

Shamba boy. (Swahili) Gardener

Shilingi yango. (Swahili) My money

Bhang. (Hindi) Leaves and flower tops of cannabis, used as a narcotic

Njugus. (Swahili) Roasted peanuts

Kikapu. (Swahili) Basket

Bus bring me to market. I ask for hospital. Askari show me *gari yako.*

Dolly and I are grateful for the extra help, but the children will not be pleased by Pennina's unexpected arrival. They mimic her strict ways, with mock announcements—*Baff time, baff time!*—as she is wont to do.

The children quickly make friends with Christine, Joe and Simon Onyango, our next-door neighbours. Holidays find them shinnying up and down mango trees, which impart an immense aerial playground, plucking guavas, playing hide-and-seek, before coming in for lunch and rest from the hot sun, and hurrying out again after teatime for a few more hours of fun.

Baths and dinner done, the kids watch television for an hour while Dolly and I dine together. The large screened-in verandah where the black-and-white Toshiba set is installed and Dolly's African violet plants line the entire window ledge, is affectionately called *the TV room.* Uganda Television programming begins at six o'clock in the evening, showcasing a combination of comedies and dramas from the UK and America and a weekly local *Uganda Playhouse* in Luganda. Saturday mornings are especially exciting with two added hours of cartoons. Dolly and I watch the nightly news as we sip our after-dinner coffee. The national anthem followed by the test card on the screen signals sign-off.

During these early months, we cannot tell if the day will end without incident or the night without gunfire. In need of camaraderie and advice, we fall back on a small cadre of people in the city as well as adjoining Entebbe. It is from our Goans we receive timely hospitality. Dolly and I regularly enjoy a quiet meal, *reichado*—a flat fish fried with piquant stuffing in its split middle—pork vindaloo, or even a simple *xit kodi*—rice and fish curry. We swap stories of Goa and plaintively air our sentiments of what will become of Uganda and what that might do to us. I never sense an element of panic in their conduct. We are an optimistic group with a stoicism that helps weather such upheavals, and our dread of the army slowly subsides; although the curfew puts a crimp on our activities, we enjoy every minute of free time.

Professor Ian McAdam, chief of the Department of Surgery, welcomes me to Mulago Hospital. There is an invigorating newness about the teaching hospital of Makerere University School of Medicine. Its physical makeup is modern and spruce, its staff imbued with a sense of mission. Doctors come from across the world, the British Commonwealth, Scandinavia, the United States, and of course

---

Gari yako. (Swahili) Your car

Uganda. This assemblage of brilliant young doctors sees its task as one of ensuring the health of the nation and focusing on newer research to unravel Africa's chronic health problems. I am honoured to be a part of the group. With twice as many surgeons as there were physicians at Lira and Gulu combined, most of my Ganda colleagues are teachers and administrators in fields as diverse as science, language, and theatre. I am eager to know them as I did the Lango and Acholi; however, a subtle aloofness precludes getting closer. Conversations consist of the usual pleasantries with little mention of anything substantially personal. While not unfriendly, it is challenging to get past a certain level of acquaintanceship.

It is difficult also to achieve rapport with patients. Being in a teaching hospital, they are examined by a string of physicians including residents, medical students and specialists. Initially pleased by the unaccustomed attention, they soon become confused by the multitude of doctors. I do not speak Luganda and they know no Swahili. Circumstances were different at Lira Hospital, where I made up the entire surgical department and was both patient advisor and friend. I rarely attain this relationship at Mulago.

Mondays are reserved for surgeries at the polio clinic. Patients mill around everywhere, limping, crawling, shuffling, hobbling with stout sticks put to use as canes, as well as homemade crutches, hoping to be ambulant one day. As the clinic becomes busier, Ron Huckstep trains more orthopaedic assistants. Help comes from abroad as well. The New York–based World Rehabilitation Fund sends Juan Munros, former popular Spanish footballer, now an ardent teacher of how to use locally made, inexpensive artificial limbs and braces for the handicapped in the third world. A down-to-earth, likable man, he persuades students in the polio workshop to stay with simple aids. It is the most practical way to extend help to a larger number of people. Workshop employees put in long hours to keep up demand, cutting leather straps with knives, pounding nails, planing wooden shanks to form crutches, sectioning slender iron rods to make metal braces that are welded to iron rings, and fashioning wooden clogs with power-driven saws. When the Professor steps in, there is more banging and welding, more planing, sawing and cutting, each one vying to be heard. Sparks fly from welding sites, and the sawing of metal sounds like the cackle of hyenas. The smell of leather mingles with wood.

A sorority of women volunteers works with rare public spiritedness in a ward at old Mulago converted into an office. Most British Embassy officials' wives are here as a matter of civic duty. After preliminary assessments, they register polio patients, obtaining a history of illness together with relevant family details. They also document their villages and regions. The volunteers deal with the nitty-gritty of medical records, placing charts in retrievable order and entering details to keep them up to date. Without the services of these good women, the clinic would grind to a halt.

Patients see the Professor, house surgeon, or me. We put them at ease, then proceed to examine and formulate treatment plans. They are x-rayed and photographed for visual documentation. Depending on our recommendations, patients are fitted with calipers, clogs and crutches by the orthopaedic assistant and referred for physiotherapy. If surgery is recommended, a date is set. Clinic records show more than 7,500 polio patients have passed through our doors.

Long before that, it becomes clear something has to be done to contain this terrible disease, and the only effective way to prevent it is immunisation. The Rotary Club, associated with the polio clinic from inception, is prepared to give it a try. It is a brave undertaking. Nothing of this magnitude has ever been done. The tasks of taking this novel idea to parents steeped in old ways and moving distraught children to unfamiliar locations are gargantuan. Our grandiose plan is widely publicised. Newspapers report extensively, radios boom the message, televisions broadcast the event exhorting parents not to miss this once-in-a-lifetime opportunity of ensuring a healthy future for their children. The City Council and Ministry of Health give their blessings. President Obote lends his patronage, and the Rotary Club even goes as far as having Lord Snowdon, husband to Princess Margaret, fly out from England to declare open what will be Uganda's first major immunisation programme.

In one day, almost 90 percent are immunised with the Sabin oral vaccine in a major district of Baganda. Again, newspapers splash the story, radios blare its success and television screens show infants and children swallowing vaccine drops on sugar cubes while happy parents look on. The ministry exhibits pride in forward thinking, the Rotary Club pats itself on its back and the orthopaedic team is overjoyed. Another two doses and they will forever be protected from the ravages of polio. Lord Snowdon leaves for England after being feted with congratulatory celebrations for supporting this endeavour.

Six weeks later, the second dose is due. Just a handful turn up. Everyone is flummoxed. *How can it be? What happened?* The reason subsequently becomes clear. Ganda villagers, in their earnest simplicity, solicit medical treatment only when ill. *Why would the government go out of its way to provide healthy children free treatment?* The elders deliberate the matter and conclude this is an insidious attempt on the part of the government to sterilise their offspring. They are convinced this is Obote's nefarious plot to settle old scores.

My heart weeps as I realise the enormity of mistrust between the two tribes and how enmity serves to deny children the sole opportunity of avoiding this crippling disease. While we continue to treat our patients, they will not reap the benefits of the vaccine, the one answer that will forever ward off their deformities.

11

WE HELD HANDS

Professor McAdam supervises the first of three surgical units, each consisting of two consultants and a senior resident. Sir Ian is always accessible, and his secretary, Zena Pereira, a young Goan, assists us in every way. She complements the Professor's personality nicely and brings efficiency to the department while remaining receptive to our constant requests.

The second unit is in the charge of Sir John Croot, a tall, lanky Englishman nearing retirement. A professor in his time and minister of health in the colonial government, he is an avuncular figure whose advice we frequently seek and whose anecdotes hold us entranced. I have the utmost respect for Sir John, who is an extremely good clinician. He is all that one can be in professional life, having reached the pinnacle in academics and politics. But what makes me take to him is, in spite of all his accolades, he remains a gentleman, never curt or haughty, treating me as an equal.

Mr. Sebastian Kyalwazi, a Muganda, runs the third unit. In his mid-forties, he is expected to take over from Professor McAdam when the time comes. Unlike other Baganda, he borders on being gregarious. A broad smile always plays on his kindly face and I have never known him to get cross. Both students and staff are exceptionally loyal to him, a phenomenon I ascribe to his being plainly unpretentious.

Work is both challenging and gratifying, dealing with patients, teaching students, pursuing research. In the weeks that follow, I pick my way carefully, doing all that is expected of me and more, until I am familiar with established routine. I have been allocated one morning a week to see private patients who include well-placed Ugandans, Indians and foreigners, as well as diplomats, senior government officials and ministers. My schedule fills rapidly, and my allotted hours extended, a welcome development. A few months later, Sir John Croot has a quiet chat with me.

Leo, I have great regard for you and trust you will handle this well. In fact, I know you will, with aplomb. Your Indian patients come to see me after consulting with you. Please don't think any less of yourself. I am from an older generation and they have known me in different circumstances.

The Indians are fond of Sir John. He understands their ways and is a good listener. They, in turn, place him on a pedestal. *Is he not a mzungu? And where could you get a better medical opinion?*

In a later conversation with Mr. Kyalwazi, I casually mention what Sir John told me.

Fortunately, I have no such problems! At least, in your case, the Indians come to you first, then go to Sir John. I wonder what will happen when Sir John retires. He chuckles softly.

We fall silent. Wrapped in our thoughts, I cannot help but appreciate he is mature enough not to feel slighted at being overlooked because of colour, even though he is a professor and will soon be chief.

He tells me his story.

When he was a student at Makerere University, his teachers and administrators were all Englishmen. He was a good student, not a rabble-rouser or disputatious. He had no problems with the establishment, but the pecking order did not escape him. It was associated with colour. As a black student in a colonial country, he was closely observed, often patronised. Would all the time and money invested in him come to naught? Would he eventually make it? In the Britisher's mind there was always a nagging uncertainty.

Mr. Kyalwazi lived through that doubt-ridden period. He was taught to regard whites as being of higher status, to revere them. It became so ingrained, he invariably rose from his seat as a mark of deference every time a white man entered his classroom. Even now, as senior surgeon in his own office, he can barely repress the impulse to stand whenever a white colleague comes in. I comprehend what Sebastian is telling me and feel a kinship with him.

Towards the end of my stay in Tanga before I left for Edinburgh, that was how I felt too. When I returned to Tanga, a young doctor fresh out of training, I would refuse to be browbeaten and could put up a fight as often as I had to. In time, tired of having to challenge a system that never let up, I was close to capitulating.

He asks me about my Tanganyikan background. It intrigues him because he knows little of the country, and there were hardly any Tanganyikan students with him in medical school.

Independence celebration in Lira, Uganda, October 9, 1962

Leo with Denis Burkitt, Lira, February 1964

Opening day: new Ward 8, Lira Hospital, April 5, 1963

Lira Hospital staff

Dolly with midwives and nurses, Lira Hospital

House at 9 Moroto Road, Lira, September 1964

Dolly and the children in her rose garden in Lira, September 1964

Eddy and Annie Moné with son, Egbert—
Leo and Dolly's godson—on January 23, 1966

Mac at Murchison Falls National Park

Vultures at Murchison Falls National Park

Back: Piero Corti with Joanna; front: Louella, Dominique Corti, Lea and Mario in Gulu, 1965

Visiting in Lacor

Larry Brown with Leo, Kampala, 1966

Larry and Jo Brown with Dolly, Lea and daughter Janine

Family, including Kevin and Janine Brown, at Kampala railway station seeing Mario and Louella off to boarding school in Nairobi, 1968

Department of Surgery, Mulago Hospital

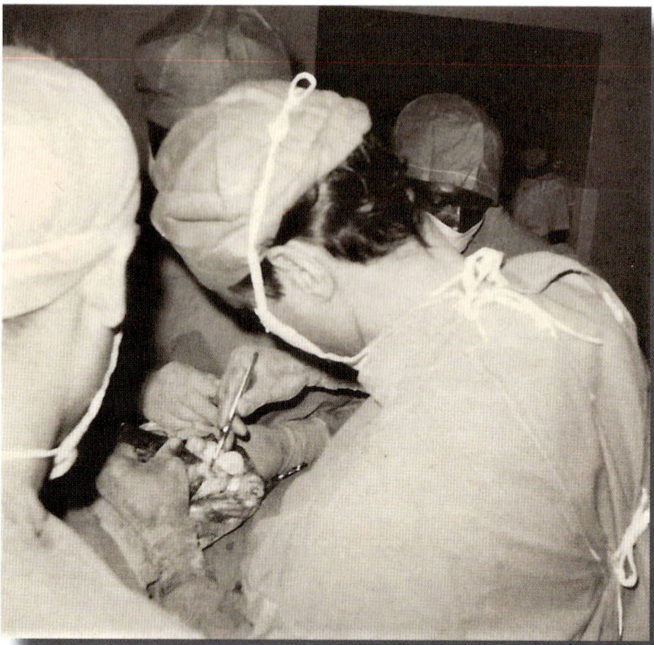

Leo in surgery at Mulago Hospital Kampala

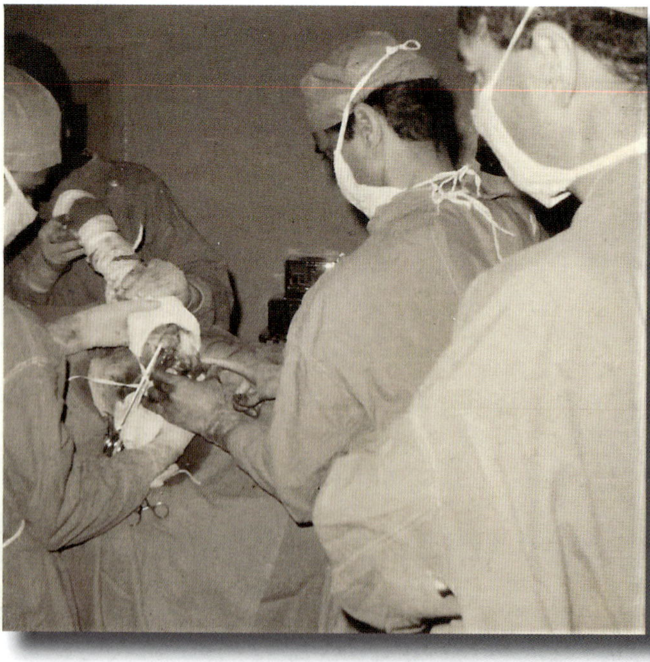

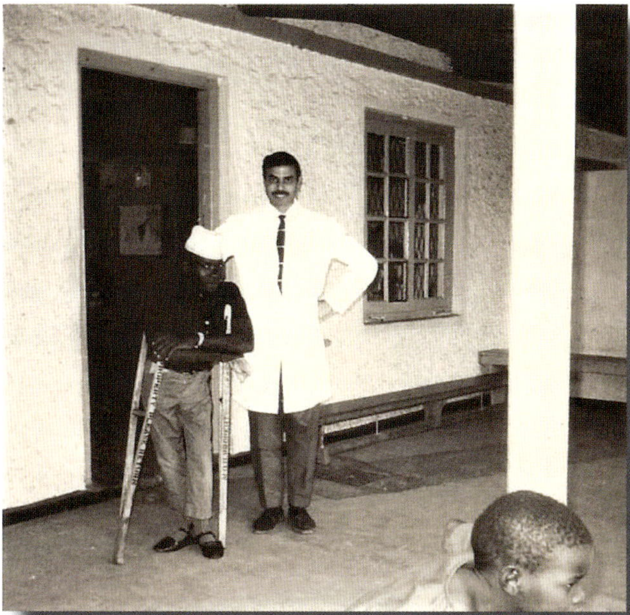

Leo with polio patient

Mulago Hospital Polio Clinic

With Mr. David Kisumba, Mulago Hospital

Polio Clinic assistants with Leo De Souza, Ron Huckstep and David Kisumba (center front)

Association of Surgeons of East Africa

Good-bye party at the Polio Clinic for Donald Gibson (right)

I take him briefly through my many milestones in Tanga, Arusha and Lindi, the many challenges and oversights, and how eventually, through Jack Darling, I found my way to Uganda.

I am truly surprised, Leo. I know we were always oppressed but I never thought of Indians in this light.

We are quiet for a while. Seated at his desk in operating scrubs and white coat, he leans back pensively. The soft whir of the overhead fan continues; a car starts in the parking quadrangle. I am not privy to what is going on in his mind, but imagine what I told him has set off a train of thought that is displacing old concepts.

Well, then, you are one of us.

Taken aback, I don't know how to express my deep gratitude. I softly say, Thank you.

We become close friends, talking often about work and politics. One morning, as we walk along the long corridor between our offices and the surgical wards, engrossed in discussing a case, Sebastian takes my hand by the fingers.

I inhale sharply! This touch, this contact, I understand is common practice among Ganda men. Holding hands is a sign of close friendship and brotherhood. It clearly establishes to Sebastian Kyalwazi I am one of his own. Aware of the luxury of his friendship, there is an imperceptible bond ensuing between us. When the time comes to leave for our respective wards, his hand disengages mine as effortlessly and lightly as he initially sought it.

A few months later, a young orthopaedic surgeon joins our unit. Mr. David Kisumba, also Ganda, has returned from Glasgow after completing his training. In time, we become friends, and before long, we too hold hands, talking over problem cases as we walk along that long corridor with the low parapet overlooking the courtyard.

12

POLIO, THE PROFESSOR AND I

Professor Ron Huckstep is reluctant to allow me to do additional surgeries; however, after a particularly trying day, he has no option but to let me have a larger role. We walk to his office where he plops into a chair and begins jotting down my added assignments. Through it all, I sense he is not particularly happy having to delegate more cases to me. He wants to remain in complete charge. I discover this facet of his personality, a propensity for garnering power while keeping me under control.

Dolly arrives in the surgical department around four driving from Kampala Clinic after work. No sooner than Mr. Huckstep sees her, his face clouds over, and before I register Dolly is at the door, he confronts her in an unusually harsh tone.

Are you here to pick up Leo? Already? You do realise he works in a big hospital now and has greater responsibilities. Which means, of course, he is not ready to go home yet.

The greeting Dolly intended freezes mid-syllable. Her smile dies. She flinches and stops abruptly, briefly scanning his face. Swallowing hard, she mumbles, I'm sorry.

Stunned by the way he addresses Dolly, a little voice urges me to restrain myself. In a raspy whisper caused by rising anger, I say, She's giving me a lift to the Fiat service station to collect my car.

Dolly drives in silence, jaw clenched, eyes moist.

Who the hell does he think he is, Leo?

My mind is a roaring storm. *Would he have done that to the wife of an English doctor? He wouldn't have dared! The wife of an Ugandan doctor? Of course not. The Ugandans are in power.* Some mzungus are the same, whether in Tanganyika or here, whether before independence or after. And there's nothing we can do about it. How could I have left without standing up to him? I am ashamed. I then know I matter little to Mr. Huckstep.

Ron continues to work at the galloping pace set for himself, for there is much to be accomplished. Never before has anything been done for the poliomyelitis patient. The Professor is the right person for such a challenge. He is in the vanguard, a man possessed with unflagging resolve, ready to vanquish the demon that is polio. In such a single-minded operation, he does not need a colleague or partner.

To his patients, the Professor is the most exceptional medicine man there ever was, one who straightens legs and restores their given purpose. The bent and twisted, having drifted into the clinic by curiosity aroused from hearsay, find themselves imbued with a new sense of direction and hope. They thank this mzungu doctor a thousand times.

Everyone wants to be part of the crusade the Professor has pioneered, no matter how small. The Round Table Club of Kampala makes the polio clinic its top priority. Newspapers are eager to write about this doctor, the architect of the clinic, who is changing lives of children. Before-and-after photographs of severely deformed children looking remarkably straightened and cheerful post-surgery alongside Mr. Huckstep help launch published stories. Statistics emphasise the fact this clinic is most outstanding and perhaps the only one of its kind in all of Africa. The Professor is deserving of the adulation showered on him, and his reputation spreads mainly by bush telegraph but also over radio and television.

Word extends abroad. His proficient work has attracted attention in Britain and the United States, and he slowly emerges as champion of the crippled in Africa. Sharad Hardikar, a young Indian orthopaedic surgeon, spends a year among us to observe the management of polio patients in a developing country. Mr. Chris Horn from Britain and Canadian doctors Robert McMurtry and Donald Gibson join the team for a year as Fellows. Dr. Gibson, who had worked at Mengo Hospital in Kampala for ten years in the early 1950s, is back to lend his services to the Professor's orthopaedic unit.

Ron Huckstep, David Kisumba and I are now senior members of the staff manning the clinic. Patients pour in from all parts of the country, more than we can tend to, leaving us physically drained. We see between sixty and seventy children and adults every week. The time has come to add another clinic day or even two. Mr. Kisumba agrees that change is necessary, and I decide to bring up the matter.

Ron, the clinic has grown too much for us to manage. So many patients. Long waiting lines before we can even get to the children. Their families travel extremely long distances. David and I were thinking it may be a good idea to have three smaller clinics, spread over the week. We can each hold a clinic on separate days with the assistance of Dr. Gibson, the registrar, and the house surgeon.

Plainly shocked, the Professor stands rigid, eyes boring into me.

Or even better, we can have two clinics to start. David can handle one and I can run the other. It would free you up to do other important things. And you could join us whenever you want.

Ron shrugs and walks away. Straight off, I know I've said the wrong thing. There is nothing the Professor is more proud of than the clinic. *His* clinic.

Before the week is out, the Professor asks that I see him in his office. Lips constricted, face taut with restrained rage, words shoot out, stiff and sharp.

I haven't put up . . . this successful place. I haven't built . . . this . . . this renowned clinic . . . for you to destroy. I will *NOT*. . . tolerate it. If you don't mend your ways, I will be forced to limit your involvement at Mulago. If I have to . . . I will break you!

What is he talking about? Is he referring to me? What am I destroying?

I realise how important it is for him to be the one running the clinic. He is its creator, its director. He takes pride in being seen flanked by his many assistants.

A long, uncomfortable silence follows. Ron does not say another word. He doesn't need to.

I have not done anything to hurt your interests, and there is no reason for you to consider me a threat. I was just suggesting a way to handle the growing volume of patients.

My attempt at rebuttal is feeble and I leave utterly deflated. It is a morning I will never forget. I cannot continue to work with the Professor. Nor can I leave the department. I find myself in a quandary.

My only option is to have Medical Superintendent Dr. Y. B. Semambo clear the air and settle this issue. A doctor who previously worked at peripheral hospitals, he occupies an impressive office to which he brings a quiet dignity and skillfully resolves problems that constantly arise with diplomacy. I apprise him of what has taken place and of the Professor's threat to limit my involvement.

Mr. De Souza, you have been appointed by the Ministry of Health as consultant surgeon at Mulago. Mr. Huckstep should respect your position as our appointee. He has no power to remove you.

I am relieved to hear you say that.

He can do no such thing, he repeats emphatically.

Although I place my trust in Dr. Semambo, I strongly believe this matter should be brought to the attention of the ministry at Entebbe. My cordial relationship and close connection with Dr. Kadama assures me he will seek redress.

If you wouldn't mind, sir, I would like to go to Entebbe to present my case.

I will take care of it, Leo. He shakes my hand warmly.

A few weeks later, I receive a letter from the ministry. It confirms what Dr. Semambo said and reiterates Mr. Huckstep would be overstepping his bounds if he carries out his threat. The ministry also commends my work at the clinic.

While the Professor is on staff at Makerere University, Mulago Hospital falls under the aegis of the Government of Uganda, more specifically the Ministry of Health. At the time of expansion, the ministry wanted to ensure it had a hand in guiding the direction of the polio clinic. However, the clinic has come to be almost synonymous with Professor Huckstep. Keen on maintaining its authority and to counter the university's influence, the ministry sees a way out. Six months later, I am promoted to senior consultant surgeon, a tangible affirmation of their earlier statement and a pat on the back.

The Professor does not expect this development. It comes as a surprise but I do not let this appointment alter our relationship. I consider the clinic to be Ron's domain and am content to let him run it the way he always has. There is no doubt what he is building greatly benefits the country and improves the lot of every polio patient. Unfortunately, I think he just got carried away.

13

SIT DOWN THERE

I need a re-entry permit stamped in my passport to ensure return to Uganda after attending a medical conference in Dublin scheduled for September. Not being a citizen, I will become an undesirable faster than it takes the immigration officer to open and shut my passport.

I have been invited to read a paper at the Eleventh World Congress of the International Society for Rehabilitation of the Disabled. My presentation, *Practical Problems in Developing Rehabilitation Services in Africa,* will relate to our success at the polio clinic, in restoring independence to our patients using minimal surgical interference and little expenditure. This distinction should rightfully be given to Mr. Huckstep, for the polio clinic is his brainchild, but he is unable to attend.

So it is with childlike eagerness I drive to the immigration office, which reopens at two o'clock after the noon break. In East Africa, everything shuts—schools, offices, shops—between the hours of twelve and two, a practice as old as the colonies. This time is set aside to recoup from the rigours of the enervating weather, torpor of the heat, or lassitude of humidity.

Between a busy morning at the outpatient clinic and a surgical case scheduled for late afternoon, I reckon I will be back in good time. My requirements are straightforward. All the officer needs to do is go through my papers, establish my bona fide status, pick up the appropriate rubber stamp, freshen it squarely on the ink pad, then come down on the first blank page of my passport with a thud of a done deal. Simple as that.

It is two o'clock. I am the first person at the immigration office. Two Muganda officials, dressed in khaki shirts and sporting brass nameplates reading IMMIGRATION, are seated behind security windows with openings for the transfer of documents. I decide to go to the one on the right, who is, at that moment, picking up the *Uganda Argus* from his desk.

He looks me up and down.

Good afternoon.

Yes? he asks gruffly.

I need a re-entry permit stamp on my passport.

Sit down there, he says, indicating with his eyes and a nod the two benches against the opposite wall. He opens the newspaper.

I didn't expect this. I take my passport and papers and sit down.

I look up. The official's face is hidden behind the raised newspaper while the other man does not look in my direction. Since I already spoke to the first official, albeit tenuously, it would be rude at this point to go to the second person.

This situation is ludicrous. *What am I doing here, sitting on a bench waiting for my passport to be stamped while the man is reading his newspaper?* I am scheduled to be in surgery in a little while.

Fifteen long minutes drag by. There is no one other than me, and these two officers are glued to their seats, one reading his newspaper and the other, as far as I can see, doing nothing. My patience is thinning and I can sit no longer. Grasping my documents firmly, I stride to the man effectively screened behind the fully opened paper.

Excuse me. Don't you want to look at my passport?

Though annoyed, I keep my rising temper in check. Acutely aware I need the re-entry permit and this is the only place to get it, I will most certainly have to return if I leave in a fit of pique.

He slowly lowers the newspaper, just enough to see me above the edge.

Did I not tell you to sit down there? he snarls.

His eyes startle me. Unmistakably narrowed to focus sharply on me, they affirm, in no uncertain terms, what he wants to say. This man, I assume from his tone, sees an Indian, an unwelcome rival in his own land.

I try to look at him but his face disappears again behind the newspaper.

I am furious yet powerless. I put my passport and papers away and walk out.

The incident stays with me for a while. *Did I not tell you to sit down there?* When I am able to talk about it without indignation, I seek help from President Obote's cousin Akena Adoko, Minister of Internal Affairs.

Send me your passport and I'll arrange to have it stamped. Another thing, Leo, why don't you put in your papers for citizenship? You've been here for more than five years. Let's get you an Ugandan passport. Then you won't need any more permits.

This is another instance of how I am compelled to seek assistance at the highest echelon of government for the smallest thing. Aware this harried government has weightier issues on its hands, I am forced to seek help wherever

I can. Within the hospital, I walk alongside friends holding hands; outside, I have to learn to brace myself against a world that does not know me, except I am neither white nor black.

14

THIS COUNTRY IS FINISHED

President Obote has visibly consolidated his power by the time I get back from Dublin. Rancour between southerners and northerners appears less strident, the familiar presence of soldiers at intersections and strategic points less obvious. It seems as though understanding between both sides can be achieved and we could have peace. But December 1969 explodes in a way we do not expect and the reverberations that follow never quite let up.

Friday, the nineteenth of December, Dolly and I are having dinner at the home of our long-time friends, the Godinhos. Their house, on the other side of Kololo Hill, is a modern residence with a swimming pool, an uncommon amenity in East Africa. I have known Carlos and Jane since college. After going our separate ways, we meet again in Uganda some twenty-odd years later. Carlos, studying law in Cambridge, England, was six months from completing the bar when his father died in 1952 of a sudden heart attack at age sixty-five. Norman owned choice real estate in Kampala, including the Speke Hotel and Norman Cinema. A dutiful son, Carlos cut short his intended career and returned to assume management of the family business.

Jane worries a great deal about the unsettled political climate, while Carlos remains optimistic and accepting. Although everything seems quiet, the Baganda have been restive ever since the overthrow of the kabaka. Carlos is pouring after-dinner drinks when the telephone rings. It is the medical superintendent from Mulago. I am on call and the hospital knows where to reach me.

Mr. De Souza, you must come right away. The president has been shot.

Aghast, I stand rooted, receiver in hand. The very worst has transpired.

Is something wrong, Leo? Jane asks. You don't look yourself.

I tell them. A chill descends. No one says anything for a while.

Jane murmurs, What's going to happen?

I don't know how badly the president is hurt. If he is shot in the arm, leg, or back, Mr. Huckstep will take care of him; he has always believed it is his prerogative to treat the influential and powerful. If Obote dies, the country will plunge into violence. Blood will flow as northerners kill southerners. The Baganda will respond. The president's men will then kill to even old scores. Vengeance will stalk the land. If he survives, there will be chaos, with trigger-happy soldiers on the loose, roadblocks, checkpoints, curfew, police interrogations. My insides are hollow from dread and misgivings. *Please God,* I plead, *spare his life.*

President Obote comes from a family of chiefs and I had the honour of meeting him during better days at Lira Hospital, when I took care of his extended family. I remember him being kind to me and recognising my work. The president had many ideas on how to govern and improve the lives of his people; however, tribal conflicts often had his back against the wall.

I take Dolly home and race down the now deserted road to the hospital. There are only heavy armoured vehicles rumbling along with deadly determination. The sight of soldiers away from barracks, heading, perhaps, to the hospital makes me slow down. I drive on, noting additional military lorries joining the road at every junction, all proceeding in the same direction. At every checkpoint and barricade I am regarded with suspicion, but upon learning of my mission, soldiers salute and send me on my way.

At Mulago, the entire senior staff, including professors, are gathered in the Department of Surgery, summoned because no one knows the extent of the trauma. It is the only way to ensure the president receives prompt and appropriate treatment.

President Obote had been shot in the mouth just as he was leaving the Uganda People's Congress Delegates Conference at Lugogo Indoor Stadium. The bullet entered the right cheek, knocked out his lower teeth, ripped through the tongue and exited the left side. It was purely fortuitous the trajectory of the bullet missed the jugular, brain and spinal cord.

The oral surgeon assesses Obote's injury while the rest of us cluster together outside the operating theatre. It is an uneasy situation as some of our physicians are Baganda. Most people hold strong sentiments but rarely speak their minds for fear of retribution. Here, tonight, the Baganda doctors open up as never before about what they think is happening to the country. Although they opt for an independent Buganda and stand by their kabaka, they do not condone an attempt on Obote's life.

We want no such killing. We are for peaceful negotiations, however long they take.

As there is very little for me to do, I decide to leave the hospital, which is filling up with army personnel, top party officials and government brass, all rallying round the president. Military vehicles dot the campus and I am concerned it will be difficult to pass them. It is fortunate I leave when I do. Those left behind are not able to vacate the hospital that night.

Following surgery, in pain and unable to speak, the president asks for paper and pen to inform Major General Idi Amin, who was not at the conference, what has occurred and apprise his wife, Miria, Akena Adoko and Police Inspector General Cryema as well. Obote declares a state of emergency, bans all opposition parties and institutes one-party rule.

Brigadier Pierino Yere Okoya, the forty-five-year-old Acholi commander of the Second Infantry in Masaka, and a few officers are dispatched to Amin's house on Kololo Hill. He cannot be found. Rumours swirl that Amin is at his private residence in Bombo. Okoya takes a dim view of his behaviour, accuses him of being a coward and wants to initiate disciplinary action. He suggests to Obote that Amin might have something to do with the assassination plot.

On the twenty-sixth of January 1970, news reports detail the shocking murder of Brigadier Okoya and his wife, Anna Akello, the previous evening at their home in Layibi, a few miles outside of Gulu. Speculation implicates Idi Amin. Obote strips Amin of most of his powers and institutes an authoritarian regime.

Everyone worries what will befall next: Will the army go on a rampage? Who will be killed? Officers? Cabinet ministers? Opposition leaders? In the ensuing months, the city is gripped by terror. *Kondos*—merciless thugs—armed with pangas break into houses, slashing, maiming, killing. Sleep becomes fitful. One ear remains cocked for unfamiliar sounds: furtive steps, whispered voices, soft ripping of window screen gauze, breaking glass, unhooking latches, dismantling locks. Every month, a few hundred innocent and unarmed people are slain.

One evening, a truck speeding towards Kampala overturns, injuring more than twenty armed soldiers. Rushed to Mulago, the wounded, immediately transferred by gurney or wheelchair, fill every examination room, spilling over into the corridor. Fractured limbs, ruptured organs, head injuries, lacerated wounds. A bloody mess! Dolly, the weekend doctor in charge of the Casualty Department, makes quick evaluations for the expeditious transfer of victims.

Patient has a ruptured spleen. Check his haemoglobin. Begin an IV and have him admitted as soon as possible. Inform the surgeon on call. Fractured femur . . . place him in traction, then admit. Dress this man's hand . . . Start an antibiotic IV . . . Apply a padded splint and admit to surgery. David, send for the surgical residents on call. We can't get to all of these men ourselves.

Amid the pandemonium, Dolly notices a large man, dressed in khaki shorts, crumpled shirt and sandals, moving among the prone troops. *That's odd*, she thinks. *Who is that funny-looking man and what is he doing here? This is a casualty department! I'm going to tell him to leave.*

David, her nursing assistant, whispers, Don't you know who he is?

Dolly does not recognise him.

He is big army chief Idi Amin. Powerful man. Can kill anyone.

Fear is etched on David's face. She takes in his cowed look and instructs the staff to carry on as usual.

Prices of Ugandan cotton, coffee and tea plunge on the world market, and increasing food shortages contribute to the rising cost of living. My patients often encounter difficulties paying for school fees and uniforms and are forced to cut back on celebrations and family observances. Indians are troubled by Obote's plans for nationalisation, which began when the Committee on Africanisation in Commerce and Industry instituted work permits and trade licenses restricting economic and professional activities. The regime now owns a little more than 60 percent share in major private corporations and banks. Additionally, Obote's insistence on Indians either becoming citizens or leaving the country has them agonising over the future.

Dr. Sahib, I not professional like you. I only have my business. If government asks me to give it to African, there is nothing for me. With Ugandan passport, I be stuck here. No one will want me.

I appreciate the struggle. While their reasoning appears somewhat self-centred, survival depends on clinging to the one thing they have and are good at—namely, business.

As soon as Louella and Mario go back to boarding school in Nairobi after the Christmas holidays, we fly to India, leaving Lea and Joanna with friends who we knew in Gulu, Dr. CM Patel and his family. Dolly's father in Bombay is in failing health, and Bai, my auntie in Goa, is losing mobility to rheumatoid arthritis.

The twenty-fifth of January 1971, the day before we return to Kampala, BBC World News reports that Milton Obote is toppled in a coup led by Army Commander in Chief Idi Amin. The president was in Singapore attending the first Commonwealth Heads of Government meeting. All flights to Uganda have been cancelled and Entebbe Airport sealed. Communication is severed, and frantic, unsuccessful attempts to telephone CM leave us in a state of panic and confusion.

After days filled with increasing agitation, on the fifth of February, we finally board Air India to Nairobi. The next day's connecting flight to Entebbe is solemn. Passengers are drawn and silently preoccupied. There isn't the normal banter or laid-back laughter. Entebbe Airport swarms with militia and tanks. Customs and Immigration clerks are uncharacteristically quiet.

CM is there to receive us. Usually ebullient, he is quiet, tense and watchful. Kampala is under strict curfew from 7:00 p.m. to 6:30 a.m., enforced by patrolling troops. We hear muffled sounds of heavy shooting and smell acrid smoke. Links to major roads are blocked.

In a hushed voice, he says, I will tell you more when we get home. My Acholi friends have told me *this country is finished.* And I agree.

15

THE BLOODY DECEPTION

When Radio Uganda announced news of the coup, there was much celebrating, singing and dancing in the streets. President Amin released more than 1,500 political prisoners, including the five cabinet ministers from Luzira Prison, Brigadier Opolot, and the kabaka's sister Princess Nalinya Mpologoma.

CM's Acholi connections tell him that less than a week after the coup, Amin sent his men north, systematically hunting down Obote supporters.

It was terrible. They ransacked Gulu, destroying houses and shops, and killing Acholi soldiers who were loyal to Obote. In Lira, they took two hundred Langi soldiers in lorries, and at Karuma Falls, shot them and threw their bodies in the Nile for the crocodiles to eat. You know, they also captured Brigadier Suleiman Hussein and took him to Luzira Prison. Leo, can you believe . . . they cut his head off and brought it to Amin.

As we near the city, the ominous rumbling of gunfire grows louder. It is unnerving. Before long, we stop at a roadblock manned by soldiers, big men dressed in shabby fatigues who do not look Ugandan. They exude unmistakable power. The metallic crunch of their boots, the reckless angle of guns slung across their shoulders, their disdain for us. I presume they are Nubians. Repressing my growing apprehension, I address them in Swahili, letting them know we are doctors from Mulago returning from holiday. They stare us down for an intimidating moment, then wave us on.

We are relieved to be reunited with Lea and Joanna and hug them tightly. No sooner we arrive at 4 Upper Kololo Terrace, they run to greet Otiri and hear his version of the gunfire.

Lea is eleven. With straight hair cut to the nape of her neck, delicate face and slim build, she appears fragile but has the pluck of a fifteen-year-old and can hold her own with an unblinking gaze from large, expressive eyes. She sits next to Joanna while we relax on the large sofa in the living room, excitedly telling us about the coup.

We were getting ready for school and suddenly, *boom, boom, boom . . .* shooting everywhere, then quiet, then *boom, boom* again. I was really frightened. We didn't go to school, Daddy. We couldn't even play outside. Uncle CM said the soldiers would kill us. Just like they killed the two Indian girls walking to school. Their parents didn't know they were not supposed to go out.

Lea is overcome by the fate of these two girls.

After a few days, Uncle CM allowed us to play in the back. We could smell gunpowder and saw smoke everywhere. We were afraid all the time, and in the night we slept under the beds. What if the soldiers came? I cried so much and wanted you to come home soon.

Nine-year-old Joanna takes over. She looks stronger than Lea but, in most cases, prefers to be taken care of by her siblings, and they enjoy doing it for her, especially Louella.

It was so boring, Mummy. We were stuck in the house. Every time someone knocked at the door, Uncle CM told us to hide under the bed. I was afraid the soldiers would come in the night with guns and take us away. I'm so glad you'll are home.

Amin tells the people all is well. No worry, he repeats on TV. He lies. What takes place in subsequent weeks, however, never makes news. The television, an extension of the Ministry of Information, informs us the British government has recognised the new regime and continues to beam assurances about how everything is peaceful and proceeding as planned. To win favour of the Baganda, Amin brings the body of Kabaka Edward Mutesa II, King Freddie, from London for a state burial with full honours at Kasubi Tombs.

A few months later, the disappearances and killings start.

News reaches us that our friend Ambhubai Patel has not been heard from since he left Lira for Kampala a week ago. He is one of the few Indian businessmen who maintain Indians need to be involved in Ugandan political life. Zealously attached to Obote's cause, he gives the fruits of his labour to the United People's Congress and has many friends among the Lango.

Summoned by Amin, his family believes he is being asked to assist the new government's standing in Lango. But when Ambhubai does not telephone by evening, they are worried. He does not return the following day, and panic turns into dread that something has happened. They are terrified. Everyone knows what happens to people who do not come home.

It is the noon hour, and I am in the operating theatre at Mulago inserting Küntscher's nails into a patient's fractured left femur. We hear loud footsteps resounding on the tile floor.

What's the noise?

Sounds like boots . . . big heavy boots.

Boots in the operating theatre suite?

More footsteps, accompanied by a cacophony of raucous voices in unfamiliar tones. Booming orders, somewhat garbled, emanate from an angry male. Scuffling and then a scream. We look at each other.

What's going on?

I'll find out, the scrub nurse says and slips out.

Again, the sound of footsteps, loud and clear, hard boots on the tile floor. They trail off, and it is quiet again except for soft whimpering.

They've taken Dr. Ebine, the startled nurse tells us.

Dr. Ebine?

Yes, soldiers came and took him away.

Dr. George Ebine, cousin to Obote, recently back from Glasgow, where he trained as an obstetrician and gynaecologist, is a colleague of Dolly's. Amin's goons believe Ebine is hiding Obote loyalist Lieutenant Colonel Emmanuel Ogwal in his home. After blowing up the house, they barge into the operating room and seize Dr. Ebine, in the midst of surgery, leaving a woman to die on the table.

Dr. Ebine's house is the same one Dr. Jack Darling had lived in. As I drive by its remains, charred, crumbled and forlorn, I think, *Therein, too, lies a bit of my past.*

In April, another brazen disappearance. This time, it is Dr. Vincent Emiru, our ophthalmologist and director of the national campaign against trachoma, a contagious bacterial eye disease blinding thousands in Uganda.

Sometime before dusk, an armoured car drives up to Emiru's residence, which is next to the hospital. They tell him their senior officer has injured his eye in an accident and he is needed in the emergency room to render assistance. Never mind it is not routine for a senior physician to come in before the doctor on call and the resident assess the case, but these are uncertain times, and he dare not tell the military personnel waiting at his door this is an irregular request. Dr. Emiru informs his wife and leaves, escorted by soldiers. Soon after, another army vehicle pulls up and abducts his wife. Hospital whisperings allude to the fact President Amin had his eye on Mrs. Emiru, who was a handsome woman. We never hear of Dr. Emiru again and presume the worst. The whereabouts of his wife, too, are lost to us.

We all know scores of people who go missing: Langi and Acholi police officers, political opponents, judges and barristers, businessmen and relatives of neighbours and friends. Among the prominent citizens arrested is former Minister of Public Service and Cabinet Affairs Joshua Wakholi, who had been in hiding since the coup but turns himself in when the lives of his wife, Alice, and baby girl are threatened. Visiting him in Makindye Prison, George Walwanyi, his brother, relays horrifying tales of atrocities—lengthy interrogations, brutal beatings, torture, mutilations and slaughter. Following prisoner executions, Wakholi and fellow inmates were made to wash blood-splattered cells using brushes and pails of water, removing pieces of skull, teeth and brain tissue from the many bludgeonings. Surprisingly, Wakholi is released in June and flees to Tanzania.

Grisly details of untimely ends at the hands of cruel men are unimaginable. Our fears mushroom. They appear when we awake. They stay with us all day. They fuel our nightmares.

16

AMIN ERASES EVERYTHING

When the big, fat, bedecked bear of a military dictator takes over, he lays waste to the entire country, the entire big, beautiful country, this entire big, beautiful God-given country.

He erases men he views as progenitors of evil, rips out their genitals. He erases women he views as repositories of evil, cuts out their fertile wombs. He erases children, for they are the offspring of evil. He erases villages until there is no scenery left, only smoke and smell and moaning.

He erases day and night, for there is no such thing as time to rest and time to work. There is time only to escape, to escape from the killing as fast and far as legs can outrun.

He erases the seasons, for there is no more planting and no more reaping, for the land is soaked in blood with no room for the green seed.

He erases the present, for there is no moment called *now.*

And he erases the future, because you can run and run and never reach safety.

In time, Amin erases everything.

17

AMIN SILENCES ME

Nearly a decade has passed since liberation, when festivities in the land were unstoppable and Ugandans couldn't contain their joy. This land of their forefathers had broken the chains of foreign domination. Although the nation had been put together somewhat askew by white self-serving foreigners, Uganda was free. The occasion, marked by days of jubilation, dance, libation, crystallised the desire for the success of their new country and better days for themselves and their children.

Those were great days in October 1962, a unique event in the time span of a nation. For a while, all was well. Then the country slowly began to fall apart. Differences, caused by uncompromising positions, separated the two peoples, northerners and southerners. The ensuing split allowed for the emergence of a schemer who took advantage of circumstances presented and struck for power. This man, Amin, invested with ill-gotten power, slowly revealed his colours, an imposter who was also an outsider, a brute and a killer.

The fine fabric of this startlingly beautiful land, caught in the aftermath of a coup and now inextricably bound to a violent lunatic, is coming undone. Its seams, once firm and invisible, are on the brink of splitting. Through the widening chinks, it is possible to glimpse into Uganda's heart and mind and sinew, none of them functioning the way they should. The heart is weakening, the mind losing its grip and the sinew beginning to spasm. Turmoil is everywhere and the air is foul. The ordinary is lost and violence reigns supreme, killings senseless and brutal. Hope gives way to despair, love turns to hate, and faith to doubt.

Within the confines of this agitated country, men and women are prisoners with no means of easy escape. Those who can slip away, do. Escaping to neighbouring Kenya or Tanzania requires connections and money, so the vast majority stay back, looking for ways to be inconspicuous and hoping the panic that now seizes them will also make them invisible.

We reel under the impact of what is taking place. Never before have there been so many premeditated murders, such bizarre slayings. There has to be an end to this. But how?

While President Kenneth Kaunda of Zambia and President Julius Nyerere of Tanzania are supportive of Obote, the rest of Africa is divided. The talk is that Nyerere, who offered him sanctuary, is organising an army to invade Uganda. The Organisation of African Unity, a consortium of African nations, concludes in its deliberations the matter of Obote's removal is outside its charge. It is disheartening they have taken such a stance. Britain is a different matter. From his early days in the King's African Rifles in Kenya, the British think of Amin as a *bloody good soldier*, a *jolly good fellow*. I am revolted the British think this way. However much I detest their colonial system, I always believed their government was honourable. But here, they are backing a frenzied autocrat, only because his predecessor had disagreements with them.

It seems we are all by ourselves to face the wrath of Amin in villages, towns and cities across the entire country. He has delegated the deadly business of selective extermination to chosen henchmen. The rest of us are imprisoned with fear, careful about what we say, what we do and with whom we associate. I thought I was careful enough until one Saturday morning.

Lea, Joanna and I arrive home from Cristos, where none of our four can ever have enough cream pastries. They are satiated. I feel good. We need to tell Mummy how much we enjoyed ourselves.

As soon as we open the door, Augie, our dog, leaps up to greet us. The children run in to tell their mother all about Cristos.

You know, Mummy . . .

But Mummy isn't in the kitchen or busy about the house in the relaxed sort of way she is wont to on a Saturday morning, humming old favourite songs from her schooldays. Dolly is seated by the telephone in the bedroom, staring into space with no greeting for us.

Mummy, Mummy, the girls continue.

Deathly pale, hands trembling, she makes no response.

What's the matter, Doll? I take the handset from her and return it to its cradle. She looks at me, trying to bring me into focus.

Lu, I'm so afraid, she whispers.

Something is very wrong. My heart starts to pound.

The telephone rang just before you came home and the person on the other end sounded Ugandan. In a very menacing tone, he said, *Are you Dr. De Souza?*

Yes.

I'm going to tell you something, and you better listen.

Who is this?

No need to know. Your husband is Mr. De Souza? Surgeon at Mulago?

Yes.

You tell your husband he is talking too much. If he does not shut up, he will disappear. Do you hear? Are you listening?

Yes.

I repeat, if he does not shut up, he will be food for the crocodiles.

The implication of the man's stark warning sinks in, making Dolly shudder.

Lu, you're in danger. Let's go as soon as possible, she pleads.

I hold her hand in a tight grip. *Someone wants to kill me and throw me to the crocodiles! What awful things have I said? Something critical of the Amin regime?* When we moved from the north in 1966, our Lango and Acholi friends in Kampala sometimes referred to me as an *Obote man.* We often discuss politics and the current deteriorating situation. Who knows? I may have said something I shouldn't have, that may have been overheard by someone it wasn't meant for.

We wonder who this man might be. Is he trying to frighten us? Or is he trying to protect me by warning us? Is this a hoax? It may also be a disguised order to leave the country. What do we do? Confide in our friends? Confide in our associates? Keep to ourselves?

For the next several days, we withdraw from everyone we know and everything we do. Our seclusion is partly shock, partly fright. But we cannot get away from the ring of the telephone, the insistence of its warning, its dire threat. My life is in jeopardy. I scrutinise every male Ugandan who speaks to me, observing eye movement and inflection of tone, looking for it to reveal any sign of complicity. Could this be the person who telephoned? Will he call again?

The decision is slowly borne in upon us there is no way out but to leave. It means abandoning all we have known, all we hold dear. We cannot remain in this country, not with Amin at the helm. The past rushes before me, and it is not one I want to give up.

Tanganyika became a lost land in 1962 when we began anew in Uganda, first in Lira, then Gulu, and now Kampala. I carried a secret hope of a homecoming to Tanga someday. As time went by, I realised the futility of cherishing that dream. I gave it up unwillingly and with overwhelming sadness. Tanga has always been home to me. It is where I was born, where I returned after becoming a doctor, where Dolly and I married, where our children were born, and where we buried

Martin. I should have been able to call it my own but burned my bridges when I turned down Minister Shaba's offer in Lindi.

Uganda was welcoming. Our years here brought family stability and professional success. Dolly and I had a wide and varied circle of friends, regularly entertaining doctors, nurses, ministers and their wives, Goan friends, as well as business associates from the Indian community. Life went on with no incident despite the curfews and political unrest. It is different now. The current unexpected upheaval and profound uncertainties, the atrocities spawning terror, the dead, the dying, the disappearances, pervade our lives, but it is the threatening telephone call that propels our decision to promptly emigrate to the United States.

Last September, prior to the Dublin conference, I was invited to read a paper in New York at a sectional meeting of the Eleventh World Congress. Dolly and I took a side trip to visit our dear friends Jo and Larry Brown in Golden Valley, a suburb of Minneapolis, where we broached the idea of moving to the United States when it was time for Louella and Mario to attend university in a few years. Larry introduced me to Dr. Richard Reiley, a prominent orthopaedic surgeon, who asked me to consider joining his practice. I thanked him profusely and told him I would not be leaving Africa quite yet.

But now everything has changed. I telephone Larry to tell him of the threat and our need for a hasty departure. I immediately contact Dr. Reiley. Can I still take him up on the offer? So the race begins, to organise what we take, what we don't. Packing, shipping, selling Dolly's car and making arrangements for mine. One thing, then another, toward getting us on the unforeseeable road to a secure future.

Breaking the news at the hospital is difficult. Sebastian Kyalwazi, my friend with whom I held hands, hopes I will reconsider my decision and, if it is a matter of citizenship, will be happy to help. David Kisumba, my orthopaedic associate, is dismayed.

Leo, you are one of us. I was looking forward to us building up the surgical department together after Mr. Huckstep is gone.

At a cocktail party hosted by Carlos and Jane Godinho, most people believe we are fools to leave, even say so.

This situation is bad now, but cannot go on forever. You'll see. It will change. It must change.

Remember, there's no place like Uganda. Not England, not even India. But you are going to America? Why?

I understand what they are saying. I am well established in my profession. I have a good practice. I teach at an academic institution. If I give this up, there is nothing comparable in the United States. At forty-five, I will have to start all over.

Many, like me, were born in East Africa. They love this land as much as we do but can't just give it up and move elsewhere. So they play down what is happening around them and bide their time until these bad times end. Dolly and I have also come closer to danger than they have. Their sentiments and concern for us are sincere, but our friends unwittingly make it more difficult for us to say goodbye.

Out of caution, we decide to slip out of Kampala quietly and separately, informing only a few people of our departure. Louella and Mario fly home from Nairobi on the eighth of April for Easter holidays. They are happy not to be going back to boarding school. For the younger two, it is different. Lea is saddened she will never see her friends again. Joanna is all right as long as she can bring Augie.

Why can't we take Augie? I can look after him, Daddy.

The world has suddenly changed for her, as it has for all of us, but her main loss is our big affectionate dog. We will all miss him, but there is a special closeness between Augie and Joanna. He stands by her side as if he were her bodyguard. Joanna, in turn, is wont to hug, almost squeeze him, eyes closed, jaws clenched with deep joy.

I told Daddy to bring you, she tells Augie, sobbing bitterly.

Dolly and the children depart for Bombay on the fourteenth of May. The house is like a cemetery with buried memories. Each morning, Otiri serves breakfast at our large, round dining table. Unsure what his own fate is going to be, his usual cheerfulness has left him and he does not say much.

My only companion at the table now is Augie, standing by my side, resting his chin on my lap. Not a sound, not the slightest movement. Every so often, he lifts his head and looks at me. It tears at my very being. I make arrangements for a Sikh family to take Augie. Jaswant Singh owns several dogs, and I am grateful.

On the eleventh of June, I fly out of Entebbe for Tanga to see Santos and family. As the East African Airways plane rises to its cruising height, I look down through misty eyes to see the land unfolding beneath me: green, pristine, beautiful. Diminished by its colonial bondage and restored by its freedom, I once believed this land was mine: its history, its struggles, its promise.

On the fourteenth of June 1971, I leave Dar es Salaam to join Dolly and the children. I am severed from all I have known.

PART IV

Epilogue

Taken from Leo's notes. A toast given to neighbours.

I'd like to thank you for being with us today, 30th June 1981.

Exactly 10 years ago, on 30th June 1971—Joanna then 9, Lea then 11, Mario 13 and Louella 15—landed on US soil—NY airport—for the first time with their migrant parents looking for a home.

We arrived in Golden Valley to a house that had been acquired by the Browns, stocked with amenities provided by neighbours. We were greeted with roses at the airport and champagne at 4200 Poplar Drive, courtesy of Ed Harrington.

I had made sure that I would be here on 30th June so that I would be able to begin work on the 1st of July at the Department of Orthopaedics, University of Minnesota. But come 1st July, I find the Chief of Ortho out of the country and nobody there knew anything about me. After an agonizing wait, meet him 2 months later—told he has no place for me.

While we went through throes of depression, it upset Larry Brown no less and he arranged a meeting with (Don) Fraser, then U.S. Congressman, to see if things could be rectified. Was decided not to fight the Professor—after a 3-month spell at Abbott-Northwestern Hospital providing an extra pair of hands to any surgeon who needed it in the operating room—January 1972 saw me in Toronto, Canada.

First 6 months—lowest ebb. Denied promised appt, without work. Went through lot of soul searching: should we go into Gen Practice? Should we leave the country? Mayo offered residence in Rehab Med—being ortho before, found it difficult to accept. Meanwhile Toronto offered appt I needed.

So, we were onto another trip to another country for 2½ years.

1974—Louella graduated St. Joseph's Morrow Park in Toronto—

that was her 13th school—1st one being in Peterborough, England. Mario was at Brebeuf (Boys School) in Toronto—that being 7th school in 6 diff countries—Started in Royston, Cambridge and finished in Golden Valley. Both Lea and Joanna finished in Golden Valley—being 6th school in 5 countries for Lea and third school in 3 countries for Joanna.

Returned from Toronto to 4200 Poplar Drive in July 1974.

1975 we moved to 1101 North Tyrol Trail—the rest is well known to you.

What might, however, not be so well known to you is that the person who held things together when they were rough, was Dolly. Elected to give up her career, now open to suggestions.

Another thing you might not know: We have also been held together by all that you've done for us. Without you we would not have able to celebrate tonight. Without your help we would have been either lost in Uganda, unwelcome in England or discontent in Canada.

So, we would like to thank you: Browns—first/foremost, Cervenkas, Mundts, Tovslands, Rotschs, Monnicks and Howells. Hayes, Knolls and Harrington. Van Konynenburgs, Parkers, Haucks and Kilners.

We thank you for joining us in celebrating our decade in the U.S. Joanna, Lea, Mario, Louella, Dolly and I would like to raise a toast:

"For all that you've done, good fortune be yours, in equal measure and more. God bless you. God bless America."

Biographies & Correspondence

Mildmay Thomas "Tommy" Boscawen

(5 February 1892 – 18 November 1958)

Lieutenant-Colonel the Honourable Mildmay Thomas "Tommy" Boscawen, youngest son of the seventh Viscount of Falmouth, served with the Rifle Brigade during World War I, receiving the Distinguished Service Order for leadership. At the end of the war, he moved to Moa, Tanganyika, where he built and managed the largest sisal growing enterprise in Tanganyika and Kenya, some 85,000 acres. He employed a large staff and was very solicitous of their welfare, often paying for the education of their children. Immersed in local mores, he always attended the feast commemorating Prophet Muhammed's birthday, made a substantial contribution to the Arab Welfare Association in Mombasa and built a mosque at Moa.

Boscawen was a legendary traveller, botanist, naturalist and hunter. He loved books and music, collected plant and animal specimens from travels in Arabia, East Turkestan and South America, and went fishing in New Zealand every year. A discerning collector of one of the finest Renaissance and Baroque bronze sculptures dating from the turn of the sixteenth century, he donated South Arabian antiquities to the British Museum, birds and skins to the Natural History Museum, and loaned a number of objects to the Fitzwilliam Museum (which, after his death, were donated to the museum). He walked from India through Tibet to Turkestan with his assistant Shaikh Abdullah Abubakr al'Amoodi in 1929.

Grace Stuart Katebariirwe Ibingira

(23 May 1932 – 8 December 1995)

From the royal clan of Ankole, the Bathinda, Grace Ibingira was born in Ibanda, Western Uganda. He studied law at the University of Wales with postgraduate work at London University and a call to the Bar at Middle Temple in London. On his return to Kampala, he went into legal practice.

A founding member of the Uganda People's Congress (UPC), Ibingira served as legal advisor. In 1961, he was appointed and, then, elected to the Uganda Legislative Council (Ankole). When Milton Obote formed his government, Ibingira was selected minister of justice in 1962, minister of state and UPC secretary-general in 1964. In 1966, Obote jailed him and four other ministers, detaining the group without trial for five years. After Idi Amin overthrew Obote, Ibingira was named the Permanent Representative to the UN, from 1971 to 1974, and information minister from 1979 to 1980. He is credited with designing the Uganda flag.

George Bikanchulika Magezi Atenyi

(1928 – 4 July 2003)

Born in Rusaka, Buhaguzi, Hoima District, Western Uganda, George Magezi was a teacher who turned to politics in 1955 when he represented Bunyoro in the Legislative Council. A founder and secretary general of the Uganda People's Union, which merged with Milton Obote's Uganda National Congress in 1960 to become the Uganda People's Congress. Magezi was elected member of Parliament in 1962 and appointed minister of state. At the time of his arrest in 1966, he was minister of housing and labour. Detained without trial until his release in 1971 by Idi Amin, Magezi was imprisoned, both in 1973 and 1974, by Amin. He escaped to Kenya in 1977, remaining in exile for two years until Amin was deposed. Magezi retired from politics in 1986 to embark on tea farming.

Balaki Kebba Kirya

(1924 - 9 August 1994)

Balaki Kirya was born in Petete, Bukedi (Pallisa District, Eastern Uganda). A soldier in the King's African Rifles, he entered politics under the Uganda National Congress. Kirya, an architect of the UPC/Kabaka Yekka Alliance and member of Parliament, was minister without portfolio and, later, minister for water and mineral resources. A fallout with Obote led to his arrest and detainment in Luzira Prison. On his release during Amin's tenure, Kirya fled to Kenya in exile. With Obote back in power, he was abducted in 1982, charged with treason for alleged involvement in rebel activities, and imprisoned until the July 1985 Okellos' coup d'état. When Yoweri Museveni and his National Resistance Army captured power in January 1986, Kirya was appointed Security Minister.

Emmanuel Bijugo Ssajjalyabene Lumu, MD

(25 February 1916 – 11 December 2019)

The sixth of ten children, Emmanuel Lumu was born in Komamboga, Kampala, and attended King's College and Makerere University. Prior to independence, Lumu was on the committee to draft plans for the secession of the kingdom of Buganda from Uganda, which was rejected by the British.

The National Assembly selected him to head the Ministry of Health because of his good record as medical practitioner at Mulago Hospital. As first minister of health, Dr. Lumu was responsible for assembling the country's superior public health infrastructure and developed a ten-year national health strategy. From 1962-66, he oversaw construction of over twenty regional referral hospitals across the country so patients could gain access to care without having to travel to Kampala for services.

A fallout with Obote in 1966 led to his arrest and imprisonment. On his release, Lumu quit politics and started his own private clinic, Dr. Lumu's Surgery, in Kisenyi, Kampala, practicing until he was eighty years old.

Matthias Mbalule Ngobi

(Dates of birth and death unknown)

Matthias Ngobi was a member of Parliament for Busoga South, then minister of agriculture and cooperatives in the first Obote regime and, again, in the short-lived Godfrey Binaisa government (1979). Arrested at a cabinet meeting in 1966, he was released with the overthrow of Obote. He was also minister of state for presidential affairs. In February 1981, he fled to the United Kingdom in exile until Obote was ousted. He returned to Uganda in 1985, where he lived at Namulesa near Jinja.

Okot p'Bitek

(7 June 1931 - 19 July 1982)

Born in Gulu, Okot p'Bitek, Uganda's most renowned and influential poet, credits his mother, a gifted singer of Acholi folklore, and his father, an accomplished storyteller, for his creative spirit and interest in literature.

He studied at the Universities of Bristol (education), Wales (law), and Oxford (social anthropology), and after returning to Gulu in 1964, he worked for the Extra-Mural Department at Makerere College and organized the Annual Festival of African Arts to celebrate the oral history, dance, and arts of the Acholi people. In 1966, he moved to Kampala serving as director of the National Theatre and National Cultural Centre, and helped create the dance group, Heartbeat of Africa.

Okot p'Bitek achieved international recognition after his epic poem, *Song of Lawino,* self-translated into English, became one of the top one hundred African books of the twentieth century, followed by *Song of Ocol* (1970) and *Two Songs: Song of Prisoner and Song of Malaya* (1971). In addition to poetry, p'Bitek wrote several essays and books on Acholi culture. He was winner of the 1972 Jomo Kenyatta Prize for Literature.

During the Amin years, p'Bitek lived in Kenya, coming home in 1982 to the Makerere University Department of Literature as the first professor of creative writing.

Eddy Moné, MD

(14 September 1926 - 15 May 2014)

Annie Moné, MD

(5 November 1926 - 20 July 2007)

July 2019 email from Egbert Moné, son of Eddy and Annie Moné

. . . We returned from Uganda in July-August 1968. At that time my father was District Medical Superintendent in Tororo. He was one way or another falsely accused of overstepping his limits as DMS and anonymously threatened to be killed, after which he wouldn't endanger us and decided to return to the Netherlands. His intention was to go back to the tropics, as his specialism was tropical medicine. Unfortunately he developed a certain type of haemofilia (Werlhof disease or ITP), after which he wasn't allowed to use sulphates and anti-malaria profylaxe anymore, so he couldn't go back to the tropics. In the meantime he started as a GP in a small village in the northeast of the Netherlands. In 1976 (after I developed the Hodgkin) he decided to move closer to the cancer hospital (at that time we only had 3 such hospitals) and changed jobs to become a doctor at the government social services. His job here was to check in how far people where able to work and/or what type of physical aid people needed to work or to be able to live independently as much as possible. He stayed until his retirement in 1991. He passed away on 15 May 2014.

After returning from Uganda, my mother picked up working as a child psychiatrist, part time working for the government mental health services for children and had her own practice as child psychiatrist. Due to the shortage of child psychiatrists she kept on working until 1995.

She passed away on 20 July 2007, just a few months after she became a proud grandmother.

Eddy and Annie's sons, Egbert and Henk-Jan, live in the Netherlands with their families.

Lucille Teasdale Corti, CM, GOQ

(30 January 1929 - 1 August 1996)

Pietro "Piero" Corti, MD, FRCSC

(16 September 1925 – 20 April 2003)

Lucille Teasdale decided, at twelve years of age, to become a doctor. She won a scholarship to the Université de Montréal Faculté de Médecine in 1950, graduating cum laude, and deciding to specialise in surgery. Piero, a specialist in paediatrics, radiology and neuropsychiatry, wanted to be a doctor in foreign lands. He travelled to India and Chad before making a commitment to the village of Lacor, Uganda. The husband-and-wife team, working side-by-side, spent thirty-five years of their lives treating patients, training new doctors and gradually developing the small thirty-bed missionary hospital into a major health complex, often under very difficult conditions.

In 1985, Lucille Teasdale was diagnosed with AIDS, having contracted the virus while performing surgery on infected soldiers. Given two years, her perseverance and determination made it possible for her to live another eleven years. She continued to care for patients and, up until several months before her death, often worked six-hour days. In her career at Lacor Hospital she performed more than thirteen thousand operations. Lucille died in Besana, Italy, but was buried on the grounds of Lacor Hospital.

Piero continued their legacy of love, hope and caring at Lacor Hospital until his death in 2003 of pancreatic cancer. He is buried next to his wife.

In 1993 the Cortis established Fondazione Corti in Milan and Teasdale-Corti Foundation in Montréal to ensure survival of Lacor Hospital. Their daughter, Dominique, who followed in her mother's footsteps, runs the foundation in Milan. In 2000, Canada Post issued a commemorative postage stamp in Lucille Teasdale's honour and, a year later, she was inducted into the Canadian Medical Hall of Fame.

To learn more about the Teasdale-Corti Foundation or to donate to Lacor Hospital, please go to http://eng.fondazionecorti.it/ and www.lacorhospital.org.

Gulu 16.2.74

Dear Friends,

We were very happy to hear from you. Thanks for your greeting and we are sending ours also even if a bit late.

We are still in Gulu as you can see. We are back from one month of leave in Italy. We went there to spend the Christmas holiday with Dominique who is now studying there. We sent her during the troubles in August '72 for a month of holiday but because the situation was not improving, we decided it was time for her to start to study in Italy . . .

The hospital is now having 200 beds and Nursing School. For one year we stayed alone, Piero and myself, because we could not get permit for new young doctor and also the young doctor were not very interested to come in this country. But now we are three, plus a temporary one doing some training in surgery with me. The work is increasing always. I did almost alone more than 800 operations in the theater last year and I saw between 60 to 80 out patients a day!

We shall go to Montreal next summer that is in July or August '74 and will try to contact you by phone.

Best wishes to all of you,

Lucille and Piero

Gulu 20.1.75

Dear Friends,

We are still in Gulu even if big part of our heart is not here any more . . .

We are presently taking the 3rd intake of students for our school of nursing training and Piero is very proud to have succeeded in spite of all problems to complete that school he was dreaming of since we arrive in Gulu.

We are now 5 doctors (but one of them is almost always borrowed by another mission hospital) 2 Italians and one Canadian paediatrician. We have now also 2 outposts to look after: one in Pabo and one in Opit. Presently they are only dispensary but they will eventually become health center with maternity and few inpatients. One of us must go each place once a week. A third one is under construction in Amuru. As you can see there is plenty of work to keep us busy. Our schedule is now from 8:30 to 2 or 2:30, then (for me) from 3:30 to 8.

Best wishes to all of you for the New Year,

Lucille and Piero

Gulu 1/11/89

Dear Dolly and Leo,

Today, All Saints Day, I have an afternoon of rest and I take the opportunity to write to you a few words. This year has been the most terrible of all our 28 years in Africa. The rebels have been disturbing us so much that in Eastern twice they reach the point of abducting one doctor (deputy Medical Superintendent) and 5 nurses. They had planned to abduct us also but we were in Mombasa for a few days' holiday and had to come back without even a swim in the sea. We had to close the hospital, send away the pupil nurses and the interns and the 5 MO all decided to go away also. One Italian expert and doctor had to leave also and we came very near to go away ourselves. The hostages came back after 1/52 unarmed and we postpone our own departure just to organize the evacuation of medical expensive equipment. But it took so long that finally the situation quiet down and we stay by ourselves, Piero and me, for 6 weeks, admitting only life threatening conditions. Also only some 12 staff nurses stayed with us, the other ran away.

Then a miracle still happened, finally the NRA soldiers started to chase the rebels and around end of May there was no more shooting heard at night and no more rebels around. Slowly 3 MO come back to Lacor and we reopened the hospital . . .

We went again for holiday end of July—long holiday because both me (for 1 1/2years) and Piero since June are without contract so without salary or obligation we left behind this time only 4 African doctors and they did so very well, it is unbelievable. Now the roads are free and safe and we are really overworked and understaffed. As of today beside the 2 of us, we have only 2 MO (one went to Italy to specialise in radiology and radiotherapy and ultrasound) and 5 interns. But yesterday for instance, there were 300 children in CWC and 180 adults in adult outpatient. The new wing with clean surgical ward with 6 2-bed rooms and 5 8-bed wards are open and working as well as the 3 new theaters. So, the hospital capacity has passed from 305 to about 350 beds but often with near 500 patients admitted. So much malnutrition in children, so much AIDS and TB in adults and so many old cases of osteomyelitis from GSW in surgery. Presently about 18 waiting for operation—one is a 10-yr girl whose mother and 8 sibs were killed and she is the one to survive, with osteo of humerus and tibia.

We have also quite a number of patients needed orthopaedic reconstructive surgery. We would like to know if you could consider coming to Gulu for a period to do those cases. I am sure you would enjoy yourself and Dolly would like the trip now the situation is very quiet and safe and even the President came to visit the hospital and kept on talking about it on TV for a few days . . .
Best wishes and greetings for coming holidays to all of you. Waiting to hear from you soon. We send our best regards.

Lucille and Piero

Gulu 31/3/96

Dear Leo and Dolly,

Thank you for your letter which arrived a few days ago. Happy to hear that you are all well and happy.

We are now in a very bad situation as far as security is concerned. In fact, beginning of February the Acholi rebels came back from Sudan because they want to sabotage the election (next May) and keep on doing horrible barbaric acts of terrorism: it is unbelievable how cruel they can be with their own tribe—men they killed in cold blood and for no reason the civilians. They burned thousands of houses often with women and children closed inside. They rape, loot, steal food, cattle, many goods etc from the poor people. They ambush the military convoys and most of the time the regular army run away without offering any resistance. They abduct children 10-15 to sell them to Sudanese as slaves or to train them as rebels. Few weeks ago they got near the hospital, shell it, but missed it fortunately.

But the worst aspect, so distressing even for me is that they now use personal mine on paths and those are doing terrible damage. Almost daily we have to amputate—2 weeks ago on a 10y child who lost both legs and one arm. Horrible wounds even for me. I feel really disturbed to see it. With 10,000 soldiers in Acholi district they do not succeed to eliminate 500 to 700 rebels.

As far as for us, Piero is doing well apart from hand arthritis. Unfortunately, I am the one in bad condition. After very long period of remission, I have start again with opportunistic disease and had episode of very high fever with extreme weakness and had to increase much therapy and restart anti TB (MAC) treatment that I had stop last summer. I keep on working OPD (Out Patient Dept) 6-7 hours daily, never missed a day but always with more difficulty.

Dominique is doing well; passed neurology and is now preparing paediatric. I doubt that I will ever see her graduate. Shall be in Montreal probably 23-25 of May and shall contact you.

Greetings to all of you.

Lucille and Piero

Mulago Hospital, Makerere University School of Medicine

Mulago Hospital or Old Mulago, as it came to be known, was founded in 1913 by missionary physician Albert Ruskin Cook and gifted by the British colonial government to Uganda on Independence Day. It had been a teaching hospital for the Makerere Medical School since 1927. Ongoing renovations and expansion led to the construction and completion, in 1962, of New Mulago, a teaching hospital and medical school that was opened by H.R.H. the Duchess of Kent. In the mid-sixties Makerere University School of Medicine and Mulago Teaching Hospital was among the best medical schools in the world. Mulago was frequented by hundreds of people from different parts of the country every day.

Sheila Patel took care of Idi Amin as a nursing sister in 1965 at Mulago Hospital. Due to the political climate, she left Uganda for England in 1969 and served as director of nursing at a teaching hospital. She left Middlesex Hospital, London, in 2000 and worked part time at British Airways Travel Clinics for thirteen years, retiring from nursing in 2014.

19.10.72

My Dear Dolly, Leo and children,

Hope this letter will find you all in good health as I am over here.

You must have heard a few days ago his Lordship (Amin) has accused Sir Ian McAdam, Prof. Trussell and Dr. David Barkham for telling people to leave the country, and asked them to leave and resign from their posts. This is shocking news as Makerere University will lose competent professional people. They will be replaced by Ugandans.

I went to spend a weekend with Sir John and Lady Croot and had a lovely time. They have settled down quite well and have a beautiful house in Sunningdale. They have remembered Leo a lot. Sir John has now retired from his work, but does part time with Pensions & Judiciary and sits on a medical committee . . .

There is a rumour that Ugandan High Commission in London will be asked to leave. I think Britishers are careful until everybody is out, then they will cut diplomatic relation with Uganda...

Look after yourselves,
Love, Sheila

17th Feb 1973

My dear Dolly,

How are you, Leo and children? Leo is very hard working. I have no doubt he will get a job soon. It must be nice for him to work with Mr. Don Gibson again. I knew Mr. Gibson vaguely, but not very well. He had a good name in Uganda.

Last week I had a surprise telephone call from Prof. Kyalwazi. He was here with the mission to recruit Ugandan African doctors back to Uganda. He phoned me three times, but I was on duty so at the end he wrote me a letter and came to see me. We had a big chat. He is obviously very upset and sad to see all people go and very sad that Medical School is at stand still and so is Mulago Hospital. He went back after two weeks. Sir John and Lady Croot send their regards to you and Leo. Now Sir John has retired, they have plenty of free time . . .

My special regards to Leo, and love to the children and yourself.

Lots of love,
Sheila

John "Jack" Singleton Darling, FRCS, OBE

(5 July 1911 - 19 July 2002)

Jack Darling was born in Lurgan, educated at Lurgan College and won a scholarship to Queen's University Belfast. After two years of resident appointments in Belfast teaching hospitals, and two years as an anatomy demonstrator, he was house surgeon at the Miller General Hospital, Greenwich, and surgical officer to the Emergency Medical Service where he met his wife, Beryl James, also a doctor.

In 1963, Jack, Beryl and their four children returned to England after his sixteen-year career in Uganda. He was appointed consultant surgeon to the Huntingdon County Hospital, where he worked until his retirement in 1976. Jack died at his home at age ninety-one.

Madeley Lodge
Hemingford Grey
Huntingdon
12-2-73

Dear Leo + Dolly,

You have been so good in remembering us each Christmas and Jack has many a time said he would write to you. But he really isn't a letter writer and he has little spare time . . .

One thing is quite certain—that you were very wise to leave Uganda. We hear such sad news of friends who have had to leave in a hurry. Prof. McAdam is at present in Rhodesia where he has relatives but we had heard he was going to work in Zambia. Prof. Trussell came back to England in a hurry and the Billinghursts left Kampala in Dec. Even missionaries who have given a life-time of service to the country have had to leave. The plight of thousands of Asians has been given great publicity and we can hardly imagine what it must be like to be without home or country. And yet it is the African peasant who is going to suffer most, though this is the person Amin professes to want to help.

We are all very well and happy to be living in such a pleasant part of England. We are only 12 miles from Cambridge and the village is on the river Ouse. Jack is the only full-time surgeon in Huntingdon County Hospital but others from Addenbrooke's do sessions there. It is a small—67 bed only—hospital, but it is very busy. He hasn't a Registrar and is not infrequently without a House Surgeon. The job suits him down to the ground . . .

We see various Uganda friends from time to time. The Burkitts are coming to stay with us in March—3 years ago we had a lovely holiday with them in Norway. Their two elder daughters are married and we were at the weddings. I keep in touch with Donald and Ysobel Currie though they live in Hampshire and I have stayed with them several times. At present they are on their annual visit to S. Africa where his parents live. Donald is working as a civilian doctor in the Army near Winchester. Ysobel has given up professional work. The tie of family, elderly parents and various elderly relatives made it impossible for her to take on a job . . .

We still look back with great pleasure on our time in E. Africa. I wonder if you would ever come to England. Please get in touch with us if you do. We would love to see you. We have a large house and could fit you all in!

Jack joins me in sending our love and best wishes.

Yours sincerely,
Beryl Darling

Hemingford Grey
10/6/98

Dear Leo,

I seem to have misplaced the nice letter you wrote not long ago but I feel it deserves a reply before next Christmas! It was nice to have something a little fuller than our usual brief Christmas communications.

I remember our working together in Tanga with great pleasure, and it's good that you do also. It is always satisfying to share work with a colleague you like and trust, and have the same standards. If I was able to be of help at that stage of your career that was my privilege. I know you would have been good without me.

It's good that you are able to ease out gradually. My efforts to do the same were frustrated after a year by painful arthritis in my 1st carpometacarpal joints. Fortunately my other joints don't seem to be suffering much …

We do hope all the family are well. Loving greetings to Dolly.

If you ever get to Peterborough again don't forget to come to see us.

Yours ever,
Jack

21 December 2009

Leo & Dolly DeSouza
1101 Tyrol Trail
Minneapolis
MINNESOTA 55416
U. S. A.

Dear Mr. and Mrs. DeSouza

I have received your Christmas card addressed to Beryl Darling.

I have the sad news to bring you that my mother died earlier this year, on 17 January, suddenly, having probably suffered a heart attack/stroke. She had been in good health, and after many years living happily in Gore Tree Road had moved in October to stay with her daughter in the village, which was a congenial household for her. She collapsed while in a shop nearby and never regained consciousness. She was 94.

It were preferable that you had received a call from her at this season, or some message happier than this one, but I know that she had felt that her time had come. I hope that your Christmas will be joyous and I wish you a happy New Year.

With very best wishes

Martin Darling

Denis Parsons Burkitt, MD, FRCSE

(28 February 1911 - 23 March 1993)

Born in Enniskillen, Ireland, Denis Burkitt, a deeply religious man, earned his medical degree in 1935 from Trinity College, Dublin, and became a Fellow of Edinburgh's Royal College of Surgeons in 1938. He applied for a position in the colonies but was rejected several times. During World War II he was posted in Kenya, Somalia and Uganda as an army physician. In 1946 he joined the British Colonial Service in Uganda as a government surgeon and began work in Lira, moving to Kampala a year later.

Burkitt used to travel around East Africa taking hundreds of photographs of children with "strange lumps" or jaw tumours. He discovered the mosquito was responsible for this fatal type of cancer, and his meticulous research and treatment led to the lymphoma being named after him.

In 1966 Dr. Burkitt left Uganda to take up a position at the Medical Research Council in London. He became known as "The Fibre Man" when he hypothesised that reduced fibre in diet led to high incidences of noncommunicable diseases such as diabetes and colonic cancer in Western countries. Burkitt was highly honoured for his work throughout the world, receiving prizes, medals, honourary degrees and fellowships. He suffered a stroke at his home in Bisley and died, leaving behind his wife, Olive, and three daughters.

D.P. BURKITT, M.D., F.R.C.S.E.

DEPARTMENT OF SURGERY
MAKERERE UNIVERSITY COLLEGE MEDICAL SCHOOL

P.O BOX 2072
KAMPALA
UGANDA

29th June 1965

Dr. Leo de Souza,
Ministry of Health,
LIRA.

Dear Leo,

I enclose copies of the negatives. May I make a few comments which I hope will be of help.

When photographing a lesion it would be better if you could fill your picture with the lesion, as 35mm cannot be enlarged indefinitely. In most of these pictures the relevant part occupies much less than a quarter of the negative. You would be better not to cut off the top of the head, but to exclude a lot of the trunk.

I was very glad of the opportunity of doing these photographs for you.

Yours sincerely,

Denis

Denis Burkitt

DEPARTMENT OF MORBID ANATOMY
ST. THOMAS'S HOSPITAL MEDICAL SCHOOL
LONDON SE1. 7EH.

PROFESSOR H. SPENCER

TELEPHONE : 01-928 9292 EXT. ~~XXX~~
2919

DPB/SK

18th May, 1977.

Dr. Leo J. DeSouza,
5000 West 39th Street,
St. Louis Park Medical Centre,
Minneapolis, Minnesota 55416.

Dear Leo,

Thank you for your letter and for the reprint on small bowel volvulus. I am so glad that you are well settled as an orthopedic surgeon in North America now after all your years of hard work and faithful service. I will certainly let you know whenever my travels bring me to Minnesota.

With best wishes to both you and Dolly,

Yours sincerely,

Denis

GEOGRAPHICAL PATHOLOGY UNIT
DENIS P. BURKITT

Chandrakant Maganbhai (CM) Patel, MB, BS

(1 February 1931 - 11 June 1989)

CM, as he was affectionately known, received his medical degree in 1957 from Grant Medical College, Bombay, and represented his college in hockey and volleyball. He obtained his diploma in dermatology in England. CM was a general practitioner (GP) in Gulu from 1958-68 before moving to Kampala to set up a consultancy practice in skin diseases.

Expelled by Idi Amin, CM went to the United Kingdom as a refugee in 1972 and helped out as medical officer to the Greenham Common camp for Ugandan Asian refugees. Later, he practised as a GP in Reading and was an active member of the Indian Cultural Society.

CM was an excellent cook and enjoyed hosting dinner parties for friends. He golfed regularly and won the medal competition in his section at Calcot Golf Club.

In the last year of his life, he was deeply affected by the death of his twenty-six-year old son and never fully recovered. CM died of a massive brain stem haemorrhage. He was survived by his wife, Pushpa, and three sons.

Reading,UK
29-7-76

My dear Leo & Dolly

Your very welcome and pleasing letter has put my mind much at rest & has relieved lots of burden from my head. I could just say Thanks a lot, my real dear friend.

. . . My work is alright—the same routine monotonous that a GP does in UK. Earning is reasonable but inflation kills me. One can't save here.

. . . Pushpa and kids have finally settled. Kids have fairly pleasing report from school considering their first year here—specially coming from India after 4-5 years. Socially, life is rather boring here but old friends & relatives in London makes it up.

Please convey my love to Dolly and all the kids. With God's wish we will meet once again. My kindest regards to you.

Yours, CM

Sir Ian William James McAdam, FRCSE, FRCS, OBE

(15 February 1917 - 4 March 1999)

Ian McAdam, born in Parys, South Africa, was educated in Southern Rhodesia, then Cambridge University in England, and trained as a surgeon at James Learmonth in Edinburgh.

He applied for a post at Mulago Hospital, Kampala, and at Makerere University. After twenty-six years of exemplary service at Mulago Hospital, Sir Ian McAdam was expelled by Idi Amin in 1972 for helping friends and colleagues leave the country.

McAdam lived in Britain before accepting a year-long appointment at the National Cancer Institute in Maryland, USA, after which he and his wife, Pamela, returned to South Africa. He practised as a surgeon at Knysna Provincial Hospital in the Western Cape until his retirement in 1992 to Oxfordshire, England.

Upon his death, as stated in his will, his remains were flown to Uganda for burial. Ian McAdam had two daughters and a son with his first wife.

Sebastian Kalule Kyalwazi, MBChB, FRCSE

(31 October 1919 - 25 January 1992)

Sebastian Kyalwazi was born in Masaka District, Uganda; studied at St. Mary's College, Kisubi; and graduated from Makerere University Medical School. In 1956, he was one of the first two Ugandans to qualify as a surgeon, becoming a Fellow of the Royal College of Surgeons of Edinburgh.

His interest in chemotherapy, oncology and research led him to the Czechoslovakia Cancer Institute as a World Health Organisation scholar. A year later, in 1968, he became a lecturer at the Department of Surgery, Makerere University Medical School, and the first African president of the Association of Surgeons of East Africa.

During the papal visit of Paul VI to Uganda, Kyalwazi was his assigned surgeon and the Order of St. Gregory the Great was bestowed on him by the Vatican.

In 1973, Kyalwazi advanced to professor and head of the surgery department. He was involved with the Solid Tumor Center, a cancer research ward affiliated with Makerere University Medical School.

Sebastian Kyalwazi died of cancer in London, England. He and his wife, Mildred Leah, were parents to six children.

Sir Horace John Croot, CBE, MBBS, FRCS

(14 October 1907 - 22 May 1981)

John Croot, born in Portsmouth, England, was trained at Guy's Hospital in London. He was appointed the new chair of surgery at Makerere University in Kampala in 1951, a few years later to the Legislative Council of Uganda and, in 1958, minister of health and labour during Uganda's interim self-government prior to independence.

Sir John returned to Mulago Hospital as senior consultant surgeon. He firmly believed in the benefits of a modern teaching hospital and saw the completion and expansion of the New Mulago Hospital and medical school during his tenure.

He was bestowed the Most Excellent Order of the British Empire Award in 1962 and knighted in 1965 for services to government and surgery in East Africa. Sir John retired to Britain in 1969, serving as member and medical chairman of the Pensions Appeal Tribunals until his death. He and his wife, Linda Burley, had no children.

Ronald Lawrie Huckstep, CMG, FTSE, Hon MA, MD, FRACS, FRCS, FAOrthA

(22 July 1926 - 10 April 2015)

Ron Huckstep, born in China, spent a large part of his youth interned in a Japanese camp. He studied at Cambridge and Middlesex Hospitals, becoming an orthopaedic surgeon. His career took him to England, Kenya, Uganda and Australia.

In 1960, Huckstep went to Uganda as professor of orthopaedics at Makerere University and was immersed in the care of patients with polio, pioneering and developing new treatments such as the "Huckstep" nail and skelecast. Pope Paul VI awarded him the Companion of the Order of St. Michael and St. George following a visit to the clinic during his 1969 pilgrimage to Uganda.

Political instability resulted in the Hucksteps moving to Australia, and in 1972, Professor Huckstep accepted the position of inaugural chair of Trauma and Orthopaedic Surgery at the Prince of Wales Clinical School of the University of New South Wales in Sydney, where he worked until his retirement in 1993. Ron Huckstep passed away suddenly from a stroke. He and his wife Ann have three children.

THE UNIVERSITY OF NEW SOUTH WALES

P.O. BOX 1 • KENSINGTON • N.S.W. • AUSTRALIA • 2033
TELEGRAPH: UNITECH, SYDNEY

DEPARTMENT OF TRAUMATIC & ORTHOPAEDIC SURGERY. PLEASE QUOTE

PERSONAL. 23rd August, 1972.

L.J. DeSouza, Esq.., F.R.C.S.,
75 Oak Court,
125 Shaughnessy Blvd.,
Willowdale,
TORONTO,
Ontario,
Canada.

Dear Leo,

Thank you for your letter of August 10th. I am sorry to hear that you were let down by the Americans in Minneapolis. I think it is nothing short of appalling and I should be grateful if you could let me know if there is anything I can do to reverse this decision.

I would, however, think that you were wise to stay on the Toronto programme especially as Donald Gibson will make sure that nothing underhand such as occurred to you in America will occur in Toronto.

I would of course be very pleased to write to the American Board of Orthopaedic Surgery and to the Royal College of Physicians and Surgeons of Canada, and these I have already sent off. Please do not hesitate to let me know if there is any further support that you will require in your future career in North America.

I was very sorry to hear about your depression which I quite sympathise with. You have one small consolation however, that your position could have been very much worse if you had remained in Uganda.

We arrived here on July 14th and I am being kept very busy starting my new Department of Traumatic & Orthopaedic Surgery. There is considerable potential for the future of this department which is independent of surgery and which involves a whole group of teaching hospitals and 200 medical students a year.

Ann and the family came out with me by sea and we have rented a pleasant house in a beautiful setting only four miles from the centre of town. We too will have our difficulties in settling in a new country, but we hope that this will not pose too many problems.

I do hope that you, Dolly and the family are keeping well and my very best wishes to you all for the future.

Yours sincerely,

Ron

R.L. Huckstep.

My kindest regards to Donald & Elizabeth –

4th September 2015

Dear Leo and Dolly,

I am writing to let you know that Ron passed away peacefully on April 10. He had a sudden severe intracranial haemorrhage and did not regain consciousness. He was surrounded by his family.

Ron had been struggling a bit over the past few years, with increasing loss of mobility following an old hip fracture. He also had some cardiac problems, but he remained cheerful and optimistic. He kept in touch with

2.

work colleagues, both in Australia and elsewhere. He took particular delight in watching his six grandchildren growing up and gave them all individual encouragement.

Ron's legacy will be the gratitude of his many students, patients and colleagues all over the ~~world~~ world.

I hope you are both keeping well.

With best wishes to you and your family.

Sincerely,

Ann (H)

World Rehabilitation Fund, Inc.

400 EAST 34TH STREET
NEW YORK, N. Y. 10016

TELEPHONE: OREGON 9-3200
EXT. 2053
CABLE: NYUMEDIC RUSK

January 14, 1974

Mr. and Mrs. Leo De Souza
125 Shaughnessy Blvd.
Unit 74
Willowdale, Ontario
Canada, M2J 1J7

Dear Friends:

Thank you very much for your Christmas card which I received when I arrived in New York from my trip to Asia and Africa. I am very pleased that finally you will be going back to Minneapolis.

While in Africa, I visited Uganda and really the situation is very bad there. It looks like a dead city and it is very difficult to find anything including, rice, bread and sugar. People are still living the same way, mostly on bananas, and everybody is afraid of the government. I saw Kisumba and some other doctors and they, too, are afraid of the Government. We cancelled the course there and instead are going to start one in Addis Ababa, Ethiopia in May, 1974. We will take two technicians from Mulago Hospital, Obonyo and another one. The Kumi Leprosy Center is sending five students to the course in Ethiopia.

I learned that Dr. McAdam is in Washington as a visiting lecturer for two years. While in Uganda, I met a Dr. Brodie. I think you met him in Kenya. He is replacing Dr. Huckstep.

I am leaving next week for Hong Kong to finish the course which I started there in September, 1973. I will then return to New York for a short stay and in February will go to South America to start another course in Sao Paulo, Brazil. In May, I go to Ethiopia, and in July, to Bangalore, India, to start a course there. So you can see I am rather busy.

With all good wishes for the New Year, I am,

Sincerely,

Juan Monros

P.D. THE ADRESS OF PROF. MCADAM
is National Institute of Health
Building 31 3A 49
BETHESDA MARYLAND 20014

Donald Armstrong Gibson, MD, FRCS, FRCSC

(15 June 1924 – 20 July 2019)

Donald was born in Kaifeng, China. He studied medicine and surgery in Canada and England, where he met and married Elizabeth in 1950.

He moved their young family to Kampala in 1952 when he accepted a surgical position at Mengo Hospital, Uganda's first hospital. In 1959 Donald moved to Toronto practicing orthopaedics at the Hospital for Sick Children.

Ten years later, during a second surgical assignment in Kampala, as an agent of the Canadian International Development Agency, Donald worked with Leo and Professor Ron Huckstep at the Round Table Polio Clinic. He also began a long association with the Leprosy Mission and the work of destigmatizing the disease. Leo and Donald became good friends and, when he returned to Canada in 1971, Donald was instrumental in supporting Leo's entry into the Toronto Orthopaedic Training Program, helping him successfully transition from orthopaedic surgery in Uganda to practice in North America.

From 1977 until his retirement in 1989, Donald was medical director of the Hugh MacMillan Medical Centre (now Holland Bloorview Kids Rehabilitation Hospital) in Toronto, which serves children and youth with disabilities and their families.

In his spare time Donald helped build one of their homes, enjoyed small and large woodworking projects, sailing and bonsai. In 1999, he and Elizabeth moved to Victoria, British Columbia, to be near family. He retained a lifelong interest in organisations that were important to him and served as a board member for several, including the International Christian Medical and Dental Association and, after retirement, Friends of Mengo Hospital.

Donald was predeceased by his son, Robin, in 1998 and Elizabeth in 2002. He leaves behind two children, Ian and Joy, and their families.

4/12/74

Dear Leo,

Congratulations and congratulations over and over again. I suspect that I understand better than most what a great effort was required to adapt from the East African scene, meet the North American Orthopaedic surgeon on his own ground and on his own terms, and come up a winner. And I am so glad for your sake and Dolly's that the story of your retaining had such a triumphant conclusion . . .

Leo – it is late – I just wanted to congratulate you, oh so warmly.

Yours sincerely,
Donald

25/1/75

Dear Leo,

It was fun to get your card and clinic association announcement. I hope very much that you find them all congenial . . .

I am busy doing plaster work on a 'retirement home' we are building 90 miles away from here. That is (a) fun (b) hard work (c) a great drain on time as it leaves no chance to catch up on the weekends.

I am still trying to get David Kisumba over for a bit. I phoned him last week and he sounded eager. I hope it works out.

TIME says your old country, Tanzania, is in real trouble, just not producing food on the collective farming bit. I hope Nyerere survives. Idi Amin still makes news all the time.

Give greetings to Dolly and the family.

Sincerely,
Donald

Family in Golden Valley, Minnesota, USA, December 1971

Santos and Queenie, Tanga, October 1975

Dr. Armando Nazareth and his wife, Lydia, Tanga, October 1975

With Larry and Jo Brown, Minneapolis, USA, 1975

Jo and Larry Brown with Sheila Patel, Golden Valley, December 1980

Aziz Kazi and Leo
in London, mid-1970s

Aziz visits Minneapolis, 1980

With CM Patel in
London, July 1982

Carlos and Jane Godinho with Leo, Vancouver, December 1989

Leo with Jane and Carlos, Vancouver

Tehmi Mulla (Dolly's sister), Dolly and Jane Godinho, Minneapolis, March 1990

With Aziz in London,
June 1993

Leo and Jack Darling,
Huntingdon, England,
June 1993

Beryl and Jack Darling with Dolly, England, June 1993

Eddie and Annie Moné, Netherlands, June 1993

With Annie, Netherlands, June 1993

With Lucille and Piero Corti, Golden Valley, June 1995

Elizabeth and Donald Gibson,
Canada, December 1995

Leo visits St. Joseph's Arpora, Goa, February 1997

Larry congratulating Leo on his graduation from Hamline University, May 2002

Leo and Dolly, November 2003

June 3, 2016

Dear Dolly,

I was so sad to receive the letter telling of Leo's passing. You and he together weathered a lot of different situations, and at least had a good long marriage together. I thought my Elizabeth and I had done well with 52, but you two did better.

Leo was a genuine gentleman, meaning a gentle man, and it was a pleasure for a while to be one of his colleagues. I am sorry we did not see more of each other. Now I like to think you are well supported by your children and grandchildren. God bless you all.

I wish you all well at this difficult time.

Yours sincerely,
Donald

David Kisumba, MD, FRCS

(1934 - 1979)

David Kisumba married Catherine Zawedde, the first woman pharmacist in Uganda, in 1962. He became head of orthopaedics at Makerere Medical School after Leo left. David's untimely death in 1979, at the age of forty-five, during the Idi Amin regime, was allegedly planned by members of the army. His car, intercepted by a miltary vehicle, was crushed. David was survived by Catherine and their four children. She continued correspondence with Leo and Dolly for many years. Catherine passed away in Muyenga, Kampala on 22 October, 2017.

Ivan Saja Kadama, MD

(Unknown birth and death dates)

In 1960, Ivan Kadama was the first African doctor appointed to Medical Headquarters in Uganda, becoming chief medical officer in 1962 and permanent secretary a year later. He was the first Ugandan to head the health sector, which he transformed into one responsive to African needs. He retired in 1970.

Carlos Placido Godinho

(4 November 1926 - 9 August 1992)

Jane Hyacinth Godinho

(17 August 1926 - 21 November 2003)

Carlos was born and raised in Kampala, Uganda, studied law at Cambridge University, England, and returned to Uganda in 1952 to take over the family business upon his father's death.

Jane was born and brought up in Goa, India. She attended St. Xavier's College in Bombay where she met Leo and became friends. Carlos was introduced to Jane at a dance while on holiday in India. They met again a few years later when Jane was visiting her sister in Uganda.

Carlos and Jane were married in Kampala in 1954, where they lived with their three children until they were forced to leave the country along with fifty thousand Indians in November 1972. Following a brief stay in the UK, they moved to Canada, settling in Vancouver, British Columbia.

After Idi Amin was ousted from power in 1979, the new government invited Carlos and other prominent businessmen to return and take possession of their businesses, but they were not allowed to have title and, therefore, could not sell their properties. Carlos went to court numerous times to get full rights to his family's assets, travelling back and forth to Uganda for years until he was diagnosed with leukemia. Carlos and Jane leave behind their three children and six grandchildren who all reside in Vancouver, BC.

Nairobi 7th Nov, 1972

My dear Dolly and Leo,

Many thanks for your recent letters. Jane and I were touched by your concern for us and we knew that if there was any help that we needed we could turn to you . . .

I could not write freely from Uganda, I felt I might as well wait until I reached Nairobi . . . It was such a relief to get out safely from the country we loved but almost grew to hate in the last few weeks. We were worried that I might be prevented from leaving even at the last minute at the airport—there were rumours circulating of my arrest! However, I survived those last few weeks and I am now here for a week or so before proceeding to Bombay. I will join the family in England for the Christmas holidays. I have got a settlement visa for Canada and am planning to come there alone first to look around . . . though life may be a struggle for us at the beginning I am sure we will be happy among a people who are welcoming us so warmly.

The latest move to send Uganda citizen Asians into the villages has made many of them to leave. Rao, my cinema manager, is the only Asian left in our organization—even the two citizen Asian accountants I had, suddenly decided to leave . . . I don't know what is going to happen.

Love to all,
Carlos

Lawrence "Larry" A. Brown

(7 September 1919 – 14 March 2012)

Alice (Jo) Kelly Brown

(b. 20 October 1931 -)

After returning to the United States in 1968, Larry worked for three years as a deputy director of the Urban Coalition in Minneapolis, and later, held other positions in the private sector. He was one of three original founders of the Ronald McDonald House in Minneapolis, which opened its first house in 1979. Larry recognized the need for housing for parents of hospitalized children when his daughter Laurie was treated for and died from leukemia in the early sixties. He was also heavily involved in the CAF Red Tail Project, which educates people about the history and legacy of the Tuskegee Airmen, America's first black fighter pilots who served with distinction in WWII. Larry passed away at home at age ninety-two. Jo lives in Wayzata, Minnesota; son Kevin and family reside in Colorado and daughter Janine and family are in Minnesota.

Further Reading

Albuquerque, Daniel (2015) *Dr. Wilfred De Souza – A Journey With An Exceptional Leader of Goa.* Panaji, Goa: Rajhauns Sankalpana PVT Ltd.

Bennet, Norman Robert (1971) *Mirambo of Tanzania ca.1840-1844.* New York: Oxford University Press Inc.

Cowley, Deborah (2005) *Lucille Teasdale: Doctor of Courage.* Montreal, Quebec: XYZ Publishing

Delf, George (1963) *Asians in East Africa.* Great Britain: Oxford University Press Inc.

Farwell, Byron (1986) *The Great War in Africa (1914-1918).* Ontario, Canada: Penguin Books of Canada

Ingham, Kenneth (1962) *The History of East Africa.* Great Britain: Cox and Wyman, Ltd.

Lewin, Evans (1918) *German Rule in Africa.* Adelphi Terrace, London: T. Fisher Unwin, Ltd.

Listowel, Judith (1965) *The Making of Tanganyika.* Great Britain: Chatto and Windus, Ltd.

Morris, H.S. (1968) *The Indians in Uganda: A Study of Caste and Sect in a Plural Society.* Chicago, IL: The University of Chicago Press

Morton-Jack, George (2018) *The Indian Empire at War. From Jihad to Victory, The Untold Story of the Indian Army in the First World War.* Great Britain: Little, Brown Book Group

p'Bitek, Okot (Reissue Edition 2013) *Song of Lawino & Song of Ocol.* Waveland Press, Inc.

Rice, Andrew (2009) *The Teeth May Smile But The Heart Does Not Forget: Murder And Memory In Uganda.* New York: Metropolitan Books, Henry Holt and Company, LLC.

Acknowledgements

I would like to thank Mary F. Rockcastle for opening the magic door to writing, to Lawrence Sutin for walking me through, to Judith Katz and Deborah Keenan for their guidance and encouragement and to Sheila O'Connor and Barrie Borrich for clearing up complexities.

Thanks also are due to Darleen Hauck for steering me into the world of writing; to Cheryl Johnson, my medical secretary, both at Metropolitan Orthopaedics and Hennepin County Medical Center, for transcribing dictation of my work and my life into typed organized pages; and finally, to my wife Dolly, who put the original manuscript together, often browbeating the wayward computer in the process.